PLACER COUNTY DIRECTORY OF 1861

The Placer County Historical Society is proud to present this reprint of the Placer County Directory of 1861. Except for the cover and this page, the Directory is reprinted as it originally appeared in 1861. A copy of the original cover has been included at the end of this booklet.

The original 1861 Directory was published by R.J. Steele, James P. Ball, and F.I. Houston. According to County records, both Steele and Ball were involved in additional publishing activities in Placer County during the 1850s and 1860s. No other mention of Houston's name has been found.

In the preface of the Directory, the publishers state that the book will be "valuable as an auxiliary to the future historian." It is our hope that we have helped preserve a unique and picturesque glimpse into Placer County's past and that the Directory can continue to be of value "to the future historian."

The Placer County Historical Society is indebted to Mrs. Victor Simpson who graciously loaned us her late husband's original copy of the 1861 Directory for this project.

Published by the Placer County Historical Society, P.O. Box 5643, Auburn, California 95604, 1989. Printed by Auburn Letter House Printers.

TABLE OF DISTANCES

FROM THE

PRINCIPAL CITIES IN CALIFORNIA.

From SAN FRANCISCO
To	Benicia	30
"	Martinez	33
"	Sacramento	125
"	Stockton	227
"	Petaluma	53
"	Alviso	39
"	San Mateo	21½
"	Redwood City	31
"	San Jose	51
"	Gilroy	85
"	Santa Clara	48
"	Monterey	85
"	San Juan	94
"	San Diego	537

From SACRAMENTO
To	Nicolaus	26
"	Bear River	29
"	Dry Creek	37
"	Marysville	44
"	Tehama	119
"	Red Bluffs	134
"	Prairie House	145
"	American House	160
"	Carey's Ranch	169
"	Shasta	226
"	Iowa Hill	65
"	Placerville	51
"	Nevada	69
"	Auburn	38½

From SHASTA
To	Tower House	12
"	Gibb's Ferry	35
"	Summit Scott's Mountain	69
"	Godfrey's Ranch	99
"	Yreka	116

From MARYSVILLE
To	Charlie's Ranch	13
"	Oroville	28
"	Bidwell's Bar	32
"	Peavine Ranch	58
"	Buck's Ranch	78
"	Honcut City	26
"	Wyandot	25
"	Nachez	30
"	Buckeye	55
"	Pine Grove	75
"	Port Wine	75
"	Onion Valley	81

To	Forest City	58
"	Downieville	66
"	Rough and Ready	32
"	Grass Valley	36
"	Nevada	40

From STOCKTON
To	Spring Valley	40
"	Campo Seco	46
"	Mokelumne Hill	49
"	Murphy's Camp	71
"	Mammoth Tree Grove	86
"	Jamestown	71
"	Sonora	75
"	Columbia	81

From SONORA.
To	Big Oak Flat	13
"	French Bar	28
"	Don Pedro's Bar	26

From AUBURN
To	Bloomer Ranch	1
"	Rattlesnake Bar	6
"	Mountaineer House	6½
"	Franklin House	10
"	Rock Spring House	12½
"	Folsom	17½
"	Morrison's Stand	1
"	Mount Pleasant House	2½
"	Ophir	3
"	Gold Hill	7½
"	Virginia	9
"	Fox's Flat	12
"	Coon Creek	20
"	Jenny Lind Flat	6
"	Stewart's Flat	8
"	Pine Grove	10
"	Neilsburg	6
"	Lisbon	12
"	Illinoistown	20
"	Dutch Flat	32
"	Iowa Hill	32
"	Grizzly Bear House	6
"	Yankee Jims	20
"	Forest Hill	23
"	Todd's Valley	20
"	Michigan Bluff	36
"	Bear River	10
"	Grass Valley	24
"	Nevada	28

DIRECTORY

OF THE

COUNTY OF PLACER,

FOR THE

YEAR 1861:

CONTAINING

A HISTORY OF THE COUNTY, AND OF THE DIFFERENT TOWNS IN THE COUNTY; WITH THE NAMES OF INHABITANTS, AND EVERY THING APPERTAINING TO A COMPLETE DIRECTORY.

COMPILED BY

R. J. STEELE, JAMES P. BULL, AND F. I. HOUSTON.

PRINTED FOR THE PUBLISHERS,
BY CHARLES F. ROBBINS, 418 TO 417 CLAY STREET, SAN FRANCISCO.
1861.

PREFACE.

The publication of a Directory for Placer County, was suggested to the undersigned by the absolute existing necessity to business men of a work of the kind, and the knowledge that if properly and faithfully gotten up, it would ever be a useful work of reference for business men, and an interesting book for the perusal of the general reader. To enable the publishers to collect the materials and pay for the printing of the book, the public of Placer County was asked to aid the enterprise by advertising and subscriptions for copies ; and it was expected that, presenting as it does, the best medium for advertising ever offered in Placer County, those engaged in mercantile, hotel, and other pursuits, would give it such encouragement as would enable the publishers to not only obtain full remuneration for the labor and expense attending a thorough canvass of the county, but also a reasonable profit upon the capital necessarily invested and the labor performed. In this, however, we have been mistaken, as our receipts will be no more than sufficient to reimburse us for the money we have expended in canvassing the county, leaving a very small amount indeed as our profits upon the enterprise. Although the enterprise was an experiment, we entered into the labor with a full determination to succeed in the work, even if no profits therefrom were derived by us further than that afforded by the convenience of the book as a work of future reference—expecting, as we did, to be opposed by the ignorant in every camp and town which we visited, knowing full well that if success attended our effort in the present, the advantage would be great to us in any similar enterprise in future.

If the work should not come up to that standard expected by its friends, we can only offer as an apology the great haste in which it was gotten up, and the vast amount of labor necessary to accomplish the collection and preparation of the materials, and the total absence of any written work from which the necessary information, statistical and otherwise, could be obtained.

The historical sketches of the towns, and the county—though not as full and complete as we would desire—may be relied upon as authentic, and will be valuable as an auxiliary to the future historian of Placer County ; and, though the matter contained in the work may not be presented in that form and style necessary to enable it to escape the attacks of literary connoisseurs and professional critics, yet we feel assured that with all the faults that may justly be attributed to the work, those who have patronized it most liberally, and whom we have the greatest desire to please, will be satisfied with and approve of it.

THE PUBLISHERS.

HISTORICAL SKETCHES

OF THE

TOWNS OF PLACER COUNTY.

AUBURN.

The town of Auburn is one of the oldest in the State, having been a "mining camp" of considerable importance early in 1849. Of the first discovery of gold upon its site, or in its neighborhood, there is at this time no reliable account; but when the writer of this article passed the spot in the first days of July, 1849, the ravines which converged in what is now the Plaza showed signs of having been wrought to some extent during the previous rainy season. The only persons at work, however, at that time (July) were two Chilenos "panning" in Rich Ravine, a short distance above where the American Hotel now stands, and a white man with a rocker upon the Main Auburn Ravine, near the present bridge on the turnpike. About the middle of July, Wm. Gwynn and H. M. House started trading-posts here, and a considerable population began to accumulate. Up to this time the place had been known as Wood's Dry Diggings; its new name of Auburn was adopted during the following winter.

In the spring of 1850 it had assumed quite an important position as a mining town, and was the trading-point of a very extensive mining district. The principal traders were Bailey & Kerr, Disbrow & Willment, Walkup & Wyman, Parkinson & Leet, Wetzler & Sutter, Wm. Gwynn, H. M. House, and Post & Ripley. Of these pioneers, Mr. Willment alone remains a resident of the town, and is doing business at the old stand.

In the first division of the State into counties, Auburn came within the boundaries of Sutter, the county seat being at Nicolaus on Bear River, some thirty miles distant. The mass of the population being in the nearer vicinity of Auburn upon the North Fork of the American, and among the various dry diggings adjacent, the removal of the county seat was demanded and an order obtained for an election submitting the question to the people. Four ambitious precincts entered the lists for the honor—Auburn, Nicolaus, Ophir and Miner's Hotel (Franklin House). The favorable location of Auburn, its preponderance of population and the inexhaustible powers of voting possessed by its citizens and partisans, decided the contest in its favor by a majority considerably exceeding the entire population of the county.

The Legislature of 1851, by an Act creating the counties of Nevada, Placer, Trinity and Klamath, cut the town off from Sutter again, bringing it within the boundaries of the new county of Placer, and declaring it the county seat. This Act also provided for the holding of a special election for the organization of the county, and appointing Joseph Walkup, H. M. House, J. D. Fry, Wm. Gwynn and Jonathan Roberts, Commissioners of said election. The election was held on the 26th of May, 1851, and upon canvassing the vote the following officers were declared elected: H. Fitz Simmons, County Judge; Samuel C. Astin, Sheriff; R. D. Hopkins, District Attorney; James T. Stewart, Clerk; Alfred Lewis, Assessor; Douglass Bingham, Treasurer.

Horace Davenport, of Rattlesnake, contested the seat of Fitz Simmons; Hiram R. Hawkins, of Deadman's Bar, that of Stewart, and Abraham Bronk, of Horseshoe, that of Bingham; and, upon a rehearing by the Commissioners, fraud in the returns was shown and the contestants were declared entitled to their respective offices.

The proceedings of the Commissioners were, however, declared void by the District Court, and Fitz Simmons held his seat as Judge, while Stewart appointed Hawkins his deputy, and Bingham's death occurring on the very day of the trial, Bronk was appointed Treasurer by the Court of Sessions. The Court House was at this time a crazy wood and cloth tenement, occupying the present site of Mrs. Roussin's residence, on Court Street, and the Jail, a small but secure structure of logs upon the rear of the same lot. The town was composed of about equal numbers of log cabins and clapboard or shake houses.

The National Hotel was the only two story building in the place. A gradual improvement in the number and style of buildings has marked each succeeding year. Two destructive fires—the first on the 4th of June, 1855, and the second on the 9th of October, 1859—have been rather improving than detrimental to the appearance of the town; better and more ornamental structures having taken the place of those destroyed. There are at present nineteen brick and stone buildings, exclusive of the jail, some of which are blocks of two or more stores, making in all thirty-two brick tenements. The residences of the citizens in the suburbs of the town are noted for their substantial character and the neatness and taste displayed in their structure. Fruit and flowers flourish in unsurpassed abundance and luxuriance, and each of these homes is surrounded by its orchard and embowered with clambering vines of almost perennial bloom. Those who recollect how bleak and barren, parched and sterile those hills appeared "in that elder day," and now cast their eyes over the bright and smiling landscape, can fully appreciate what it is to "make the wilderness blossom like roses."

MINING.

Although once ranking among the first mining towns in the State, Auburn can at this time hardly be accounted as such. The diggings in the vicinity were of a superficial character, being confined almost exclusively to the beds of the numerous ravines, and to the "flats" at their sources. Among the latter, Spanish Flat, half a mile from town, and Rich Flat, at the head of Rich Ravine, were the most important and yielded abundantly for many years. Both are now considered "worked out." Spanish Flat is now a fertile garden spot, and Rich Flat is an unsightly desert of quartz boulders. New ravines and flats have been opened up of late years in the adjacent country, composing an area of fifteen to twenty miles square, giving employment to a large population, for whom Auburn is the market for sale of dust and purchase of supplies. The North Fork of the American is but a mile distant, and is year after year flumed almost from source to mouth. No deep coyote or tunnel diggings have been opened in this district. The country is thickly veined with quartz ledges, but as yet that branch of mining has been prosecuted with but indifferent success.

LYNCH LAW.

Resort to the tribunal of Judge Lynch has been had in but few instances· The first subject of this summary code was one Sharp, an Englishman and an ex-ship captain, who murdered a man in the vicinity of Auburn on Christmas day, 1850, by shooting him through the chinks of his cabin. He surrendered himself to the Sheriff, but was taken from his custody by the people, tried by a Lynch jury, and hung upon a large oak tree on the present site of Norcross' jewelry store.

In 1852 the people of Yankee Jim's hung one James Edmondson, familiarly known as "Jim Ugly." The precise circumstances of his case are unknown, or forgotten by the writer.

In December, 1854, one William N. Johnson, somewhat notorious under the name of "Long Johnson," was hung by the people at Iowa Hill.

In February, 1858, a negro named Aaron Bracy murdered a popular and prominent citizen of Auburn. He surrendered himself to the Sheriff and was committed to jail. That night the jail was broken open and the negro taken out and hung upon a tall pine about half a mile from town.

POLITICAL.

In the first election, at the organization of the county, no party lines were drawn, and the offices of the county were held by men of both political parties. In the fall of 1851, in the election of members of the Legislature, conventions were held and party nominations made, the Democratic party being successful, and that party has since been the dominant one in the county, except on very few occasions.

In 1854, the Democratic party being divided into the Broderick and Gwin factions, the Whigs elected a full county ticket. Again, in '55, the American party elected their Legislative candidates. In 1858 the same party elected their Tax Collector, all the other offices being filled by Democrats. And in 1860 the Republicans elected one Assemblyman and the County Recorder, the latter beating his strongest Democratic opponent by only two votes, there being four tickets in the field.

The present District Judge (Hon. B. F. Myres, Dem.) was elected on a local, and not on a political, issue, and his predecessor (Hon J. M. Howell, Whig), upon his own merits and popularity, having been elected by a majority of 1,000, in the face of a general Democratic majority in the District of over 1,500.

H.

MICHIGAN BLUFF.

BY DR. K. FAVOR.

This flourishing mining town is situated in latitude 39°, among the Sierra Nevada Mountains, or as the words signify in English, the Snowy Saw Mountains. It is built on the top of a hill, at the bottom of which, some two miles distant, runs the North Fork of the Middle Fork of the American river, or of the Rio de Los Americanos, as it was called by the Mexicans.

It is situated at an altitude of nearly 4,000 feet above the level of the sea. The climate for the greater portion of the year cannot be excelled for its beauty and salubrity.

The atmosphere is cool, bracing and exhilerating. No noxious gases are wafted upon its wings. No invisible poisonous malaria forms a part of its composition.

Innumerable springs of water flow from our mountain sides, clear as crystal and cold as the banks of snow from which it was formed. It is generally impregnated with iron, which gives it an agreeable taste and tonic properties which the water of the valleys does not possess.

In summer the days are very warm, the thermometer frequently rises as high as 100° in the shade, and in low situations it has occasionally reached 120° in the shade, yet the nights, fanned by gentle breezes from the snow-clad Sierras, are always cool and refreshing.

The sky, for eight months of the year, is clear and serene. No dark clouds obstruct the rays of the sun by day, nor of the moon by night. This is the appearance during the dry season. But when the wet season arrives, what a change ! Then winter sometimes pounces upon us suddenly like the eagle upon its prey. Then our mountain forests present the appearance represented by pictures of the high latitudes. The forest trees are principally evergreens ; the damp snow adheres to their branches in large quantities, causing them to droop and point downwards toward the earth, as if attracted by the snowy carpet which covers the ground and everything upon it to the depth of several feet.

A sight of this scene, especially when the large feathery snow-flakes are falling thickly all around, is indeed the most dreary and the most sublime which I ever witnessed.

And while this dreary aspect is exhibited on our mountains, it is remarkable that by going a distance of four or five miles, to the valleys of some of our deep cañons, you will find a summer climate, where the ground is bare, and mules and other animals live and fatten upon the growing vegetation.

To breathe our mountain air, free from fogs, from clouds and from malaria, to drink our pure water, distilled by the hand of Nature from banks of snow in the mountain tops, and distributed to us in sparkling rivulets, which flow from their sides ; to ride over our hill-tops and gaze upon the beautiful scenery, which Nature in her wildest mood has painted in the most romantic colors, is an enjoyment which would well repay our friends below who live in the smoky, dusty, impure, foggy atmosphere of the cities, for making our mountains a visit.

APPENDIX.

Two years have elapsed since the above sketch was penned.   Mule loads of gold have been taken from our gulches, placers and hills. Water is now brought into our town for mining purposes from thirty miles distance further up in the mountains. Wheelbarrows for removing rocks, and sledges for breaking them have given way to derricks; some of which are propelled by water power. Wrought iron pipes are superseding flumes. Improved methods of saving gold have been discovered. Mountains have been leveled, the glittering treasure precipitated and the alluvion sent to Sacramento, to be deposited in bars, or to reclaim tule lands, according to circumstances. Ground which a few years ago was not worth working, is now, in consequence of improvements in mining, very valuable.

But like all Californians, we have had our drawbacks. In July, 1857, a devastating fire swept over the whole town like a mighty wind, and almost as rapidly, destroying the labor of years in a single hour. The town was rebuilt on the same site, but the tunnels which everywhere run under the streets and houses, together with the rapid removal of the earth around it by the miner in search of gold, with the water which flows through a score or more hydraulics, has been rapidly undermining its foundation, and causing the ground upon which it was built to slide, thus compelling its removal to another site. A new site has been selected and most of the business houses removed to it, and new ones erected thereon, while fully 80 acres of land, including the old site, is, Cottonocracy-like, in a state of active secession, intent on dissolving the Union.

The night previous to the present day (March 28th) was a sleepless one with many of our inhabitants. The whole secession district moved about two feet during the night, and what made it worse was, that some portions of it, South Carolina-like, moved faster than the rest. Timbers cracked over people's heads like South Carolina rifles, causing many fears, but hurting nobody. Sectional cracks run under many houses, causing one part to secede to the south, while the other remains with the north, thus seriously endangering the union. But the foundation of the secession district is very unstable and good judges think it cannot hold together long. The superstructures erected thereon are tottering and falling, threatening to envelop the occupants in total ruin. Many of the inhabitants of the secession district are, like Southern Yankees, moving northward where things are more stable.

But while secession movements are unsettling everything in the south, the "more perfect union" at the north stands firm. Two stone fire-proof stores bid defiance to the devouring element. Two clothing stores provide for the wants of the outer man, while five provision stores make good provision for his interior, and provide him with mining implements and other necessary articles. Three hotels and two restaurants cater to the appetites of citizens and strangers, two expressmen and four barbers get a good living by shaving, two limbs of the law profit by the moral ills of man, and three disciples Esculapius relieve his physical ailments. Two bakers furnish the staff of life, and fourteen grogsellers life itself. Five shoemakers, armed with hammer and lapstone, pegs, flax and bristles, labor industriously to produce a good understanding in the neighborhood. Two German tailors, grow fat upon cabbage, as Germans and tailors generally do. Six sons of Vulcan smite at the anvil, do dirty work, and make clean money. One watchmaker teaches how to go upon tick, an art the people are not slow to learn. Five billiard and gaming saloons furnish recreation, and some of them show greenhorns that "here's the place to get your money back." Two livery stables contain fast horses for the use of fast men. Two tinmen make tinware for the tin and sell hardware for hard money. Two druggists sell pukes and physics, paints and perfumes; also sarsaparilla which cures all the diseases flesh is heir to, except coughs, colds and consumption, and they are abundantly provided for with their Cherry Pectoral. Over 40 Free Masons scribe their acts by the compass and measure them with the square. More than 60 Odd Fellows teach the duty of relieving the distressed, visiting the sick, burying the dead, comforting the afflicted, assisting the widow, and educating the orphan. Over 100 Sons of Temperance, under the banner of Love, Purity and Fidelity, are loud in their praises of cold water, and severe in their denunciation of grog. One Methodist preacher expounds the gospel to an average congregation of about 50 persons, and administers the emblems of the Savior's body and blood to about 20 communicants. One school teacher labors assiduously to teach the young ideas of 40 or 50 scholars how to shoot. One musician tries equally hard to teach how to sing. Two justices gravely explain what is the law, and one sheriff and two constables attend to its execution. The hammer of the auctioneer strikes one, two, three—everything is going, going.

YANKEE JIM S.

Gold was first discovered at Yankee Jim's by Yankee Jim, a Sydneyite, who built a corral in 1849 upon the flat or bench of land where the town afterwards was located, and now stands. The name, Yankee Jim's, has often caused the town to be mistaken for the locality known to early pioneers as "Yankee Jim's Dry Diggings," which latter place is a gulch which heads at the Forest Shades Hotel and empties into the Middle Fork of the American River. A few logs of the old cabin in which Yankee Jim lived during the winter of '49, may yet be seen at the "Gardens," about one half mile east of Forest Hill, where he lived and mined, using the corral at Yankee Jim's to hide his stolen horses until he could get an opportunity to run them from the neighborhood. This notorious character's real name was Robinson. He suffered the extreme penalty of the law, for horse-stealing, in 1852, in one of the lower counties, and the State was thus relieved of his ravages.

Among the first permanent settlers of Yankee Jim's, were B. F. Gilbert, G. W. Gilbert, N. F. Gilbert, and Thomas Farthing, all of whom are yet residents of the place, and continue their vocation as miners, in which they have ever been successful. These gentlemen were emigrants from the State of Missouri, and drove an ox team into Yankee Jim's early in the fall of 1850, loaded with their winter's provisions, mining tools, clothing, etc., it being the first wheeled vehicle that ever came to the place. A short time after the arrival of the Gilbert brothers and their companions, a store was started by Thomas Adams, James Cartwright, and Ben. Thomas, a company of Tennesseeans, who came from Illinoistown, with a large stock of miner's supplies.

Soon after the store was established and the settlers had prepared themselves suitable cabins for the winter, operations in mining commenced in Devil's Cañon and the gulches emptying into it, which, proving very remunerative and easily worked, caused large numbers of miners from surrounding camps to flock to the spot, and soon the place grew to a large town—what gamblers were wont to call a brisk place. In the month of June, 1852, the place was almost totally destroyed by fire ; but was again rebuilt, and in the fall of that year, rivalled in size any town in the county. The *Placer Herald* of September, in giving a partial history of the place, at that time, says : "The town is nearly as large as any in the county, and contains several fine buildings that will compare favorably with any structures in this part of the State."

In March, 1851, the diggings on Georgia Hill, opposite the town on the south side of Devil's Cañon, were discovered by a company of Georgians. The discovery of this rich deposit of gold was purely accidental, and is said to have occurred in the following manner : The discoverers were four in number ; were unsuccessful gold-seekers, on their return from a prospecting expedition in the mountains above Yankee Jim's, and were making their way slowly to some of the old camps in El Dorado County, with the intention of going to work in some of the old dry diggings. After passing Yankee Jim's, and reaching the top of the hill, one of them vowed he would proceed no further until he had rested ; and, throwing his blankets, tools, etc., upon the ground, he laid down in the shade of a tree to rest. The others of the party proceeded a few yards, and also came to a halt, to rest themselves and wait until their companion got ready to proceed upon their weary journey. While lying upon the ground, the one who first stopped discovered particles of gold upon the surface. Informing his companions of his discovery, they returned to the place, and, in a few minutes, the wash-pans were filled with dirt, and each of the prospectors proceeded to the cañon to wash it. The result of the washing was ascertained, and the supposition among them was that the gold had been lost or buried there by somebody, and scattered by the gophers ; but the washing of a number of pans of the dirt from different places, with equally good results, soon convinced them that the deposit was natural, and sufficiently extensive to warrant them in locating, and working the claims. The diggings thus discovered were the richest surface diggings, perhaps, ever discovered in the State. The discoverers made large fortunes, and it is said that when the party left the place for their native State, a few months after, they loaded these mules with clean gold dust. The claims changed hands several times, the purchasers each time paying large sums for them, and each party thus purchasing, made money by their investment, until the claim was worked out.

It is claimed that the first ditch ever cut to convey water upon a mining claim from a cañon in this State, was constructed by H. Starr and Eugene Phelps, at Yankee Jim's, in 1851, to convey the water from Devil's Cañon to wash the dirt upon their claims, in a "Long Tom." It is known to be the first ditch of any extent cut in the county, and, we doubt not, is the pioneer one in the State. Hydraulic washing was first introduced at Yankee Jim's, in June, 1853, by Col. Wm. McClure, who had heard of this mode of washing being practiced in Nevada County, and being a large stockholder in a ditch which was then supplying the diggings in that neighborhood with water, he traveled to Nevada to witness the operations by this mode, and upon his return to Yankee Jim's procured hose, built a "telegraph," and put the first hydraulic claim in operation.

Colonel McClure is also the pioneer fruit-grower in the eastern part of Placer County. He purchased his trees in Philadelphia, in the fall of 1852.

They were shipped around Cape Horn, and arrived in time to be planted in his orchard in March, 1853. His first planting consisted of about five hundred trees of all kinds.

Many important events have occurred at Yankee Jim's, which the limited space allowed for this sketch preclude the possibility of their receiving even a passing notice ; the object of the sketch being more to relate facts which are valuable as being a part of the history of the place worthy of preservation, rather than to write a thrilling story. The brief mention therefore made of each occurrence, it is hoped, will be considered sufficient to answer the purpose designed by the writer.

During the flush times of Yankee Jim's, which, as has been shown, was from the winter of 1851–'52 until 1855, the place was not exempt from those popular outbreaks of the people, which, in the early days of California, occasionally occurred in almost every town of any note, where desperate characters congregate, and where daring deeds of violence were committed. During the time mentioned, there were a number of men killed in fights and street brawls, and one or two persons charged with murder, or theft or both, hung by the people. But these matters do not compose any part of the history of the place which should be preserved, but rather should be forgotten, and such scenes never re-enacted where the semblance of civilization exists, particular mention of them is omitted.

The first newspaper printed at Yankee Jim's, the *Mountain Courier*, was published during the winter of 1856–'57, by Messrs. Parker and Graves. It was continued three months, and died for want of patronage On the 4th of July, 1857, E. B. Boust issued from the same office the first number of the *Placer Courier*, which was continued by him until November, 1858, when he was succeeded by R. J. Steele, who issued the paper regularly in that place until April of the following year, when the office was removed by him to Forest Hill, where its publication has been continued by him and his successor to the present time.

Although Yankee Jim's has gradually decreased in importance since 1856, yet its downfall is not attributable so much to the failure of the mines as to the building up of towns immediately adjacent. Since that time the trade has been diverted from it to Forest Hill, and Todd's Valley, leaving it dependent solely upon the mines in that immediate locality for the support of its trading population. The wealth and trade of the place is not lost, but merely transferred to a more favored locality. There are now being worked at Yankee Jim's a number of hydraulic claims, which yield large amounts of gold, and will last for a number of years.

DEADWOOD.

The town of Deadwood is situated upon a high narrow ridge of land, or promontory it might be called, high up in the Sierra Nevada Mountains, in the eastern part of Placer County, between El Dorado Cañon on the north, and the north fork of the Middle Fork of the American River on the southeast, at an altitude of 4,000 feet above the level of the sea.

The town is isolated, the country surrounding it not admitting of any settlements nearer than El Dorado Cañon and Michigan Bluff on one side, and Devil's Basin and Last Chance, on the other. There is no wagon road leading to the town from the valleys and settlements below, except that leading up the main divide by the Forks House and Secret Springs, and around the head of El Dorado Cañon, and down the narrow ridge, to the town, making a circuit of some seventy miles from Michigan Bluff to reach the town, seven miles distant. There is a good trail leading across the cañon from Michigan Bluff to Deadwood and Last Chance, over which the supplies of the settlers are transported on the backs of mules.

Mining at Deadwood is carried on extensively by both tunneling and by the hydraulic process ; and the yield of gold is considerably more than the average yield for the same amount of labor performed in the generality of mining settlements. The number of inhabitants amount probably to 160 or 175. The mines are supplied with an abundance of water, by means of ditches brought from the cañons, and the people are independent, prosperous, and happy.

The name of the place originated from this circumstance : "Deadwood" is a California provincialism, and signifies a sure thing. In 1852, some miners found a rich prospect here, and exclaimed "though unsuccessful hitherto, we have now got the *Deadwood.*" Other miners flocked into the place, a town was built and christened Deadwood. The sides of the ridge upon which it stands are so steep, that rocks rolled from the top in some places would continue their motion until they reached the bed of El Dorado Creek on the one side, or of the north fork of the Middle Fork of the American River on the other, a mile distant from the place where they were set in motion. In the wet season, when the warm rains are falling in the valleys below, the falling moisture is here precipitated in the form of snow, which sometimes falls to a great depth. About Christmas of the present winter, (1860), we had one of those terrible snow storms which annually fall upon the snowy mountains, and as is usual every winter with such storms, its history is a history of great suffering and loss of life.

On the 24th day of December, Mr. David Davis and Mr. John Williams left Deadwood, for the purpose of attending to a ditch, which brings water into town from a cañon some miles higher up in the mountains. Snow was falling when they left, and continued to fall until the ground over which the ditch runs was covered to a depth of six feet. They were never seen alive afterwards. The body of Mr. Williams was found twelve days after he left, in the ditch, where it is supposed he had sunk exhausted. He had lain himself upon his back, folded his arms upon his breast, and given himself up to die. But the savage coyotes had found the body before human eyes had rested upon it, and by their tracks had directed the persons in search to his snowy bed. Their voracious appetites had been glutted upon the flesh of the face and hands and other parts of the body which were not covered by the clothes. The Masonic fraternity, of which he was a worthy member, took charge of the body, removed it to his place of residence, and respectfully committed it to its final resting place.

The body of Mr. Davis still remains undiscovered, securely hid from human view ; wrapped in a heavy mantle of snow, it will probably sleep quietly where it lies, until the powerful rays of an April sun remove its covering, and point out the dying bed, unless the wild beasts previously scent it, and appropriate it to themselves.

But while these unfortunate individuals were struggling for dear life in the snow, or their bodies sleeping quietly beneath it, a more thrilling, but fortunately not fatal scene, was transpiring at Deadwood.

On one side of the hill, about 80 rods from town, stood the house of Mr. A. J. Felch. Two live oaks on the lower side afforded a sure foundation for the sleepers upon which the floor was laid, while their spreading branches shut out from the verandah the oppressive rays of a summer's sun. A stream of pure mountain water gurgled at the door, conducted from a spring near by. Thirty or forty rods higher up the mountain side, runs a ditch, which conveys water for mining purposes. Mr. Felch's family consists of himself, wife, and Willy, a sprightly little boy about eight years of age. Fortunately Mrs. Felch was at the time at Michigan Bluff, receiving medical treatment for her eyes, in consequence of which, she was not in the house. It is now Christmas eve. The snow covers the ground to the depth of several feet, clings in huge masses to the leaves and branches of the evergreens, and fills the air with the large feathery flakes which are rapidly falling. The wind whistles through the trees—the swollen rivulet near by, roars over its rocky bed, and masses of falling snow from the trees ever and anon splash upon the roof. But the father and son are comfortably seated, each in a chair, by the warm stove, Willy with his feet on the hearth. "Come, Willy," says Mr. Felch, "you had better hang up your stockings, and go to bed, and perhaps Santa Claus will bring you something before morning." "O, I know what you want!" says Willy; "you want to get me to bed, and then you will put something into my stockings." "Why, it is late as you generally sit up, Willy." "Yes, but I'll bet that when I get up to-morrow morning, I shall find a candy rooster or something else in my stockings, that you have put there."

These were the last words spoken. In a moment afterwards, quick as thought, crash went the house. Another moment, and Mr. Felch found himself in the open air, up to his waist in the snow, the tempest roaring around him, and volumes of snow and water rushing down the mountain side. "Where am I!" "Is this a dream, or a reality?" thought Mr. Felch. It seemed to him, he says, as though he had just returned to a state of consciousness, from a state of insensibility. He looked all around to see where he was, not noticing the gash on his head, nor the bruise on his shoulder, which afterwards told that the falling timbers had struck him. There stood the live oaks—there is the mountain side—there the canon? This must be the very place where my house stood. But where is my boy? Carried off into the canon by an avalanche along with the house. "William! William! William!" No answer. O, what an anxious moment was that, to that father! From the position of the oaks which stood by the side of the house, he calculated the place which his boy occupied before the catastrophe; there he commenced digging with his hands in the snow, Two men living near by, having heard the crash, soon came to his assistance. The work of removing the snow from the spot designated, now progressed rapidly. Calls were made to the boy, but no answer was returned. A few moments will tell whether he is carried off into the canon along with the beds, trunks, dishes, furniture, and wreck of the house; whether his body lies lifeless and mutilated beneath the snow, or whether he is buried alive with the avalanche. "William! William!" "Sir!" was faintly responded from beneath the snow. "Thank the Lord! the boy's alive;" was the heartfelt response of the father. A moment after, two strong arms pulled him from his snowy bed uninjured, although the chair upon which he had sat, and the stove upon the hearth of which were placed his feet, were broken to pieces. "William, are you hurt?" said Mr. Newell. "No! but my pa is gone, sure!" was the reply of the noble little boy. The question now arose, whether they should go into the tunnel and stay. there till morning, or endeavor to wade through the snow, up the hill, to town. The latter course was decided upon, and half an hour later, they were in a warm house, in the hospitable town of Deadwood, receiving the congratulations of the people that the whole family had escaped with so little injury from the avalanche, which had swept the house and its contents into the canon.

BATH.

The settlement at Bath was first made in the summer of 1850, by a man named John Bradford, a merchant, at that time doing business at Stony Bar. His attention was first drawn to the place by the excellent pasturage it furnished for his mules, and the beauty of the location for a stock ranch. He therefore built a cabin in which to reside and store his goods upon their arrival from Sacramento in wagons, to be packed to the store at Stony Bar as they were required or as occasion served, and also built a brush fence around the cove, claiming it as a ranch. Some time during the fall of the year 1850, the place attracted the attention of some miners from the Middle Fork of the American River, who purchased the place of Bradford for a small sum, and located there for the winter, intending to hunt deer, and mine in the dry gulches which debouch into Volcano Cañon. Among this party was D. P. Marshall, and Thomas Creagh, who are now residents of Forest Hill. By this party gold was discovered in the gulches, and, gradually, as the news of the existence of gold in paying quantities became known, miners flocked to the place and formed a settlement, and who dignified the place by giving it the name of Volcano.

The following year, in consequence of the discovery of rich "hill diggings" by the Blakeman brothers, who located the "Mint Drop" claims, and by Isaac Snodgrass, who took up the "Snodgrass claims," large numbers of miners flocked to the place, and rapidly built up a town. There being another town of the same name on the opposite side of the Middle Fork of the American River, at that time of equal importance, and considerably its senior, it was thought proper to change its name, which was done at a town meeting, called for the purpose, and it was afterwards known as Sarahsville, which name was given it in honor of the wife of a man called "Blaze." Her christian name being Sarah, and she being the first lady settler of the place, the gallant pioneers considered the place honored by bearing her name. Early in January, 1858, the citizens of Sarahsville conceived the idea of having a Postoffice at that place; a town meeting was called, the name of the place changed from Sarahsville to Bath; a petition drawn up and numerously signed, asking the Postoffice Department to establish a Postoffice at the town, was immmediately forwarded; and in a short time a weekly mail route was established from Yankee Jim's to Bath, which had the effect of rendering the new name permanent if the town itself was not.

2

From this time, owing to the rapid growth of Forest Hill, a flourishing camp, one mile and a half distant, Bath commenced to decrease in population and importance, until at the present time it is but a small village, boasting of one hotel, one store, a butcher's shop, one blacksmith's shop, and one saloon. The mines, however, are rich, and will continue to support its present, and perhaps an increased population, for a number of years. It is a pleasant place to live, and a large number of the miners have located there with their families, and appear perfectly satisfied with it as a permanent home.

DUTCH FLAT.

Dutch Flat is situated in the north-eastern part of Placer county, upon the ridge which divides the waters of Bear river from those of the North Fork of the American. The first permanent settlement at this place was made in the spring of 1851, by Joseph Doranbach. The name "Dutch" is derived perhaps from the nationality of the gentleman who has the honor of being called the pioneer settler of the place, and those who were his companions at the time ; but it is difficult to conceive of why "Flat" should be added to the word "Dutch," in giving the name to the then embryo town, except it is to fully carry out and demonstrate the Californian custom of perverting names.

Of the early history of Dutch Flat, but little is known that would be considered of very great interest to the general reader, except that the place was considered, in 1854, by persons then thought to be visionary individuals, of sufficient importance as a mining locality to warrant the construction of a water ditch, to convey the waters of Bear river upon the tops of the ridges for mining purposes. The commencement of operations upon the ditch known as the "Placer County Canal," gave quite an impetus to the settlement of the place, and it continued to increase in population and importance until, at the completion of the ditch, in May, 1859, it was about the fifth town in the county in population. Since the completion of the Placer County Canal, the Bartlett & Thomas ditch, and other ditches which convey water into the mines in the vicinity, the town has steadily increased in population until its voting population is greater than any other town in the county—the number of votes polled at the Presidential election in 1860 amounting to five hundred and one.

On the 29th day of May, 1860, the first number of the "*Dutch Flat Enquirer*," a weekly newspaper, was issued, and is yet continued, seemingly well supported. The town may now be said to be in a flourishing condition, and with a prospect of growing in size and importance. According to the last census returns, Dutch Flat contained nearly one-tenth of the whole population of the county. There are in the town and its surroundings 140 families, 7 provision and grocery stores, 17 saloons, 8 clothing and dry goods stores, 2 breweries, 3 blacksmith shops, 2 hardware stores, 2 tin shops, 2 hotels, 1 drug store ; also a carpenter shop, a cabinet shop, a restaurant, 2 butcher stalls, a bakery, 3 schools and a church.

The mineral resources of Dutch Flat are extensive, and the product of the gold mines in the vicinity probably amounting to about $20,000 per week, including the diggings at Lost Camp. The mining is principally carried on by the hydraulic process; the supply of water furnished by the ditches being ample to enable a large number of men to keep constantly employed the year round upon their claims. The yield of gold is steady and remunerative to the operatives.

A company was organized the present year, called the "Lake Pass Turnpike Company," which has in contemplation the construction of a turnpike road from Dutch Flat to Virginia City, Utah Territory, by the way of Lake Pass. The completion of this road, it is expected, will add much to the future prosperity and importance of the place, it being claimed by its friends as the lowest pass in the Sierra Nevada Mountains, the easiest grade and the shortest route that a road can be run from Sacramento to the Washoe silver region, and intersecting with the Great Central Overland Emigrant Road.

Dutch Flat is situated high up in the mountains, is surrounded with extensive forests of excellent timber for building purposes; has numerous springs of excellent water, and the timber for fuel abundant and convenient. In consequence of its elevated position, the town is regarded as a pleasant place for a summer residence; and the snows never fall to such great depth as to prevent travel to and from the place for a great length of time during the winter season.

TANYARDS.

In our general statistics of the county, we purposely omitted giving any notice of this branch of the mechanical pursuits of the people of the county, as we intended to give the only tanyard in the county more than a passing notice. Observing that saw mills, water ditches, turnpike roads, toll bridges, quartz mills, etc., formed the main feature of the report of the County Assessor of this county, and no mention whatever was made of this important branch of industry, we think it worthy of more than a passing notice.

The Iowa Hill Tanyard is situated upon Indian Cañon, about two and a half miles above Iowa Hill. Although it might be considered a small concern, yet the proprietor, JOHN RUTHERFORD, being himself a tanner and currier, informed us that he was fully satisfied, from past experience in the business, that he can make the business at that place self-sustaining. He states that with his present facilities he can turn out two thousand sides of sole and harness leather per annum; and can furnish leather to customers at a small advance upon prices paid for a similar article in the markets of the Eastern States.

Spruce, balsam and oak barks are used by the proprietor in tanning, a sufficient supply of which can be had in the forests contiguous for a number of years to come, even should the business increase to twenty times the capacity of the yard at the present time.

This experiment in the tanning business in Placer county, when found to be successful, as it must, cannot fail to draw the attention of tanners and induce them to enter into the business upon a more extensive scale, and eventually check the present extensive exportation of hides from, and importation of leather in return to this State. Hides can be procured at a low price; bark is easily obtained convenient to the yard; natural water exists in the cañon in great plenty, and there is nothing that one can conceive of except the high price of mechanics' wages to prevent the manufacture of leather in that locality as cheap as in any part of the United States.

OPHIR.

In the fall of 1850, a log cabin comprised the prospective town of Ophir, situated two and a-half miles below Auburn, on the Auburn Ravine, which during the succeeding winter grew into the fair proportions of three or four frame buildings, several log houses (?) and an indefinite number of tents and canvas coverings. The summer of 1851 nearly skeletonized the little village, but the fall and winter rains resurrected, or recreated it, and the year 1852 saw it the largest and most prosperous town in Placer county. The mining was all of placer character, and very rich ; and money was had almost for the picking it up. The town flourished. At the Presidential election of that year 500 votes were cast in the precinct.

On the 12th of July, 1852, the whole town was consumed by fire. Although great efforts were made, Ophir never recovered from the shock. The surface diggings were deemed nearly worked out, and it was thought she had no other resources. Other points below her on the Auburn Ravine came into notice, and drew away her population and means. She presents now to the eye but the shadow of her former appearance.

A not very distant future may, and not very unlikely will, reinstate Ophir in her former glory. The quartz in the district is rich, and its value is being rapidly developed. Quartz mills are springing up all round the place, and quartz mining promises soon to be the principal business of that section.

CHURCHES AND SOCIETIES.

CHURCHES.

Methodist Episcopal Church of Auburn, organized in June, 1852, by Rev. James Hunter, P. C., and Rev. J. D. Blain, P. E. Present Pastor, Rev. N. R. Peck. Number of members, 15. Cost of church building and furnishing same, about $4,000.

The Sunday School of the M. E. Church of Auburn was organized in October, 1852, by Rev. James Hunter. Present number of members, 93 ; average attendance, about 40 ; number of volumes in the library, 600 ; No. of teachers, 7. The officers for the year 1861 are :

H. HAZELL...*Superintendent.*
J. R. CRANDALL...*Assistant Superintendent.*
H. N. CUMINGS...*Librarian.*
MISS JANE ELLIOTT..*Chorister.*

The Methodist Episcopal Church of Dutch Flat was organized in 1857 ; Rev. G. B. Hinckle, P. C., and Rev. S. B. Simonds, P. E. Present Pastor, Rev. T. H. McGrath ; present P. E., Rev. J. B. Fish ; number of members, 40 ; cost of church building and furnishing the same, about $3,500 ; completed April, 1861 ; cost of Parsonage, $600.

The Sunday School denominated the M. E. Sunday School of Dutch Flat, was organized on the 13th of September, 1857. No. of registered names of scholars, 75 ; average attendance, 40 ; No. of teachers, 8.

H. DAVIS...*Superintendent.*
NICHOLS BOKE..*Assistant Superintendent.*

The Library contains 500 volumes. School in a growing and healthy condition.

MASONS.

GOLD HILL LODGE, No. 32, F. AND A. M., was organized May 5, 1853 ; 19 Master Masons ; regular time of stated meetings : First Saturday in each month.

LIST OF OFFICER :

JAMES E. STUART.. *W. M.*
HENRY W. STARR... *S. W.*
JULIUS MALSH .... *J. W.*
SAM. McCLURE... *T.*
ISAAC STONECIPHER... *S.*
D. V. MASON.. *S. D.*
L. B. DANIELS.. *J. D.*
M. WALDRON... *Tyler.*

EUREKA LODGE, No. 16, F. AND A. M., of Auburn, was chartered in 1851. The officers for 1861 are :

E. H. VAN DECAR. .... *W. Master.*
BENJ. C. ALLEN.. *S. Warden.*
ALVIN S. HIGGINS .... *J. Warden.*
JNO. C. BOGGS.. *Treasurer.*
GEORGE JOHNSON... *Secretary.*
THOS. P. HARPER }
PETER HARRISON } .... *Stewards.*
E. G. SMITH.. .... *Tyler.*

Regular meetings : Monday of each month, or preceding the full moon of each month. Number of Master Masons, 42.

DELTA CHAPTER ROYAL ARCH MASONS, U. D. The officers for 1861 are :

E. H. VAN DECAR.. *H. P.*
BENJ. F. MYERS... *K.*
HENRY GOODING.. *S.*
D. C. SCOTT... *C. of H.*
J. R. CRANDALL... *P. S.*
WM. WELD.. *R. A. C.*
WM. TIMSON... *M. 3d V.*
A. SPINKS.. *M. 2d V.*
L. KULLMAN... *M. 1st V.*
JAS. E. STEWART.. *Treasurer.*
H. R. HAWKINS.. *Secretary.*
E. G. SMITH... *Guard.*

Thirty R. A. Masons.

CLAY LODGE, No. 101, F. AND A. MASONS.—Chartered May 8, A. D. 1859, A. L. 5856. Night of regular meetings : Saturday of, or next preceding full moon ; number of members, 37 ; location of Hall, Main street, Dutch Flat, frame building ; cost of Hall, fitting up and furnishing, about $4,500. Officers of present term :

S. B. HARRIMAN .... W. M.
THOS. PATTINSON..S. W.
L. D. KOPP...J. W.
E. L. BRADLEY..Treasurer.
B. F. MOORE...Secretary.
J. S. BLOOM..S. D.
J. C. LILLIE...J. D.
J. MOULTER... Tyler.
L. D. KOPP   ⎫
B. F. MOORE ⎭ ....Past Masters.

Have a Masonic Library, for members and others.

RISING STAR LODGE, No. 83, F. AND A. M., at Todd's Valley, was organized in 1856. Officers of the present term :

JOSEPH S. FOLLANSBEE.. W. M.
N. BENEDICT.. S. W.
H. OTT..J. W.
S. S. WILLARD.. Treasurer.
R. O. CRAVINS... Secretary.
W. R. LONGLY... S. D.
J. F. SMITH...J. D.
A. BAKER,   ⎫
P. POWELL. ⎭ .... Stewards.
G. W. DECKER... Marshal.
W. S. SHIELDS.. Tyler.

OLIVER CHAPTER, No. 23, F. AND A. M., at Todd's Valley, was instituted May 6, 1859. The officers for the present term are :

J. W. HARVILLE... M. E. H. P.
G. W. DECKER. ....E. K.
N. BENEDICT...E. S.
W. R. LONGLY...C. H.
JOSEPH S. FOLLANSBEE..................................P S.
J. R. GLOVER..R. A. C.
T. N. HOSMER.. M. 2d V.
J. M. MINER... M. 3d V.

I. O. OF O. F.

OLIVE LODGE No. 81.—Instituted December 8, A. D. 1858 ; meets in Masonic Hall each Wednesday night ; number of members, 36. Officers of present term :

L. GROSS ....N. G.
JNO. BOKE..V. G.
B. F. MOORE..R. Secretary.
M. DAVIS..Per. Secretary.
R. HUDEPOHL..Treasurer.
REV. T. H. McGRATH.....................................Chaplain.
N. W. BLANCHARD, ⎫
P. B. HOLMES,   ⎪
A. HART,   ⎬ ....Past Grands.
E. B. BOUST,   ⎭

AUBURN LODGE, No. 7, I. O. O. F., was instituted October 2, 1852 ; night of meeting, Saturday ; number of members, 70 ; location of Hall, Washington street, Auburn ; brick building ; cost of Hall, fitting up and furnishing, $5,000. Officers of present term :

S. B. WOODIN..*N. G.*
C. T. PALMER..*V. G.*
E. D. TUTTLE.... ....*R. S.*
ISAAC B. LEACH...*P. S.*
H. STONE..*Treasurer.*
J. L. BROWNE..*J. P. G.*
H. HAZELL.................................*D. D. G. M. of District No. 4.*
H. HAZELL,
THOS. JAMISON, } ....*Trustees.*
JACOB FELDBERG,

AUBURN ENCAMPMENT, No. 20, I. O. O. F.—Instituted July 10, 1860 ; nights of meeting, first and third Tuesdays of each month ; number of members, 18. Officers of present term :

S. B. WOODIN........ ....*C. P.*
T. B. HARPER...*H. P.*
J. B. LANGDON..*S. W.*
N. DODSWORTH..*J. W.*
W. TOWLE ....*Scribe.*
C. T. PALMER...*Treasurer.*
J. L. BROWNE...... ....*P. C. P.*
H. HAZELL..*P. H. P.*

ODD FELLOWS' LIBRARY ASSOCIATION, organized January, 1861 ; present number of volumes about 100, and about $100 in Library Fund. Library Committee : J. L. Browne, H. Hazell, Wm. Towle. This Association is not confined exclusively to the members of the order, but will be accessible to all persons, on liberal terms. At present located in Odd Fellows' Hall.

MINERVA LODGE, No. —, I. O. O. F., at Todd's Valley, was instituted March 20, 1856. The officers for the present term are :

W, H. BALL...*N. G.*
J. B. RUSSELL...*V. G.*
WILLET WAKEMAN...*Secretary.*
A. B. BROWN..*P. S.*
J. R. WILLY..*Treasurer.*

THREE PILLAR ENCAMPMENT, No. 16, I. O. O. F., at Todd's Valley, was instituted January 16, 1859. Officers for present term :

H. LONG..*C. P.*
H. M. CONSTABLE..*S. W.*
J. B. RUSSELL...*Scribe.*
UGO GOBEL..*Treasurer.*
N. BAKER..*J. W.*

I. O. OF G. T.

NEW YEAR LODGE, No. 14.—Instituted December 27, 1860, by D. S. Cutter, D. G. W. C. T. Time of meeting, every Wednesday evening, in

Sons of Temperance Hall, Auburn; number of members, 31. Officers of the present term:

R. C. POLAND... *W. C. T.*
MRS. H. J. CRANDALL.. *W. V. T.*
H. HAZELL... *W. R. S.*
B. R. WELLS.. *W. T.*
MRS. MINNIE FRENCH... *W. F. S.*
MRS. A. E. GUIOU...*D. D. G. W. C. T.*

SONS OF TEMPERANCE.

VIRGINIA TEMPLE OF HONOR, No. 15, was organized in Gold Hill, on the 12th day of April, 1855, by Ben. E. S. Ely, D. G. W. T., with 16 charter members. The present officers are:

J. A. BOND.. *W. C. T.*
WM. HILTON.. *W. V. T.*
H. W. STARR.. *W. R.*
H. GREEN.. *W. A. R.*
J. MORRIS.. *W. F. R.*
I. J. UNDERWOOD... *W. T.*
L. E. HARRIS.. *W. W.*
W. M. WINTERS.. *W. D. W.*
E. ROSS... *W. G.*
A. P. HENDON... *W. S.*

Whole number of members 24.

AUBURN DIVISION, No. 25, S. OF T.—Instituted October 24, 1859; time of meeting, every Friday evening; location of Hall, on the hill near the Court House; number of members, 25; cost of building and furnishing, about $475; building wood. Officers for the present quarter:

J. R. CRANDALL... *W. P.*
S. G. ELLIOTT.. *W. A.*
H. HAZELL... *R. S.*
WM. K. PARKINSON.. *A. R. S.*
CHARLES BAYARD.. *F. S.*
C. W. FINLEY... *Treasurer.*
THOMAS JAMISON.. *P. W. P.*
J. R. CRANDALL... *D. D. W. P.*

BEN FRANKLIN DIVISION, No. 212, meets in Masonic Hall each Friday night; organized November 14, 1859; number of members, 75. Officers of the present quarter:

N. W. BLANCHARD.. *W. P.*
M. H. CALDERWOOD.. *W. A.*
GEO. CASSIDAY.. *R. S.*
J. L. HERBERT... *A. R. S.*
N. MENTING... *F. S.*
J. S. COLGROVE... *Treasurer.*
R. SPEAK.. *C.*
J. H. BURKE.. *A. C.*
HENRY LILLY... *I. G.*
A. BRANDER.. *O. G.*
T. H. McGRATH.. *Chaplain.*
W. H. HARRIMAN... *A. P. W. P.*
H. DAVIS... *D. D. W. P.*

TODD'S VALLEY DIVISION, No. 111, S. of T.   Officers :

GEO. GRAY .... *W. P.*
WM. HOUSTON .... *W. A.*
P. Y. BAKER .... *R. S.*
C. MARKS .... *A. R. S.*
A. LONGLY .... *Treasurer.*
B. WOODARD .... *C.*
S. JOHNSON .... *A. C.*
WM. BROWN .... *Chaplain.*

HISTORICAL SKETCH OF PLACER COUNTY.

The County of Placer was organized by act of the Legislature approved April 25th, 1851.   Its boundaries are described in said act, as follows :
"Beginning on the Sacramento River at the northwest corner of Sacramento County, and running thence up the middle of said river, to a point ten miles below the junction of Sacramento and Feather rivers ; thence in a northerly direction in a straight line to a point in the middle of Bear Creek, opposite Camp Far West ; thence up the middle of said creek, to its source ; thence due east to the State line ; thence southerly on the State line to the north-easterly corner of El Dorado County ; thence westerly on the northerly line of El Dorado County to the junction of the North and South Forks of the American River ; thence westerly on the northerly line of Sacramento County to the place of beginning."
The act of the Legislature also fixed the county seat at Auburn.   The first election for county and township officers of Placer County took place on the 26th of May, 1851, which resulted in the choice of the following gentlemen to fill the various county offices : H. Fitzsimmons, County Judge ; Samuel C. Astin, Sheriff ; R. D. Hopkins, District Attorney ; James T. Stewart, Clerk ; Alfred Louis, Assessor ; Douglas Bingham, Treasurer ; A. Bronk, Public Administrator.   Of the number of votes cast at this election, we can obtain no authentic account.   The vote at some of the camps and towns, however, was surprisingly large ; especially at precincts which had started one or two favored individuals who aspired to official honors.   The election was contested by several of the defeated candidates, but by the death of one of the contestants, and compromises made between the remaining contestants and their more fortunate opponents, the incumbents were permitted to hold the positions to which they had received certificates of election, for the remainder of their terms in peace.
The first settlements in Placer County were made at an early period of the golden era, and many places became famous for the rich gold deposits discovered in their vicinity.   In the summer of 1848, the principal tributaries of the American River were explored by a company of Oregonians, and rich prospects obtained upon almost every bar, as far up the Middle and North Forks as they proceeded.   At this time the bars were generally explored as high up the Middle Fork as Rector's Bar, which, proving as rich as any dig-

gings the explorers expected to find, and it being difficult to travel further up the river with horses, they ceased traveling, and worked the mines until the winter season sat in, or their provisions gave out, when they returned to the settlements in the valley, or to their homes in Oregon.

Early in 1849, the system of washing the auriferous dirt with the common rocker was introduced upon the Middle Fork of the American River, and was regarded as a great improvement in gold mining. During this year, miners flocked to the bars upon the rivers in large numbers, from the "Old Dry Diggings" (Placerville), "Sutter's Mill" (Coloma), the settlements in the valleys, and elsewhere; wheresoever the news of the rich discoveries had reached, contributed laborers for the gold fields, and during the summer, settlements were formed in many parts of Placer County, including Auburn and Ophir, in the foot hills; Rector's Bar, Stony Bar, Oregon Bar, and Poverty Bar, on the Middle Fork; and Barnes' Bar, on the North Fork of the American. The population upon the rivers was quite sparse, and depredations were frequently committed by the untamed savages upon the stock and camps of the whites.

During the winter of 1849–'50, the population of the now rich and populous townships 5 and 6, consisted of Dr. Todd and three or four companions, at "Todd's Ranch;" Yankee Jim and his companions, six in number, at Yankee Jim's Dry Diggings, near where Forest Hill is situated; six young men, one of whom was named Lewis, near the head of Mad Canon; two men at Bird's store; and about thirty persons at Stony and Rector's Bars. The whole white population in the two townships mentioned, amounted to not more than fifty persons.

The hardships endured by the few individuals who remained upon the river at Stony and Rector's Bars during the memorable winter of 1849–'50, can never be half told. The writer of this sketch, being one of the unfortunate individuals whose reduced fortunes forced him to remain upon the river, at Stony Bar, in order that he might eke out a scanty subsistence by working in the banks and on the high bars, when a temporary cessation of the falling rain and snow permitted him to venture forth from the canvas tent which served him and his companions as a winter dwelling, cannot, at this day, after a lapse of more than ten years, repress a shudder, when revolving in his mind the many incidents attending his residence during that winter, upon the Middle Fork.

The rains, which had set in towards the last of December, continued to fall almost constantly until the second week in February, covering the mountains on either side of the stream to the depth of four feet with snow, blocking up the trails, and so completely destroying every trace of them, that none, except in the last extremity, could be prevailed upon to venture to break a trail to Georgetown or Coloma, the nearest points at which supplies could be obtained. To add to the hardships of the little settlement of pioneer river miners, they not only had not comfortable houses in which to live, but ere the winter was half gone, their supplies of flour, pork, coffee, sugar, salt, beans, etc., were totally exhausted, and they were reduced to the necessity of living upon fresh venison, without salt or bread. But starvation was not the foe most to be dreaded by the unprotected settlement. The temporary shanties, or huts of the men were scattered along the river for a distance of two miles; in each of which lived from two to five persons. No guard was kept at night, and in case of an attack by the Indians, the men, scattered and poorly armed, as they were, could have offered but a feeble resistance. The heavy snows, higher up in the mountains, had forced a band of Indians to venture down the canons to the vicinity of the camp of the whites, in search of horses, mules, cattle, or any thing else which could serve as food for their starving squaws and children. They were discovered by the whites, and a meeting was called of all white men known to be upon the river, in reach, for the purpose of ascertaining the number and condition of the guns, and the amount of ammunition in the hands of the miners. The number of guns on hand amounted to one to every three men, and among the whole number there were not more than three pounds of powder. An organization was immediately effected, and men were started out with directions to proceed down the Middle Fork of the American River, until they had reached a point where supplies could be purchased, and to procure all the arms and ammunition they could obtain, and bring into the camp. The relief party, after scrambling over the rocks for two days, reached the Big Bar, in El Dorado county, where they purchased some powder, lead, caps, salt, and tea, and one rifle gun, and returned to their companions.

With these additions to the stock of arms and ammunition on hand, after making a show of strength by sending small parties out in search of the Indians, one of which came up with a party of the red skins, and attacked and killed some of their number, the whites felt quite secure from an attack, and remained quiet the balance of the winter.

Toward the last of February, '50, the weather turning warm and the news of rich discoveries having been made the fall previous, between the head waters of the Middle and North Forks of the American, having been spread among the miners of Hangtown (Placerville), Weavertown, Coloma, Georgetown, Kelsy's, and other thickly settled places in El Dorado, a general stampede took place, and the men came in hundreds, making Bird's store (Bird's Valley) their place of rendezvous, until the number of men gathered at that point amounted to two or three thousand. Here they were compelled to remain until the snow settled sufficiently for them to penetrate the mountains and canons higher up on the slope of the Sierras. Early in the spring good prospects were obtained in El Dorado Canon, and companies were soon engaged in mining in the bed and banks of the creek from its junction with the North Fork to its head.

During the spring of 1850 the whole country on the western slope of the mountains was explored by prospecting parties; some even crossing over the Sierras to Carson Valley. It was during this spring that the famous "Gold Lake stampede" took place, and thousands of men left good diggings, where they were quite certain of making an ounce of gold for each day's work, to join in the general stampede to the wonderful lake. Although these prospecting expeditions proved disastrous to nearly every individual engaged in them, yet the developments made caused the immediate and permanent settlement of the upper region of Placer County, where so many hundreds of rich tunnel claims are yielding their thousands of ounces of gold daily in the way of remuneration to the miners for the years of labor they have applied in penetrating through the bed rock deep into the bowels of the mountains.

From the spring of 1850 may we date the beginning of permanent improvements and permanent settlements in Placer, for from that time men commenced to have settled habitations, and some even then commenced pre-

parations for building permanent homes for themselves and families. During
the summer and fall of that year the county became blessed with the presence of a number of families, some of whom came to the country overland
from the States; others from the old States and foreign countries; and
others, again, from El Dorado and other counties where they had become too
thickly settled to thrive well, or at least where there were not as good inducements offered for permanent settlements as this county afforded. Each year
since that period has marked a perceptible change, not only in the increase
of the permanent population, but also in the manners and morals of the people, and of the agricultural, mineral and other products. The taxable property has also increased in a regular ratio, until there are few counties that
can boast of surpassing it, either in the amount of property assessed for taxes,
grain, hay, cattle, horses, etc., raised, or excel it in the number of ounces of
gold dust shipped from its mines.

Like all other localities in the State, it has not been exempt from losses by
fire and flood, those great scourges of California, which have done more to
retard the development of the vast resources of the State than all other
causes combined. On June 4th, 1855, Auburn, the county seat, was almost
totally destroyed by fire, the loss of property amounting, in the aggregate,
to several hundred thousand dollars. In October, 1859, another fire broke
out in the place, destroying all the buildings in the upper part of town, and
entailing a loss upon its citizens of about $200,000. Yankee Jim's, Michi-
gan Bluff, Todd's Valley and Iowa Hill have each suffered a like scourge,
Yankee Jim's being destroyed in June, 1852; Iowa Hill on the 2d of February, 1357: Michigan Bluff in the summer of 1857; and Todd's Valley in
the summer of 1859. The property destroyed by fires alone at the times
mentioned amounted to more than $2,000,000.

The census returns of 1852 show the whole amount of money then invested in mining enterprises of every kind, including ditches for conveying
water from the rivers, canons, etc., to the flats, gulches, etc., to amount, in
the aggregate, to $1,427,567, divided as follows : $858,037, classed as
"Temporary Investments," which was in flumes, dams, canals, etc., on the
rivers; $13,530 invested in quartz mines, and $556,000 in water ditches,
classed as "Permanent Investments." It will be seen that these estimates
of amount of capital invested in ditches and other classes of mining property were based upon calculations of absolute cost of enterprises then completed and in course of construction. At the present time there is no data
from which the amount of money invested in all the various branches of
industry can be ascertained, hence we make no attempt at an estimate, except upon a single class of mining investments, which, it will be seen,
exceeds the aggregate investments in every species of property in the county
reported in the census return of 1852. By a pretty close canvass of the
region of the county in which the tunnel mines are located, we find the number of feet of tunnel run to amount to 186,990 feet, which cost $2,716,200.
This vast expenditure of tunnel mining is in a section of the country composed of townships five, six, seven and eight, and perhaps does not embrace
more than one-fourth of the whole amount of money invested in other classes
of mining enterprises and improvements subject to taxation.

The increase of population, as shown by the census returns of 1852, and
those of 1860, is less than three thousand. The number of votes cast in
the county at the Presidential election in 1852 was 5,144, and the number

cast at the Presidential election in 1860, was 5,837, showing an increase of votes in eight years of only 693.

The political history of Placer County, if given in detail, could not fail of being interesting; but the limited space allowed for this sketch will not admit of our entering into minor particulars, hence we must be content with giving such facts as are deemed of most importance and necessary to show the political complexion of the public men of the past times, and the circumstances, as near as they can be ascertained, under which they were elected to the various offices which they filled.

The vote of the people since the organization of the county to the present time shows the sympathy of the majority to have been uniformly with the Democracy, excepting only the year 1854, when, there being a division in the Democratic party, the Whigs succeeded in electing their entire legislative and county ticket.

The following is a list of the county officers and members of the Senate and Assembly elected each year from the organization of the county to the present time;

At the election in 1851, Gen. Fry was chosen Senator, and P. Canney and ——— Assemblymen; County Judge, H. Fitz Simmons; Sheriff, S. C. Astin; District Attorney, R. D. Hopkins; Clerk, James T. Stewart; Assessor, Alfred Lewis; Treasurer, Douglas Bingham.

In 1852, Joseph Walkup was chosen Senator, and P. Canney and B. F. Myres, Assemblymen. The county officers elected were: District Attorney, P. W. Thomas; Sheriff, S. C. Astin; Clerk, Wm. A. Johnson; Treasurer, E. G. Smith; Assessor, Gunn; Coroner, Pinkham; Surveyor, Hinnman; Public Administrator, Barnes.

In 1853, C. A. Tuttle was elected Senator, [Joseph Walkup holding over,] and Myers, Fairfield, Van Cleft and O'Neill, Assemblymen; Surveyor, Finley; Assessor, McCarty; Public Administrator, Jordan.

In 1854, Hawthorne was elected Senator, [Tuttle holding over,] T. Mooreland, H. Gregg, Wm. Corey and Moses Andrews, Assemblymen. All but the hold-over Senator, Whigs, and all the county officers Whigs, which were: Sheriff, Wm. T. Henson; Clerk, A. S. Grant; Treasurer, J. R. Crandall; District Attorney, M. E. Mills; Public Administrator, J. R. Gwynn.

In 1855, Thos. Westmoreland was elected Senator, [Mr. Hawthorne holding over,] and Silas Selleck, Lansing Stout, T. H. Read and R. S. Williams, Assemblymen; all Americans.

In 1856, Joseph Walkup was elected Senator, [Westmoreland holding over,] and Caperton, Safferd, Wyman and O'Neill, Assemblymen; Sheriff, Chas. King; Clerk, Tabb Mitchell; District Attorney, P. W. Thomas; Treasurer, Philip Stoner; Assessor, Spann; Public Administrator, Gaut; Surveyor, Phelps; Coroner, Hause; Superintendent Common Schools, P. C. Millette.

In 1857, J. H. Baker was elected Senator for full term, and James Anderson to fill the vacancy occasioned by the resignation of Joseph Walkup; D. B. Curtis, A. P. K. Safford, N. Kabler and W. C. Stratton were elected Assemblymen; and P. C. Millette, Superintendent Common Schools; S. G. Elliott, County Surveyor; Thos. Coffey, Public Administrator; W. J Esmond, Coroner.

In 1858, James Anderson was elected Senator, [J. H. Baker holding over,] Wm. C. Stratton, Wm. P. Barclay, Philip Lynch and W. P. Wing, were elected Assemblymen ; County Judge, E. H. Van Decar ; Sheriff, L. L. Bullock ; Collector, M. Kimball; Treasurer, G. W. Applegate ; Clerk, Henry Gooding ; District Attorney, P. W. Thomas ; Assessor, T. B. Harper ; Surveyor, S. G. Elliott ; Coroner, James M'Burney.

In 1859, S. T. Leet was elected Senator, [James Anderson holding over,] and S. W. Lovell, D. S. Beach, J. N. Makins and J. W. Harville, Assemblymen ; S. S. Greenwood, Superintendent of Common Schools ; Recorder, Geo. L. Anderson, and M. P. H. Love, Public Administrator.

In 1860, P. W. Thomas was elected Senator, [S. S. Leet holding over ;] Assemblymen, W. J. Harrison ; L. G. Smith, P. Munday and W. D. Harriman ; Sheriff, L. L. Bullock ; Clerk, Henry Gooding ; Treasurer, E. M. Banvard ; Recorder, W. A. Selkirk ; District Attorney, Jo. Hamilton ; Surveyor, S. G. Elliott ; Coroner, Joseph Platt ; Public Administrator, Rufus Smith.

In 1854, in consequence of the division in the Democratic party upon the Senatorial question, there were three tickets—two Democratic and one Whig—run in Placer county, and the Whigs elected their county ticket by a small plurality. Upon the Senatorial question in 1854 the politicians of Placer occupied a position directly the reverse of those of any other county in the State. Although the same dissensions between Northern and Southern existed in Placer that divided the party in the balance of the State, yet they assumed a position in Placer which differed with those of every other locality in this respect :—While the Southern men united upon Gwin and opposed the election of a United States Senator by the Legislature of 1854 in every other county, and the Northern men united upon Mr. Broderick, and favored the election at that session, in Placer county the Southern men favored Mr. Broderick, and the Northern men supported the Gwin faction. Thus we see the astute and far-seeing Southern Democrats of that day assisting Mr. Broderick in carrying out the " great Northern sentiment" which he professed to represent, and the Northern men opposing him and his party, and advocating and expressing the same sentiments and opinions that Southern men did in other counties.

The causes which led to the defeat of the Democratic party were numerous, yet the disaffection of the year previous had much to do with it, and perhaps we would not be far wrong should we assign that division in the party as the principal weak point in the party. Early in 1855, the Americans organized thoroughly by establishing secret councils in every town and mining camp in the country, where a suitable room could be procured in which to hold their meetings ; and, by well directed efforts among the citizens " to the manor born," made fresh accessions to the party at every meeting. The members of the two wings of the Democratic party had, in the meantime, become so embittered against each other that it was late in the campaign ere a compromise could be made, and a union of the two wings effected. The consequence was, the election of the whole of the Know Nothing or American ticket.

The success of the American party gave the leading members such encouragement, and the organization was so complete, that notwithstanding the members of the party knew they only held the balance of power, yet, at almost every election, by superior management, the party continued to elect one or two of its candidates to the best paying offices.

Notwithstanding the many hard fought battles in which the Democratic party has proved victorious since its signal overthrow in 1855, yet the seeds of dissension sown the year previous have taken such deep root in the organization, that no efforts upon the part of the ever consistent men who stand by the party principles, and are guided by the platform, can eradicate the troublesome canker, or prevent its influence from occasionally causing the defeat of a part or the whole of the ticket.

Closely connected with the political history of Placer County, and partaking greatly of the nature of the party which each affected to represent, and professed to be or was really the mouth-piece of, the various newspaper enterprises of the county claim some notice in this sketch; and, in fact, it would be incomplete without it. The *Placer Herald* is the oldest newspaper in the county. The first number was issued on the 11th of September, 1852, by T. Mitchell & Co., under the most favorable auspices, as we judge by the introductory remarks of the editor, and the liberal advertising patronage extended to it by business men and public officers from its first issue throughout the whole of its first volume. The following is an extract from the introductory of the editor, and is a declaration of principles, which, if they could be carried out—the paper at the same time being ably conducted—could not fail to secure the success of any newspaper enterprise in a community so appreciative as are the people of Placer. The editor introduces his paper "To the Citizens of Placer County," as follows:

"Through the partiality of friends, we have been selected to the responsible position of publishing the first journal in Placer County. Although somewhat diffident of our abilities, the strong promptings of our inclinations urge us to the task.

" In becoming a candidate for popular favor, a declaration of principles is due to the public. This time-honored usage we have no desire to disregard, but will state, briefly, the principles which will guide us in the conduct of the *Placer Herald*.

" In all matters of religious or political concernment the *Herald* will be FREE and INDEPENDENT. The peculiar advocate of no sect or party, we shall strive earnestly to do 'equal and exact justice' to all."

Doubtless the editor of the *Herald* commenced his career with more than usually virtuous intentions, but perhaps the temptations held out by the ever-changing fortunes of political parties and aspirants for political and official honors were greater than human nature was capable of withstanding, and hence a change of circumstances produced a corresponding change in the sentiments or policy of the conductor of the *Herald*. Through all its changes, however, the *Herald* has been a useful paper, and, as a newspaper enterprise, a success—profitable to its publishers and advantageous to its readers.

The next newspaper started in Placer County of which we have any account was the *Placer Democrat*, which was born in Auburn, April 19th, 1854. The paper being started by the Broderick faction, and fostered by the kindness of that eminently liberal party (in promises), it survived the campaign, perhaps, not exceeding two weeks. The proprietor and editor of the *Democrat* was John Shannon, late of the Visalia *Delta*, and it is said that Philip Lynch, now editor of the *Placer Courier*, also owned an interest and had much to do with its management. To give the reader some idea of the usefulness of the *Democrat*, the following article, copied from the *Auburn Whig*, which has very much the appearance of an obituary, is republished:

"The *Placer Democrat*, a paper representing the so-called Broderick wing of the Democracy of this county, has been discontinued. Its publication commenced April 19th of the present year, and ended about two weeks since. It has had the effect of causing rather stormy times in the Democratic party during the late political canvass; but whether or not the object which it had in view has been entirely accomplished we do not know. That portion of the party whose organ it was was badly beaten here by the Anti-Electionists, as well as throughout the State. The resignation of their County Central Committee, and the withdrawal of Milton S. Latham, one of their nominees for Congress, were undoubtedly serious drawbacks to their success, though, without these obstacles, the result might have been the same. The reasons given for the discontinuance of the *Democrat* is, that "it will not pay," which, unquestionably is quite a satisfactory one to all interested. We wish Mr. Shannon better success in his private enterprise than has, in this instance, favored his political ones."

The next newspaper enterprise started in the county was the Auburn *Whig*, published by Chas. Winkley and A. L. Stinson, and edited by M. E. Mills, which, like its predecessor, was not destined to live forever. The political predilections of the *Whig* were what its name indicates; and to say that the paper was conducted, during the whole of the brief period of its existence, with marked ability, would but be doing justice to the gentlemen who had the management of it, and who prepared the matter which filled its columns. The *Whig* lived under the editorial conduct of Mr. Mills for three months, when he passed it over into the hands of H. R. Hawkins, who also continued it until it arrived at the age of thirty-one weeks; when the *Whig*, like its predecessor, the *Democrat*, without previous notice ceased to exist. Its demise occurred on May 19th, 1855; and on June 2d, of the same year, the *Placer Press* was started by H. R. Hawkins, A. L. Stinson, and C. Winkley; Hiram R. Hawkins, editor, as before. The *Press*, through all the changes of its proprietorship during the succeeding 29 months which it was under the editorial conduct of Mr. Hawkins, was a neatly printed and interesting paper, being looked anxiously for each recurring Saturday morning by its appreciative readers. On October 31st, 1857, Mr. Hawkins sold his interest to A. S. Smith, who became editor, and continued the paper, in connection with Jas. P. Bull, as a partner in the publication, until May, 1858, when Mr. Bull retired from the concern and "the editor (has) assumed the entire control." The *Press* from this time until its demise was the organ of the Anti-Lecompton party, and was accused of being strongly tinctured with Abolitionism. The *Press* continued to make a regular weekly squeeze for a short time, under the direction of A. S. Smith; but eventually falling into the hands of J. W. Scoby, who assumed the editorship, was conducted by him until December 4, 1858, when he took "ANOTHER GLANCE AT THE FIELD" and incontinently retired, the *Press* becoming a defunct institution.

In the latter part of 1855 or early part of 1856, the Iowa Hill *News* was started at Iowa Hill, by Olmstead & Miller. The *News* advocated a division of Placer county, which was one of the questions of the political canvass of 1856, but the advocates of the measure did not succeed in making sufficient converts to their cause to continue the struggle after the election, and the question became a dead issue. Sometime in the winter or spring of 1858 the *News* office was removed to San Juan, Nevada county, and the *Hydraulic Press* was started by the proprietors.

Sometime during the winter of 1857, the 30th publication of the *Mountain Courier* was commenced at Yankee Jim's, by Messrs. Parker and Graves, who continued its publication for the space of three months precisely, when creditors becoming clamorous for numerous small amounts due from the concern, attachments were sued out, and levied upon the office, and its issue stopped.

On the 4th day of July, of the same year, E. B. Boust, having purchased the press and printing materials of the *Mountain Courier*, published the first number of the *Placer Courier*, which was successfully conducted by him until November, 1858, when he withdrew from the concern, and the paper was taken charge of by R. J. Steele, who published it at Yankee Jim's, until the following April, when the office was removed to Forest Hill. The *Courier* is now published by P. Lynch, who succeeded Mr. Steele as publisher in December, 1860.

In January, 1859, the *Iowa Hill Patriot* was started in that town by E. B. Boust, and was continued there until May 1, 1860, when the materials were removed by him to Dutch Flat, and the *Patriot* was merged into the *Dutch Flat Enquirer*. Mr. Boust continues the publication of the *Enquirer*, and is doing an excellent business.

The *Democratic Signal* was started as a Democratic campaign paper at Auburn, at the opening of the campaign of 1860, by S. T. Newell & Co., publishers, and edited by R. C. Poland. The paper espoused the cause of Stephen A. Douglas, and its publication was continued by Newell & Co. until the 10th of December of the same year, when it went into the hands of R. J. Steele, who continued its publication.

Of the agricultural and grazing portion of Placer county, but little can be said in addition to the facts found in statistical tables in another part of this book. When we consider the small district of country embraced within the limits of the county susceptible of cultivation, we find by comparing its products with those of agricultural counties, that the lands under cultivation in Placer are unusually productive, yielding on an average better than the lands of some of the most famous agricultural counties in the State. We will take Napa county for an instance, and compare its products of wheat with that of Placer. We find that in Napa county there are 26,114 acres of land cultivated in wheat, which produced last year 652,850, or 25 bushels to the acre. In Placer the number of acres cultivated in wheat the same year was 5,000, producing 170,000 bushels, or an average yield of 54 bushels to the acre. In Alameda, another agricultural county, we find that there were last year 20,000 acres of land cultivated in wheat, which produced 440,500 bushels, or an average of 22 bushels to the acre.

The above facts are sufficient to show that the soil of the agricultural portion of the county is not inferior to that of the best agricultural districts in the State, and that the land is in a high state of cultivation. A large portion of the county is well adapted to the raising of the various kinds of fruits, grapes, etc., and during the summer and fall our markets are abundantly supplied with every variety, at prices which defy competition by other fruit districts.

All that portion of Placer county lying west of the foothills, between the American, Sacramento and Bear rivers, is rapidly being put under cultivation, or enclosed for grazing purposes. The prairies are dotted all over with

3

the habitations of the settlers, and the public highways for miles, in many instances, are run through a continuation of lanes.

Rich mineral discoveries were made at an early period of the county's history, far down in the foothills, bordering on the plains, which, during the winter and spring seasons, afford employment to a large number of men at from two to four dollars per day each ; and in many places, in the gulches and ravines, miners are making double and even treble that amount, on an average.

Of the towns in the lower part of the county, Gold Hill, Virginia, Rattlesnake, Pine Grove and Stewart's, are the most important, each of which are noticed separately in this work.

STATISTICS OF PLACER COUNTY.

According to the County Assessor's report, there were in Placer County, in 1860, 40,740 peach, 23,360 apple, 7,521 pear, 6,436 plum, 6,036 cherry, 1,836 apricot, 1,000 quince, 1,400 nectarine, 400 fig, 700 almond, 80 English walnut, 30 mulberry, 60 pomegranate, 20 chestnut, 16 orange and 2,000 currant trees and bushes ; strawberry vines, 100,000 ; raspberry bushes, 7,000 ; blackberry bushes, 800 ; grape vines, bearing, 135,532 ; grape vine cuttings, 135,532 ; and gooseberry, 400.

In 1860 there were 11,748 acres of land in cultivation, upon which were grown 303,800 bushels of grain, besides potatoes, vegetables, and 1,877 tons of hay.

The live stock of the county in 1860 consisted of : horses, 2,175 ; cows, 2,241 ; oxen, 510 ; stock cattle, 8,490 ; mules, 470 ; jacks and jennets, 18 ; hogs, 11,488 ; sheep, 17,589 ; two-year old cattle, 750 ; one-year old cattle, 1,120 ; lambs, 7,945 ; calves, 673 ; goats, 52. The aggregate value of which is estimated at $545,914.

The total number of barnyard fowls amounts to 11,035.

The total of land taken up amounts to 102,503 acres.

WATER DITCHES AND CANALS.

Owl Creek Ditch takes water from Devil's Canon; length, 3 miles; capacity, 150 inches; value, $500.

Paradise Ditch takes water from Todd's Valley to Paradise and Spanish Bar Bridge. Length, 10 miles; capacity, 200 inches; value, $800.

Union Water Company's Ditch takes water from Shirt Tail and Brushy Canons. Capital stock, $90,000 ; value, $15,000.

Independent Ditch takes water from Volcano Canon. Length, 8 miles ; capacity, 250 inches; value, $10,000.

Pine Flat Ditch. Length, 1¼ miles ; capacity, 120 inches ; value, $500.

Brown and White's Ditch takes water from Volcano Canon. Capacity, 150 inches; length, 12 miles; value, $7,000.

Miner's Ditch takes water from South Shirt Tail. Length, 18 miles; capacity, 400 inches; cost, $40,000; value, $9,400.

El Dorado Ditch. Capital stock, $60,000; takes water from El Dorado Canon; length, 18 miles; capacity, 400 inches; value, $20,000.

Black Canon Ditch takes water from Black Canon to Deadwood. Value, $600.

North Shirt Tail Ditch takes water to Elizabethtown. Length, 11 miles; capacity, 300 inches; value, $5,500.

Grizzly Ditch takes water from Grizzly Canon to Wisconsin Hill. Length 4 miles; capacity, 200 inches; value, $900.

McKee's Ditch takes water from South Fork of Shirt Tail Canon to Iowa Hill. Length, 18 miles; capacity 800 inches; value, $5,000.

Rich & Co.'s Ditch takes water from Indian Canon to Iowa Hill. Length, three miles; capacity, 100 inches; value, $500.

Hill's Ditch takes water from Indian Canon; supplies Iowa Hill and vicini y. Length, 10 miles; capacity, 400 inches; value, $5,600.

Parkison & McCoy's Ditch takes water from Deep Canon to Last Chance. Value, $1,000.

Jamison & Co.'s Ditch takes water from Indian Canon to Iowa Hill. Length, 3 miles; capacity, 150 inches; value, $1,700.

Why Not Ditch takes water from Dutch Flat Ravine to Why Not Claims. Length, 1 mile; capacity, 150 inches; value, $1,100.

Dutch Flat Water Company—five ditches—takes water, from Little Bear River and Canon Creek, and supplies Dutch Flat and Indian Hill; value, $40,000.

Bartlett & Thomas' Ditch takes water from Bear River to Dutch Flat and vicinity. Length, 13 miles; capacity, 500 inches; value, $3,000.

Indian Ditch Company conveys water from Canon Creek to Indian Hi'l. Length, 7½ miles; capacity, 500 inches; value, $2,000.

Bear River and Auburn Water and Mining Company. Capital stock, $600,000; takes water from Bear River, above Illinoistown, and supplies the lower part of the county. Whole length of ditches, 200 miles; value, $50,000.

American River Ditch Company takes water from the American River at Tamahran Bar to Sacramento County. Length in county, 22 miles; capacity, 200 inches; value, $75,000.

Gold Hill and Bear River Ditch takes water from Bear River, and supplies Gold Hill and Virginia. Length, 14 miles; value, $12,000.

Total number of miles of water ditches, 394; total amount of water run, 7,220 inches; total value, $217,600.

SAW MILLS.

Pioneer Saw Mill—situated two miles below Yankee Jim's; steam power; vertical saw; capacity, 1,000,000 feet per annum; value, $3,600.

Spring Garden Mill—Water power; vertical saw; product, 250,000 feet per annum; value, $1,000.

Devil's Cañon Mill—Located at Yankee Jim's; water power; vertical saw; product, 200,000 feet per annum; value, $1,000.

Todd's Valley Mill—Located in Todd's Valley ; steam power; circular saws ; capacity, 1,000,000 feet per annum; value, $2,500.

Brushy Mill—Located on Third Brushy Cañon ; steam power; vertical saw ; product, 500,000 feet per annum; value, $2,000.

May Flower Mill—Located near Forest Hill; steam power; circular saws; product, 1,000,000 feet per annum ; value, $4,500.

Forest Hill Mill—Located at Forest Hill ; steam power; circular saws ; capacity, 2,500,000 ; cuts 200,000 feet per annum ; value, $300,000.

Volcano Mill—Located near Michigan Bluff; steam power ; vertical saw ; capacity per annum, 1,000,000 feet ; value, $3,000.

King's Old Mill—Located near the head of Shirt Tail Cañon ; water power ; vertical saw ; product per annum, 400,000 feet ; value, $1,500.

Parkinson & McCloy's Mill—Located at Last Chance ; water power; circular saw ; cuts 250,000 feet per annum ; real capacity, 1,500,000 feet ; value, $1,000.

Mt. Pleasant Mill—Located near Iowa Hill ; steam power ; real capacity, 1,200,000 feet ; actual amount produced, 600,000 feet ; value, $200,000.

Little Bear River Mill—Located at the head of Little Bear River ; water power ; sash saws ; capacity, 400,000 feet per annum ; value, $7,000.

Dutch Flat Steam Mill—Located at Dutch Flat ; steam power ; circular saws ; capacity, 1,000,000 feet ; cuts 750,000 feet per annum ; value, $2,000.

Cañon Creek Mill—Water power ; located on Cañon Creek ; vertical saws ; capacity, 200,000 feet ; value, $1,000.

Allen & Co.'s Mill—Located at Dutch Flat ; water power ; capacity, 400,000 feet per annum; value, $1,000.

Burton & Williams' Saw Mill—Located on Cañon Creek, near Dutch Flat ; water power ; sash saw ; cuts 400,000 feet per annum ; value, $1,000.

E. J. Brickell's Mill—Located at Illinoistown ; steam power ; two sash and two lath saws ; capacity, 1,500,000 feet ; product, 500,000 feet ; value, $4,000.

Mountain Mill—Located four miles below Illinoistown ; steam power ; circular saw ; capacity, 1,500,000 feet per annum ; product, 500,000 feet ; value, $2,500.

New England Mill—Located four miles below Illinoistown; steam power; circular saws ; capacity, 1,200,000 feet ; product, 700,000 feet; value, $1,000.

Empire Mill—Located eight miles above Auburn, on the Illinoistown road; steam power; sash saws; capacity, 1,000,000 feet ; product, 550,000 feet per annum ; value, $500.

O. N. May & Co.'s Mill—Located at Lisbon; steam power ; circular saw ; capacity, 1,000,000 feet per annum ; value, $2,000.

C. S. Preble's Mill—Located on Bear river ; water power ; capacity, 400,000 feet per annum; product, 200,000; value, $1,600.

Lath and Shingle Mill—Owned by C. J. Garland ; located at Forest Hill ; steam power ; capacity, 100,000 lath and 500,000 shingles per annum.

QUARTZ MILLS.

Pioneer Quartz Mill—Located near Damascus ; steam power, 45 horse ; runs 9 stamps, 1,400 pounds each ; two 12 feet arastras ; crushes 24 tons per day ; employs 15 hands the entire year ; value, $2,500.

Union Quartz Mill—Located near Bald Hill ; water power ; with 8 stamps and 2 arastras ; value, $1,800.

Eastman & Co.'s Quartz Mill—Small mill, located at Ophir; water power; 7 light stamps ; value, $500.

Decker & Co.'s Quartz Mill—On Dutch ravine ; water power ; with 5 stamps and 2 arastras ; crushes 5 tons per day ; value, $1,500.

Peterson & Keiser's Mill—Location at Bald Hill; steam power, 14 horse; 11 stamps and 2 arastras ; value, $1,500.

FLOURING MILLS.

Cataract Mill—Location on the Illinoistown road, four and a half miles from Auburn ; water power ; value, $4,000.

Auburn Steam Mill—Steam power, 12 horse ; one run of stone ; grinds 17 barrels in 24 hours ; value, $1,500.

TURNPIKES AND BRIDGES.

Stony Hill Turnpike—One mile in length ; macadamized the entire length ; level road ; value, $2,500.

Mile Hill Turnpike—Toll road between Auburn and Yankee Jim's ; one mile in length ; macadamized one-quarter mile ; value, $5,500.

J. A. Mattason's Toll Roads—Two roads—one leading from Baker's Ranch across Volcano Cañon to Michigan Bluff ; length 2 miles—the other from Forest Shade House to Michigan Bluff by the way of Bath ; new road five and a-half miles ; cost of construction, $12,000 ; value for the two, $6,000.

Yankee Jim's and Wisconsin Hill Turnpike—Crosses Shirt Tail Canon ; length of grade, 8 miles ; value, $3,500.

Indian Cañon Turnpike—Road crosses Indian Canon from Wisconsin Hill to Iowa Hill ; length two miles ; value, $900.

Mountain Springs Turnpike—Road leading from Mountain Springs to within 5 miles of Illinoistown ; length 2 miles ; value, $4,600.

Mineral Bar Bridge and Road—From Iowa Hill to Illinoistown, crossing the river at Mineral Bar ; length of road 7 miles ; value, $13,500.

Eastern Extension Turnpike Co.—Road commencing near Gold Hill and completed to the Nevada road on Dry Creek—the intended termination near the California House—7 miles completed ; length contemplated 11 miles ; value, $1,000.

Auburn Turnpike—Road leaves the old Sacramento and Auburn road at the Oak's House and intersects the Illinoistown road at the Junction House, 2½ miles above Auburn ; value, $10,000.

Auburn and Yankee Jim's Turnpike—Road crosses the North Fork above and near the junction of the North and Middle Forks of the American river ; value, $16,000.

BRIDGES.

Ford's Bar Bridge—John Calloway, proprietor bridge across the North Fork of the American river at Ford's Bar ; value, $1,000

Bear River Bridge—Across Bear river ; value, $3,000.

Murderer's Bar Bridge—Wire Bridge across the Middle Fork of the American river at Murderer's Bar ; one-half assessed in this county, the other in El Dorado ; value, $5,000.

TUNNELS IN PLACER COUNTY.

Name of Tunnel.	Locality.	Length.	Cost.
Old Colony Bed Rock Tunnel	Spring Garden	850	$9,500
Gone-In Tunnel	Spring Garden	1,000	——
Valley Bed Rock Tunnel	Todd's Valley	1,000	30,000
North Star Tunnel	Near Todd's Valley	1,100	24,200
Mountain Tunnel	Todd's Valley	1,300	19,500
Todd's Valley Tunnel	Todd's Valley	1,750	31,500
Chesapeake Tunnel	Todd's Valley	1,200	12,000
Oro Tunnel, bet. Todd's Valley and	Forest Hill	1,800	32,400
Green Spring's Tunnel, bet. Todd's	Val. and For. Hill	2,000	70,000
Baltimore Tunnel	Forest Hill	1,700	62,000
Forest Hill Slope Tunnel		1,400	30,800
Hoosier and Telegraph Tunnel	Todd's Valley	1,000	6,000
Hope Tunnel	Forest Hill	3,200	40,000
Independent Tunnel	do do	1,700	34,000
Independent Slope Tunnel	do do	1,200	60,000
Missouri Tunnel, Devil's Canon, near	Yankee Jim's	2,000	40,000
India Rubber Tunnel	Forest Hill	1,100	11,000
Alabama Tunnel		1,600	16,000
Eagle Tunnel	do do	1,200	9,600
Garden Tunnel	do do	1,300	9,100
Maus Company's Tunnel	do do	2,300	60,000
Kate Hay's Tunnel	do do	600	13,000
Lone Star Tunnel	do do	700	14,000
Deidesheimer Tunnel*	do do	2,000	24,000
Rough and Ready Tunnel	do do	3,800	60,000
Jenny Lind Tunnel†	do do	2,200	25,000
Gore Tunnel	do do	2,400	25,000
Pioneer Slope Tunnel	do do	1,450	65,000
Orono Tunnel	Bath	1,600	25,000
Humboldt Tunnel	do	600	5,000
Watson & Nevit's Quartz Tunnel	do	300	20,000
Old Rip Tunnel	do	500	10,000
Golden Gate Tunnel	do	900	15,000
Rough Gold Tunnel	do	1,000	15,000
Little Dorrit's Tunnel	do	1,000	20,000
Dewey Tunnel	do	2,000	8,000
A. Snodgrass & Co's Tunnel	do	1,000	6,000
New York Co.'s Tunnel		1,200	20,000
Sebastopol Tunnel	do	600	15,000
New Jersey Tunnel	Forest Hill	2,000	40,000
Sneider Tunnel	do	1,500	10,500
Northwood & Fast's Tunnel	do do	1,500	15,000
Boston Tunnel	do do	4,000	14,000
Know Nothing Tunnel	do do	1,100	6,600
Iowa Tunnel	do do	900	4,500

* This claim has paid upwards of $300,000 above the expense of working.

* A new tunnel is being run in this claim, and has been pushed forward 500 feet, at a cost of $12,500.

Name of Tunnel.	Locality.	Length.	Cost.
Tiger Tunnel	Forest Hill	500	$2,500
French Tunnel	do do	750	5,250
Rochester Tunnel	Yorkville	1,000	4,000
St. Louis Tunnel	do	700	3,000
Small Hope Tunnel	do	1,800	5,000
Iowa Tunnel	do	1,000	6,000
New York Tunnel	do	900	5,500
Washington Tunnel	do	1,100	7,000
Backus Tunnel	do	1,000	6,000
Pike County Tunnel	do	850	5,000
Oriental Tunnel	do	1,700	6,000
Brushy Slide Tunnel	do	1,500	20,000
Dutch Washington Tunnel	do	1,600	20,000
Oriental No. 2, Tunnel	do	500	5,800
San Francisco Tunnel	do	500	2,500
Texas Tunnel	do	1,600	12,800
Sacramento Tunnel	do	1,000	30,000
Independent Tunnel	do	1,500	15,000
Naugatuc Tunnel	do	400	4,000
Green Mountain Tunnel	do	400	1,200
Green Horn Tunnel	do	600	5,000
Dardanelles Tunnel	Forest Hill	2,400	150,000
Bay State Tunnel	do do	600	6,000
Ohio Tunnel	do do	600	5,000
Big Spring Tunnel	do do	1,800	20,000
Red Sea Tunnel	Yankee Jim's	509	13,000
Swindle Hill Tunnel	do do	1,200	17,000
Mameluke Tunnel	do do	900	15,000
Yankee Jim's Tunnel	do do	1,200	16,000
Ben Franklin's Tunnel	do do	700	7,000
Bald Eagle Tunnel	do do	800	11,000
Buchanan Tunnel	do do	450	3,000
Chucky Slide Tunnel	Volcano Canon	300	45,00
Volcano Slope Tunnel	do do	400	8,000
Maine Tunnel	do do	500	7,500
Cape Horn Tunnel, near Forks House		400	1,600
Lola Montez Tunnel	Green Valley	600	24,000
Oro Tunnel	El Dorado Canon	1,000	6,000
Huffacre Tunnel	El Dorado Canon	400	1,500
Craig & Co's Tunnel	do do	210	6,000
Bull Tunnel	do do	300	2,500
Dead Horse Tunnel	do do	200	3,500
Dix's Tunnel, Salome Hill District, near Forks House		300	1,500
Dix's Slope	Salome Hill Dist.	130	4,000
Arkansas Tunnel	do do	200	2,000
Faunce & Wisinger's Tunnel, near Fork's House		150	15,000
Jack Hay's Tunnel	do do	300	6,000
Bay State Tunnel	do do	500	3,000
Garibaldi Tunnel	Deadwood	700	6,000
Hooking Bull Tunnel	do	800	nominal

Name of Tunnel.	Locality.		Length.	Cost.
Cement Tunnel	Deadwood		300	$1,000
Snug Harbor	do		300	4,000
Belle of the Mountain	do		280	4,000
Mohawk Tunnel	do		800	8,000
Rattlesnake Tunnel	do		250	5,000
Jenny Lind Tunnel	do		500	4,200
Golden Age Tunnel	do		300	1,000
St. Lawrence Tunnel	do		200	8,000
Jerusalem Point Tunnel	do		160	6,000
Gibraltar Tunnel	do		250	2,000
Kayler's Tunnel	do		300	1,500
Wabash Tunnel	do		150	1,100
Shipwreck Tunnel	do		150	600
Whirlwind Tunnel	do		300	750
Elkhorn Tunnel	do		500	1,500
English Tunnel	do		500	1,500
Belvidere Tunnel	do		200	1,600
Van Zandt's Tunnel	do		170	500
Cusick's Tunnel	do		100	500
Howe's Tunnel	do		350	9,000
Old Gravel Tunnel	do		200	1,250
Crumwall's Tunnel	do		80	250
Mississippi Tunnel	do		630	3,500
Sebastopol Tunnel	do		200	800
Flying Dutchman's Tunnel	do		300	6,500
Quartz Point Tunnel	do		500	2,500
Douglas's Tunnel	do		150	300
El Dorado Tunnel	Last Chance		700	30,000
Long Tunnel	do	do	1,000	20,000
Wolverine Tunnel	do	do	400	8,000
Henson Tunnel	do	do	700	3,500
Nigger Tunnel	do	do	200	5,000
Fiddler's Green Tunnel	do	do	500	25,000
Slab Tunnel	do	do	300	5,000
Scandinavian Tunnel	do	do	500	2,500
Fanny Hill Tunnel	do		500	2,500
Pennman's Tunnel	do		300	1,500
Hope Tunnel	do	do	100	900
Root Hog or Die Tunnel	do	do	160	4,000
Morning Star Tunnel	do	do	150	1,200
North Star Tunnel	do	do	60	2,000
Hell's Delight Tunnel	do	do	400	3,000
Viola Tunnel	do	do	150	500
Light Foot Tunnel	Bird's Valley		600	2,000
Oneida Tunnel	do	do	600	4,000
Star of the West Tunnel	do	do	400	5,000
Exchange Tunnel	do	do	500	4,000
Buckeye Tunnel	do	do	400	4,500
Yankee Tunnel	do	do	400	1,300
Bird's Valley Tunnel	do	do	1,500	6,000

Name of Tunnel.	Locality.	Length.	Cost.
Specimen Tunnel	Bird's Valley	800	2,000
Washington Tunnel	do do	700	6,000
Mt. Cosumnes Tunnel	do do	1,000	30,000
Stony Bar Tunnel	Stony Bar	600	10,000

IOWA HILL DIVIDE.

Name of Tunnel.	Locality.	Length.	Cost.
Old Michigan Tunnel	Wisconsin Hill	900	5,400
Louisiana Tunnel	do do	900	8,100
Mississippi Tunnel	do do	300	2,700
Auburn Tunnel	do do	400	2,800
Cincinnati Tunnel	do do	1,000	8,000
Washington Tunnel	do do	200	1,600
Sacramento Tunnel	do do	800	8,000
Lone Star Tunnel	do do	500	7,500
West Point Tunnel	do do	500	7,500
Hoosier Tunnel	do do	400	4,000
Pennsylvania Tunnel	do do	500	5,000
Bennett Boys' Tunnel	do do	350	3,500
Selden Tunnel	do do	400	4,000
Ohio Tunnel	do do	1,000	15,000
New York Tunnel	do do	600	6,000
Morning Star Tunnel	do do	900	9,000
Mammoth Tunnel	do do	500	4,000
Valencia Tunnel	do do	700	4,900
El Dorado Tunnel	do do	800	8,000
Coloma Tunnel	do do	1,000	25,000
Sailor Tunnel	do do	350	3,500
Buckeye Tunnel	do do	400	4,000
Monticello Tunnel	do do	800	6,400
Hawkeye Tunnel	do do	200	1,600
Golden Gate Tunnel	do do	600	12,000
Jenny Lind Tunnel	do do	300	3,000
Bennett Tunnel	do do	300	3,000
American Tunnel	do do	350	3,500
Hope Tunnel	do do	600	6,000
Monumental Tunnel	do do	400	4,800
Nevada Tunnel	do do	500	5,000
Harris Company's Tunnel	do do	500	5,000
Forest Rose Tunnel	do do	150	1,200
Findley Tunnel	do do	150	1,200
Wisconsin Tunnel	do do	500	4,900
Silver Grey Tunnel	do do	500	4,500
Refuge Tunnel	do do	950	9,500
Washington Tunnel	do do	300	3,000
Virginia Tunnel	do do	400	4,400
Iowa Tunnel	do do	900	9,000
Invincible Tunnel	do do	500	4,000
Atchison Tunnel	do do	300	2,700
Elizabeth Tunnel	do do	300	3,000

Name of Tunnel.	Locality.		Length.	Cost.
Philadelphia Tunnel	Wisconsin Hill		100	600
Lebanon Tunnel	do	do	1,300	45,500
Chicago Tunnel	do	do	900	9,000
Placer Tunnel	do	do	700	8,400
San Francisco Tunnel	do	do	900	10,800
Judge Berry Tunnel	do	do	900	8,100
Prospect Tunnel	do	do	1,000	9,000
Bay State Tunnel	do	do	1,150	11,500
Humboldt Tunnel	do	do	1,200	12,000
Illinois Tunnel	do	do	500	6,000
California Tunnel	do	do	800	9,600
Volcano Tunnel	do	do	500	6,000
Caledonia Tunnel	do	do	800	8,000
Hopkins Tunnel	do	do	300	2,400
Rough & Ready Tunnel	Grizzly Flat		400	8,000
Vigilance Tunnel	do	do	400	10,000
Simon Peter Tunnel	do	do	200	5,000
Sam Slapp Tunnel	do	do	300	2,000
Ben Franklin and R'h and R'y T'l	do	do	1,500	15,000
McKennon's Tunnel	do	do	200	3,000
Rip Van Winkle Tunnel	do	do	700	6,000
Know Nothing Tunnel	Grizzly Canon		500	6,000
Defiance Tunnel	Sucker Flat		800	9,600
Sucker Flat Tunnel	do	do	600	7,200
Mountain Echo Tunnel	do	do	250	2,000
Indiana Tunnel	do	do	400	4,000
Golden Hope Tunnel	Elizabethtown		1,000	60,000
Caroline Tunnel	do		1,000	20,000
Wolverine Tunnel	Roach Hill		1,800	20,000
Empire Tunnel	do	do	1,300	10,000
Glencoe Tunnel	do	do	263	1,600
Mount Holyoke Tunnel	do	do	500	7,500
Pacific Tunnel	do	do	1,700	20,000
Roanoke Tunnel	do	do	2,000	18,000
Columbus Tunnel	do	do	2,000	28,000
Dayton Tunnel	do	do	1,800	29,000
Shelby Tunnel	Monona Flat		1,200	18,000
Medford Tunnel	do	do	600	6,000
San Francisco and Stockton Tunnel	do	do	1,400	38,000
Vigilance Tunnel	do	do	1,400	17,000
Penn Valley Tunnel	M't Pleasant Flat		900	15,000
North Star Tunnel	Iowa Hill		2,400	50,000
Sailor Union Tunnel	do	do	1,800	20,000

The whole number of feet of tunnel run in the county amount, in the aggregate, to 186,990, at an aggregate cost of $2,716,200. Nearly the whole of this great outlay of money has been made by comparatively poor men, who earned the money thus invested by their labor in surface or hydraulic claims. A portion, however, was invested by capitalists, but there is only an occasional instance of tunnels having been run by capitalists where they have received any return from their claims for the money thus invested.

ADDITIONAL HISTORICAL SKETCHES OF TOWNS.

IOWA HILL.

Immediately connected with the history of Iowa Hill, is also the history of Independence Hill, Roach Hill, Bird's Flat, Monona Flat, and Grizzly Flat. The rich hill diggings at those places, the discovery of which was first made at Iowa Hill, in 1853, and soon after extended to all the places above named, caused the large, populous, and flourishing town of Iowa Hill to spring up like magic, and in two years to become the principal town in the eastern part of Placer County.

The first discoveries of gold made where the town of Iowa Hill now stands, was upon the ground known as the Jamison claims, first called the Kennedy claims. These claims lie upon the north side of the ridge, in the head of a gulch leading into the North Fork of the American river. The claims are now worked on an extensive scale by the hydraulic process, and are rapidly ascending the hill towards the principal street of the town, which is destined eventually to be washed away; tunnels driven through the hill having demonstrated the fact that the whole of the ground upon which the town stands is auriferous; also, that rich and extensive deposits of gold exist at a great depth immediately under where are now the principal business houses. The Jamison and North Star claims are the principal claims at this place, and each have yielded sums of money to their lucky owners almost incredible to relate. The North Star is said to have yielded three hundred thousand dollars for the first twelve months' work done in the claim after pay dirt was reached. This statement in regard to the yield of the North Star claims, is authentic. Mr. John C. Coleman is the business manager of the North Star Company; and under his management, notwithstanding the quality of dirt washed is not what would be denominated rich, it pays good dividends to the shareholders. A tunnel has been driven clear through the hill, from the north side of town, a distance of 3,000 feet, to Indian Cañon, on the south side of town. At the mouth of the tunnel, on Indian Canon, there is a mill for crushing the stone and cement, similar in structure and upon the same principle as the common quartz mills. The dirt being a hard cement, it was found impossible to separate the gold from it by the ordinary process of washing, and the experiment of crushing was made with cheap machinery, which, upon a fair trial, was found to answer the purpose. The North Star cement crushing mills, are the first works of the kind erected for that purpose in the State, and as they have proved so eminently successful in this instance, can scarcely fail to come into constant and universal use wherever the dirt in which gold is found is of a similar character.

The principal tunnel diggings of Iowa Hill are situated above the town, at Roach Hill, and extend a distance of near three miles up Indian Canon. Many of them have been driven into the hill to the centre, a distance of

1,000 feet, and some of them even as far as 2,000 feet. According to a calculation made upon authentic information obtained from an undoubted source, the tunneling upon the Iowa Hill divide, on both sides of Indian Cañon, including Wisconsin Hill, Grizzly Flat, and Elizabethtown diggings, amounts to 62,460 feet, at a cost of $827,300. By far the most costly, and at the same time the most productive of these tunnels, are those at Iowa Hill proper, and Roach Hill, and Monona Flat. The amount of money which has been taken out of those which are now worked and are paying, cannot be correctly ascertained; but it far exceeds the cost of running the tunnels, and yet the riches of the hills are only just commenced to be developed.

The business of Iowa Hill consists of three large grocery stores, four hotels, five drygoods and clothing stores, one fancy store, three variety stores, one brewery and soda factory, two hardware and tinware stores, and two butcher shops; besides the usual number of bowling alleys, billiard, and lager beer saloons. Iowa Hill also has a splendid Catholic Church building, a Methodist Church edifice, a Masonic Lodge, and a lodge of the I. O. of O. F.'s; also a public school, and a theatre.

On the 2d of February, 1857, the whole of the business part of the town was destroyed by fire; the loss to the citizens by which was estimated at a half million of dollars. Notwithstanding this severe loss, the town was immediately rebuilt with better buildings, presenting a better appearance than before the conflagration. The buildings of Iowa Hill are principally of wood, yet there are some of brick and stone. There is a daily stage, running from Iowa Hill to Illinoistown, connecting with the California Stage Co.'s stages to Dutch Flat, Grass Valley, Auburn, and Sacramento.

Iowa Hill, like all other old towns in California, has been the scene of many of those outrages upon law so common in this State, and which have rendered our people subject to the charge of an inclination to take the law into their own hands, and execute it without the sanction of judge or jury. But whatever may have been the habits, customs, and morals of the inhabitants of the town in former years, the citizens of the place at the present day are as religious, moral, and intelligent, as those of the average of small towns in the State.

There have been two newspaper enterprises started in Iowa Hill. The *News*, by Olmstead and Miller, in 1855, and the *Patriot*, by E. B. Boust, in 1859; both of which practically demonstrated the fact that the business resources of the place were not sufficient to support a respectable newspaper. Both of the papers mentioned, were conducted with the average ability of similar publications in country towns, and both were worthy of support; but notwithstanding their deserts, and the high appreciation in which they were held by the citizens of the town and vicinity, the publishers were forced to seek a larger and better field in which to display their genius and talents with a reasonable hope of obtaining a living.

A great deal of the ground upon which the town is built, having been undermined, it is observed that it is gradually sinking, rendering brick or stone structures unsafe to live in. This doubtless has an injurious effect upon the value of property, and will, eventually, as was the case with Michigan Bluff, cause the buildings to be removed to where there is a more stable foundation upon which they may stand.

WISCONSIN HILL AND ELIZABETHTOWN.

Wisconsin Hill and Elizabethtown are situated on the southerly side of Indian Cañon and about two miles from Iowa Hill. The two places are about three-fourths of a mile apart, and, were it not for a deep ravine which separates them, and the two different appellations which distinguish them, they might be considered as one village. Elizabethtown was settled by miners early in the fall of 1850, and took its name from the wife of one of the early settlers, who moved with his family to the place and opened a boarding-house, his wife, Elizabeth, being the first white woman who ever visited the place. The diggings at Elizabethtown were good, and soon after their discovery the place grew to be a considerable town, sporting several provision stores and drinking saloons, the requisite number of hotels to furnish accommodations to travelers, prospectors and the sporting men who favored the place with their presence—this class being looked upon at that day, in California, as being as essential acquisitions to a town as "round tents" and grocery stores, and without whom no place could flourish. The place grew rapidly, and was the most noted place north of Shirt Tail and south of the North Fork, until it was eclipsed in 1854 by its rivals, Wisconsin Hill and Iowa Hill. The era which marks the rise of the latter places also marks the downfall of "Elizabeth," it dwindling down until nothing remained to mark the spot where it stood but a few scattered miners' cabins and an apology for a hotel, dignified by being called "the boarding-house."

Wisconsin Hill took its rise in 1854, and gained immense accessions to its population, caused by reports of rich and extensive hill diggings being discovered in the hill upon which the town was built, and those adjacent. About this time there was quite a mania for tunneling, and about one hundred companies were formed, who staked off claims and commenced running tunnels into the hills in the vicinity of the town. The operatives in the tunnels were men who owned shares in the claims in which they worked, yet, as every claim was owned by joint stock companies, the wages received by the working men in each was sufficient to keep up the assessments upon their own shares and supply them with sufficient means to pay their board, purchase their clothes and leave them a handsome allowance for spending money. The laboring population of Wisconsin Hill proper perhaps never amounted to more than one hundred and fifty men ; but there were a number of miners on Shirt Tail and the tributaries of Indian Cañon who resorted to the place weekly for the purpose of purchasing their supplies and indulging in a Sunday's recreation, and as this class usually had plenty of money and there were plenty of inducements offered them for investment, they managed always to deposit enough in the different institutions to keep up some half dozen saloons, two hotels, several restaurants, clothing establishments, grocery stores, etc., until the spring of 1856, when the tunnels commenced to reach the center of the hills, and no rich deposits being struck, capitalists ceased to furnish the wherewithal to pay men for driving the tunnels, and claims were "laid over" to wait for future developments. From this time they commenced to dwindle ; but soon again the hopes of the business men and property-holders were revived by the completion of a turnpike road across Shirt Tail Cañon, connecting the place with Yankee Jim's, and another across Indian Canon, connecting it with Iowa Hill. But instead of these roads inducing an increased population, by rendering the place easy of access, they furnished the superabundant population with an easy mode of transit from it to some more favored locality, where men could invest their labor to better advantage, and so the place continued to decline until the completion of several ditches leading water to the place furnished such increased facilities for washing that the few miners remaining, by washing away the hill-sides by the hydraulic process, could make mining a paying business, since which a slight improvement in the business appearance of the place is perceptible. It now supports two provision and grocery stores, two butcher shops, two boarding-houses, a hotel, and several drinking saloons. The residents have also, within the last twelve months, renovated a number of the old dilapidated buildings upon either side of the street, which gives the town an improved appearance.

GOLD HILL.

Among the prominent towns built on the banks of the Auburn Ravine, is that known as Gold Hill. As the name indicates, it is a mining village ; although it receives considerable support and trade from the agriculturalists who reside below and contiguous. The town received its name from the fact that gold was discovered on the hill, which rises in a conical shape a few yards west of the main street. In the spring of 1851, about simultaneous with the discovery of gold on various hills of the State, a party of Georgia miners set out from the town of Ophir, four and a half miles above the place now known as Gold Hill, on a prospecting expedition. They passed down the Auburn Ravine from bar to bar, looking for some place where they might make a "rich strike," as others had done before on the bars above and below Ophir. Our party of prospectors little dreamed of finding "hill diggings," but were anxious to discover some locality in the bed of this rich stream, where the sands had not buried the bed rock beneath the hope of a prospect in the dry season. As this party reached a low point making off a hill in the Auburn Ravine, just below an extensive flat, gold was discovered in the rich and dark alluvial soil. This lead or deposit was traced by the usual mode of pan prospecting, until it was decided that the hill "would pay." The spot or elevation of ground at once was, as a matter of necessity, designated "Gold Hill," and by common consent it has been since known by this name. Two large mining companies were soon after organized, their claims staked off, and preparations made for bringing water from the ravine, about one mile and a half above, to the top of the hill. These companies were respectively known as the "Georgia" and the "Ohio," and the members of each immediately commenced the survey of the ditches, which were, and are still known by the same names, and which were completed and conducted water upon the hill early in 1852. The Georgia ditch was first completed, and the company commenced the work of "ground sluicing" on the southeast point of the hill, which is now marked and covered by the building belonging to Hill & Devane. About the same time, the point opposite, on the south side of the ravine, distinguished at this time as "Gardner's Hill," was discovered and mined by Castle & Co.; also, a point of land of less altitude, off the northwest section of Gold Hill. Both these localities afforded the richest yields of gold ever discovered in the town.   A small blind ravine winds and turns immediately north of the base of Gold Hill, and which has been known since 1853 as "Humbug."   This was prospected in pits, later in 1852, by Dr. J. A. Bond and Charles Sprague; but in the year following, A. S. Smith made further discoveries, and staked off the ravine for a quarter of a mile, dividing the ground into one hundred feet claims among the miners.   These claims proved quite rich, and Dr. O. K. Levings, Spruance Brothers, and Mariner, Willard & Co., during the summer of 1853, took from the same a large amount of gold dust.   This mining led to further and later discoveries, and to the final opening up of "Humbug Flat," into which this little stream of water emptied and lost itself; and which is finally being worked out by Chinese miners.

During the same year, rich gold deposits were discovered in the vicinity of Gold Hill, which all contributed to build up rapidly the town.   Half a mile north of the town Doty's Ravine makes its way towards the plains. Bars were opened along this little stream, which proved to be very productive.   Peters Brothers, in the year 1853, with the use of the common rocker, took out over ten thousand dollars, in coarse gold, on this stream.   Their successors, in the latter part of the same year, also re-worked the same claim with a "tom," and made another fortune.   Dutch Ravine, which also runs parallel with the Auburn Ravine, and empties into it immediately below Gold Hill, was partially opened by miners the same year, and is yet yielding up the precious metal.

The site of this town being among the foot hills, the topography of the vicinity is one continuous succession of hills and ravines—one day, perhaps, an extensive table land, but by the action of water at the annual floods, during a period of generations, the face of the country was cut up into ravines and hills.   The locality is also thickly interspersed with quartz ledges, which generally follow the northeast and southwest points of the compass, and crop-out on many of the highest hills.   Some of these ledges have been prospected, but they have been found to be "spotted," and generally their working has not proven remunerative.   A small quartz-mill was erected on Shipley's Ravine, in 1857, by Stewart & Co., but the rock failed to prove remunerative.   The same mill was subsequently worked by J. W. Spann & Co., but after a more thorough trial, again abandoned.

Soon after the discovery of gold on Gold Hill and the surrounding hills, parties of miners began to agitate the feasibility of working the Auburn Ravine, in the vicinity.   Although that which was denominated "pay dirt" was deeply buried in sand and gravel, washed by the floods from the *debris* of the miners, then and before laboring for miles above, it was determined by the enterprising people who settled at this camp, that the ravine might be opened by long drains, and the worthless dirt removed by the shovel or wheelbarrow.   Consequently, in the year 1853, the Auburn Ravine for miles was located, and a company opened a frail and shallow ditch through the sand.   But from inexperience and want of perseverance, little effectual mining was done, though several of the companies "got down," and found good prospects.   However, at the upper end of the flat, opposite Gold Hill, one company (Bedford & Co.), worked successfully for two or three months, and made fine wages, until driven out by the winter rains; since which time the Auburn has been opened up annually by mining companies; and from year to year the mining has been retired down the stream, until the same has been opened for a distance of five or six miles. At this time, the best general paying claims in the county, estimating comparative expense of opening, are found on the Auburn Ravine, between Virginia and Walkup and Wyman's old ranches.

While all these mineral discoveries were being made, another class of people were attracted to the new El Dorado. The merchant and mechanic were assured a field for trade and labor was being developed ; and during the first years of this new mining *furor*, a town of no small pretensions was laid out and erected. In June, 1852, the present streets of Gold Hill were laid out and quickly built over. The pioneer merchants were Messrs. Hill & Devane, and the pioneer "mine host" was Augustus Foost. Both of these structures were originally cloth houses, and Hill & Devane's was erected nearly oppositr their present location, The hotel occupied the ground now covered by Hill & Devane's building.

Subsequently other merchants located in the town, and other hotels were erected. Flagg, of Ophir, opened a branch in 1853, the successors of whom are Crocker & Co. Morgan Bros. also opened a store next door east of Decker's Bakery, (then Marshall's) ; but the boys failing to have a " California sense " of doing business, they closed out after about one year's hard struggle. May their shadows always be less ! They were succeeded by Douglas & Pendleton, who opened in the old wooden building built by Perry Clark and Alexander Mills, and which was so long and profitably occupied by their successor, T. Ross. This old California "shake and pole " erection was supplanted in 1859 by a brick building, the only one in the town. Other improvements, however, have been made in all parts of the town, and but a few remnants of 1852 now remain to mar the general appearance.

Perhaps the writer of this brief sketch ought not to pass by unnoticed the first case of " secession " which occurred in this town in the year 1852. It is an incident of importance, from the fact that Oro City owes its birth to the " rebellious movement."

The good people of Gold Hill, like all other communities at an early day, entertained jealousies, resulting from prospective trade and difference about which direction the streets should run. Two formidable parties arose, and they very nearly equally balanced in numbers, and " prospective" wealth. The first party was anxious the main street should run east and west, and the second party stubbornly in favor of a street running north and south. They could not agree, and the result was that the east and west-streeters lost their temper, and " seceded " down the ravine about half a mile, among those romantic native oaks, and to that beautiful flat, and builded up " Oro City." This is a brief history of the rise of this city, now unfortunately in the hands of the Celestials.

The prosperous and healthy growth of Gold Hill was greatly retarded in 1852, from the want of water for mining purposes. The two small canals, Georgia and Ohio, afforded only a small quantity of water, during the rainy season, and the town, in the summer of 1852, was almost entirely deserted for the want of this element. Several other important canals were consequently surveyed in 1852–'53. The McMartin ditch was commenced in 1853, and conducted water from Sailor's Ravine to Gold Hill in the latter part of this year. O. K. Levings, also, surveyed and constructed a canal leading to this section on a higher grade, taking water from the Auburn

Ravine half a mile above the other canal privileges. This new and valuable canal was finished in 1853, and lay idle from pecuniary embarrassments and opposition brought to bear by the Auburn and Bear River Water and Mining Company—by which company it was finally bought. A flume from this canal is the only one now running water upon the brow of old Gold Hill, all other canals having withdrawn through the force of competition. The first canal of importance brought into Gold Hill and its vicinity was the Gold Hill and Bear River canal. This work was also finished in 1853, and on the introduction of its waters, a large mining population was attracted to Gold Hill, Virginia, and contiguous mining localities. Old ravines were then reworked during the dry season, when they could be mined with greater advantage and profit, and other ravines where "natural" water could not be obtained before, were opened to the labor of the miner. From this period to 1856, the prosperity of this mining community was at its zenith ; and the mining population was larger than during any former or subsequent years. A lively competition in water springing up between the Auburn and Gold Hill canals through the purchase of the Levings canal, water was offered to the miners at low prices, to the advantage of the consumers, but seriously to the detriment of the Gold Hill Company. The price of water was not only reduced, but the finances of the Gold Hill Company were seriously affected. Other causes, beyond the control of the managers of this canal, conspiring, this enterprise failed to remunerate its stockholders, though the community in general have reaped a rich reward therefrom.

This town organized a civil government in the spring of 1852, by the election of James Bedford to the office of Justice of the Peace, and a Mr. Waggoner, Constable. These gentlemen were the first judicial officers of the town. Mr. Bedford resigned after about one month's service, and a Mr. Green, resident of Oro City, was elected to fill the vacancy. Mr. Waggoner served as constable for two years.

The limits of this publication would not permit the writer to give as full a description of this town as he desired. He would have alluded to its former normal and healthy condition from its settlement to the year 1856, and to other prominent physical changes, and the causes of the same. Thus much has been written without notes or memoranda, and from bare recollection ; and which, though mainly correct, cannot be free from errors in facts, and perhaps conclusions.   S.

FOREST HILL.

Forest Hill is situated upon the divide between the Middle Fork of the American River and Shirt Tail Canon. Its altitude is about 3,600 feet above the level of the sea. The location is beautiful, the atmosphere is pure, the water good, and the people are healthy and prosperous.

The first settlement at Forest Hill was made in the fall of 1850 by M. Fannan, James Fannan and R. S. Johnson, who located there and established a trading-post. During the winter of 1850 and '51 they built the house now known as the "Old Forest House." The place, at the time they made the location, being a dense forest of pine, spruce, fir and oak timber, they gave the place the name of "The Forest House," from which the

4

town derived its name, Forest Hill. At the time of the building of the
Forest House no mining was carried on in the vicinity, except at the gulch
diggings at "the Gordons" in Yankee Jim's Gulch, the canon diggings in
the Jenny Lind Canon, the diggings at Sarahsville (Bath), and other localities at a greater distance. The Forest House being on the road leading to
Bird's Valley, Humbug, Horseshoe and Stony Bars, and the mines on the
upper divide, made it a good stand for teamsters, packers and travelers to
stop at, and so the enterprising proprietors added the business of hotel-keep-
ing to their mercantile business. They succeeded so well that other houses,
built with a design to carry on business similar to that of the Forest House,
were erected in the fall of 1851, at short intervals upon the road, the nearest
of which was the Middle Fork House, by W. T. Henson, Brown & Co.
Both these houses were liberally patronized by the traveling and mining
communities; the proprietors made money, and their property became valuable.

The rich deposit of gold at Forest Hill, like the celebrated silver mines
of Potosi, were discovered by one of those accidents that it is impossible
for man to foresee, but which all are willing to take the advantage of. The
discovery led to the running of the numerous tunnels which pierce the ridge
on which the town of Forest Hill is built, and eventually, as the mines
became developed, to the building up of the town. During the heavy storm
in Dec., 1852, and Jan., '53, (which the citizens of Sacramento and Stockton
perhaps hold in remembrance), a slide took place at the head of the Jenny
Lind Canon. just above the claim of Snyder, Brown & Co. Upon going to
their claim in the gulch, when the storm was over, the company was surprised to find that a large part of the hill had slid down, covering up their
claim and burying their tools. They were still more surprised, when walk-
ing over the mass of dirt which had thus fallen down to learn the extent of
the damage they had received, to find that chunks of gold were plainly visi-
ble in the bank and loose dirt which had slid off from it. The company
procured tools and set to work removing the rubbish and washing the pay-
dirt in sight, and were reported at the time to wash out from $2,000 to
$2,500 per day.

The discovery thus made was the cause which led to the development of
the rich deposits of gold in the hill, as, by washing up the pay-dirt which
had slid off the hillside and following the vein of pay-dirt into the hill, it
was found to be merely an outcropping of an extensive deposit, and immediately tunnels were started along the base of the hill for miles above and
below where the discovery was made. The next company which penetrated
through the rock to the auriferous gravel was the Deidesheimer Company,
whose claim was located about three-fourths of a mile further up the ridge,
and near where Yankee Jim's Gulch forms a flat, from which claim it is said
upwards of $300,000 have been taken in about one year. The Independent
Company was the next which reached pay-dirt, which claim also proved
very rich, yielding immense sums of money.

Although the rock in most of the tunnels was very hard, costing in some
instances as high as $40 per foot for running the tunnels, yet the miners
received fresh courage from each discovery, until the existence of an
immense deposit of auriferous earth in the centre of the hill became an
established fact in the minds of the miners, and each one considered the
probability of his becoming a millionaire as being a question of time only;

each being satisfied that the gold was in his claim, if he could only reach it. Time wore on, and at intervals the news was spread abroad of one claim after another having penetrated through the rim-rock and obtained prospects similar to those already mentioned. As nearly all of these claims are well known, to many persons at a distance from the scene of these rich discoveries, it will not be amiss to mention some of them in the order in which they were worked through the rock, and reached the gravel containing the gold. The Jenny Lind, the Northwood & Fast, the Rough and Ready, the Jersey, the Dardanelles, the Alabama, the Eagle, the India Rubber, Garden, and others of equal richness, were gradually opened, and made to add to the wealth of the country, by furnishing constantly large sums of gold to supply the wants of trade. It is needless to say that each new discovery added fresh courage to the weary miner who had toiled for years, day and night, in blasting through the rock ; and, although a large number of them have been engaged for nearly eight years in running bed-rock tunnels, at a cost in some instances of forty or fifty dollars per foot of tunnel run, yet one can read upon their countenances no signs of discouragement, all seeming confident of eventually being successful.

After the Jenny Lind, Rough and Ready, Jersey, Northwood & Fast, and Gore companies had reached pay dirt, the increased demand for laborers caused such a rapid influx of population, that a considerable town was soon built up under the hill. A store, well stocked with miner's supplies, and a number of saloons had been established, and the place assumed that brisk business appearance characteristic of new mining towns in the mines of California.

In November, 1856, the Forest House and Ranch, embracing the land on which the town now stands, was purchased of the original proprietors by Messrs. Hardy and Kennedy, who built a store-house near where their brick block now stands, and commenced business upon a large scale. In 1857, they sold to J. W. Phillips the old Forest House, and the south half of the ranch, who immediately laid off the ground into suitable sized building lots, and offered them for sale. In January, 1858, he laid the foundation and commenced the erection of the building now known as the Forest House, which was completed the following May. At about the same time that Phillips commenced building the Forest House, other parties purchased lots and also built, and soon a considerable town had sprung up, and an extensive trade was established.

In the summer of 1858, the first fire proof building built in Forest Hill was erected by Messrs. Hardy and Kennedy ; and many other buildings, though not of such substantial materials, were erected and opened as business houses.

The building of the town where it now stands, not only drew large accessions to its business population from the surrounding towns, but those doing business under the hill moved up into the new town, where the whole business of the place was soon concentrated ; and soon a heavy trade was drawn to the place from the rivers and towns, and camps surrounding it ; being situated on the main thoroughfare leading to Michigan Bluff, Last Chance, Deadwood, Forks House, and the whole upper divide.

We have taken considerable pains to ascertain the amount of tunneling done, and the cost of running the same upon the Forest Hill and Michigan Bluff divides, and give the following as the result : We find that there have been 124,530 feet of bed rock tunnel run, at a cost of $1,888,300. A very large proportion of this immense outlay of capital has been made immediately in the vicinity of Forest Hill ; and by far the greater proportion of those now paying, are within three miles of that place. The resources of Forest Hill are perhaps greater than those of any other mining town in the county. In addition to its vast mining resources, its extensive forests are supplying not only sufficient lumber for the wants of its people, but the mills in the vicinity are sending large quantities to Auburn, Sacramento, and the ranches in the agricultural districts. Lumber is so cheap upon the Forest Hill divide, that notwithstanding the great distance it has to be hauled to market, it can be furnished at Sacramento at prices as low as from any other part of the country.

ILLINOISTOWN.

This place is situated in a small, though beautiful valley, upon the divide between the North Fork of the American and Bear river, about eighteen miles from Auburn, and seven miles from Iowa Hill. Illinoistown is on the direct stage road from Auburn to Iowa Hill. From Illinoistown to Iowa Hill there is one of the most important turnpike roads in the county. The road is known as the "Mineral Bar" road, the grading of which could not have cost less than from $60,000 to $75,000. The hills are precipitous, and in many places the track is blasted out through solid granite of the hardest quality. The road is under the supervision of Chas. Rice, Esq., one of the principal stock-holders, and as the whole of the travel and freighting from Sacramento and other places below for Iowa Hill and all the rich mineral region of country lying between the North Fork of the American river and Shirt Tail must necessarily pass over this road, it pays a reasonable profit upon the cost of its construction.

The mining at Illinoistown was never extensive, and no rich developments were ever made there sufficient to make the town worthy of note as a mining camp, but the situation is an important one in many other respects, and although there are few inhabitants in and about the place, the trade in lumber, miners' supplies, etc., has always been considerable and profitable. The circumstances attending the first settlement of the place, and the ceremony of its christening we find graphically described in a historical sketch of the place, published in the *Placer Herald*, on the 18th of September, 1852, from which we extract the following as the most reliable information in regard to its early history that we can obtain :

" This beautiful valley was first occupied by a few traders in 1849. At that time there was but little mining done within several miles of the place, but discoveries of rich deposits soon after caused hundreds to settle there. [The writer evidently means that the " discovery of rich deposits" were made upon the rivers, and not immediately in the vicinity of the town.—ED.] The bars, and not unfrequently the banks of the North Fork of the American and also of Bear river proved very rich, added to which, many of the immigrants arriving by the Truckee route halted there. Although immense piles were not often made, yet few portions of the mines ever paid better on the average. The settlement at first had as many names as the heroine of a modern romance ; but in the month of October, '49, the miners had a grand dinner in the *town of four houses*, and as the residents and miners were mostly Illinoisans, they, by acclamation and a bottle of whisky, named the place Illinoistown."

From the same sketch we learn that there was at that time—1852—a nursery of fruit trees, and some excellent gardens at the place ; it being the only account we have of an attempt being made, at that early day, to raise fruit in that portion of Placer county.   Illinoistown was at that time considered the "head of wagon navigation," from which to the mines on the rivers, and between the North Fork and Shirt Tail, all the supplies of the inhabitants had to be packed on the backs of mules.

One great source of wealth to the residents of the town is the extensive forests of excellent timber which abounds in the vicinity.   There are two steam saw mills here, which produce yearly millions of feet of lumber, which is sold to the miners in the vicinity, and to the people of the towns in the foothills, at a good price.

RATTLESNAKE.

The village of Rattlesnake is situated on a beautiful flat, on the North Fork of the American River, about seven miles below Auburn.   It is located near Manhattan, Horseshoe and Rattlesnake Bars.   The mines in the channel, banks and bars of the river were worked in 1849, and were exceedingly rich ; and large numbers of miners flocked to that portion of the river to work during the summer and fall seasons, but left again as soon as the winter rains set in, and no permanent settlements were made until after the discovery of the rich diggings in the flat on which the village now stands ; which discovery was made by John C. Barnett & Co., on the 19th day of April, 1853.   The first pan-full of dirt washed by the happy discoverers, after they reached the bed-rock, contained $15 27.   They then washed a bucket-full of the dirt, and obtained $20.

The discovery of these rich diggings in the flat created great excitement among the miners in the vicinity on the river, and at Auburn, Ophir, and other towns in the region round about, and hundreds of men were to be seen daily flocking to the place to secure claims.   Many persons who visited the claim of Barnett & Co. would obtain leave of the company to wash out a pan-full of the dirt, and were often surprised to find a pan-full of the gravel to contain several dollars' worth of gold.

The pay-dirt in the flat was from twenty to sixty feet deep, and so extensive as to give employment to a large number of men.   During the summer of 1853, the travel to and from the place was so great, that a stage line was started between it and Auburn, which ran daily, and did a good paying business.   Substantial buildings were put up, and the place grew rapidly, soon becoming one of the important towns of the county.   The location being one of the prettiest of any town in the county, it became the pride and boast of its inhabitants.   Gardens, orchards and vineyards were planted, and handsome and comfortable cottages were built; showing that, if the people had not confidence in the permanence and stability of the town as a business place, they were satisfied that by a proper cultivation of the generous soil they would receive handsome returns for their labor.   The superior advantages possessed by the place induced many miners to cease digging for gold, and to become tillers of the soil.

The village of Rattlesnake, since its first rise from a river mining camp to the dignity of a town, has ever been considered of sufficient importance to keep up a post office. It is not, however, now considered a brisk business place, and has been gradually declining for several years, but still shows that it was once a place of greater pretensions than at the present day. There are several ditches that convey water to the mines, and those engaged at mining in the vicinity make average wages, there being a plentiful supply of water the year round.

YORKVILLE.

The village of Yorkville is situated on a narrow ridge running down betwen First and Second Brushy Canons, about one mile and a half northeast of Yankee Jim's. At this place there are both tunnel and hydraulic diggings, some of which are very rich and have yielded immense sums of gold. The place has an average voting population of about ninety. The diggings were first discovered in 1853, by Ben. Moss, Frank Emmens and Henry Ewer, who sunk a shaft from the surface to the bed-rock on top of the ridge just below where the village now stands. The hill has been pierced by a large number of tunnels, some of which run entirely through it from one canon to the other. The business houses, at the present time, consist of one store, one billiard saloon and a boarding-house, each of which is doing a good business. There have been a large number of tunnels run into the hills at this place, some of which cost as high as thirty thousand dollars.

Attempts have been made by large capitalists to penetrate the rich deposits in the Forest Hill Divide, by tunnels run through the bed rock from the Brushy Canon side of the ridge, but up to this time, although tunnels have been run a great way into the hill, at a very great expense, none of them have ever reached the main gravel deposits supposed to exist in the center of the hill. A great many, however, have obtained good paying dirt upon the rim rock, and although they failed in the main object of their enterprises, lost nothing by their investments. Some companies even yet, after six years of constant labor in running these tunnels, do not despair of yet reaching the " main lead," and at once becoming millionaires.

PINE GROVE,

Sometimes called "Smithville," is the centre of a large mining district, composed principally of placer diggings, and known as "Secret Diggings." These mines were first struck in 1850, by Messrs. Post & Ripley, and Wm. Gamble, and the first work done was in the neighborhood of " New Castle," which is now defunct as a town. Gradually the miners worked further down towards the plains, where was built a new town, which was named Stewart's Flat ; but, like most mining towns of an early date, it has gone into a decline.

Pine Grove was established about the same time as Stewart's Flat, and has improved very gradually, until it is now the centre of a population of some 1,500 inhabitants. Very many of the residents of the district are permanent, having large farms fenced in and under cultivation. The mines will without doubt last for a long term of years, and the town has a fair prospect of a lengthened existence.

Among our business men we count one of our old pioneers, L. G. Smith, at present one of the representatives of this county in the Legislature, who was the first to establish a trading post at this place. Another is Wm. D. Perkins, familiarly known as Dana Perkins, proprietor of the Pine Grove Hotel. He has a fine race track near his house for quarter racing, as well as one of the finest dancing-halls in the State. A large proportion of the mining population are "forty-niners."

We have a Dashaway Association at this place, which has been in existence since the 20th of January, 1860. It consists of some thirty-five members. The officers are: John F. Weaver, President; C. A. Mullen, First Vice President; B. W. Neff, Second Vice President; J. W. Belden, Recording Secretary; W. Becker, Financial Secretary; Wm. Vosburgh, Treasurer. They have now a library of two hundred and eighty volumes. The Post Office address for Pine Grove is Secret Ravine Post Office; Edward Cook, Postmaster.

The officers of the township of which this is the centre are: John B. White, Collector, office at Pine Grove; G. C. Harmon, Assessor, office at Stewart's Flat; Edward Cook, Justice of the Peace, office at Pine Grove; Samuel Ray, Justice of the Peace, office on the Auburn Road, two miles from Pine Grove.

GENERAL DIRECTORY

OF THE

COUNTY OF PLACER.

A

Anderson Geo. L. attorney-at-law,	Commercial st, Auburn
ALLEN B. C. banker,	Main st, do
Addrian A. baker, Eagle Bakery,	Main st, do
Andrews M. watch-maker and jew'r,	Commercial st, do
Atkinson John, laborer,	California st, do
Armitage J. laborer,	bds Am. Hotel, do
Ambrose William, steward,	American Hotel, do
Arkwell John, miner,	Ophir
Abbott A. J. livery stable,	Main st, Virginia
Aldrich Geo. D. merchant,	Main st, do
Aldrich E. K. clerk,	Main st, do
Anderson B. D. hotel-keeper,	Mt. Pleasant House, Turnpike Road
Applegate George W. farmer,	Lisbon
Averal W. laborer,	Applegate's Ranch, Lisbon
Aitken B. engineer,	Massachusetts Mill
Atckinson R. farmer,	Rock Creek
Atckinson Thomas, miner,	do do
Arnold John, miner,	Gold Hill
Anderson Andrew, miner,	do do
Airs L. B. miner,	Horse Shoe Bar
Andrews N. miner,	Rattlesnake
Atwood N. teamster,	bds Crescent City, Auburn
Annibal William, miner,	Mugginsville
Anderson Thomas, miner,	Grizzly Bear House
Albrecht E. C. W. merchant,	do do do
Atkinson J. W. miner,	Forest Hill
Acker E. M. carpenter,	do do
Ash H. teamster,	do do
ANGELL A. J. saloon-keeper,	do do
Andrews George W. saloon-keeper,	do do
Awart Chas. miner,	do do
Arras Conrad, boot-maker,	do do
Aikins H. D. tinsmith,	do do
Armstrong Adam, ranchman,	do do

ARMSTRONG'S
LIVERY STABLE.

The undersigned begs leave to inform his former patrons and the public generally, that he can always be found at the Old Stable, on

MAIN STREET, DUTCH FLAT,

where he is prepared to accommodate his friends with Good Saddle and Harness Horses, Carriages, Buggies, &c., &c.

☞ Horses groomed and boarded, by the day, week or month.

JOHN ARMSTRONG.

ANGELL'S
NEW BILLIARD SALOON,

In Old Post Office Building, on North side of Broadway,
FOREST HILL.

WINES, LIQUORS AND CIGARS of the very best quality. ☞ FANCY DRINKS MIXED TO ORDER.
Two New Tables, with Phelan's Improved Cushions.

A. J. ANGELL, Proprietor.

GEO. BISHOP.   M. DODSWORTH.   A. SEIFERT.

BISHOP & CO.
MEAT 🐑 MARKET

MAIN STREET, AUBURN.

☞ The Finest Supply of MEATS kept constantly on Hand.

Allen T. miner,	do do
Allen John, miner,	do do
Arthur William, miner,	do do
Adams Samuel, butcher,	do do
Atwill J. M. miner,	do do
Allington John, miner,	do do
Adams S. S. miner,	do do
Avens John, miner,	do do
Alers William, miner,	do do
Alix Joseph, miner,	do do
Arthur James, miner,	Todd's Valley
Arthur James, Jr. miner,	do do
Allison J. G. tinsmith,	do do
Anderson L. miner,	do do
Adams Samuel, butcher,	Forest Hill
Atwill J. M. miner,	do do
Alexander Andrew, lumberman,	Michigan Bluff
Adams Samuel, saloon-keeper,	do do
Armstrong John, stage-driver,	do do
Aldrich J. M. miner,	do do
Allen E. miner,	do do
Albeck Charles, miner,	do do
Ashley James, miner,	do do
Abrams L. miner,	do do
Anderson — miner,	do do
Allen "Old Grizzly," packer,	do do
Armstrong A. S. miner,	do do
Addison William, miner,	do do
Ailsworth Daniel, carpenter,	Last Chance, Michigan Bluff
Arnott James, miner,	do do do do
Abernethy G. L. miner,	do do do do
Allen Fred. miner,	Long Cañon, do do
Appleton Ned, miner,	Michigan Bluff
Amstrong Robert, miner,	do do
Arnold A. J. miner,	do do
Andrews B. H. miner,	do do
Andrews Mathew, miner,	do do
Ash James, miner,	do do
Ayres Lorenzo, miner,	do do
Amesberry James, miner,	do do
Adriano F. miner,	do do
Anderson William, (colored) porter,	Yankee Jim's
Ambriester S. miner,	do do
Adams George, miner,	do do
Adams L. miner,	do do
Adams Timothy, miner,	do do
Armsden Joseph, miner,	do do
Andrews Joseph, miner,	do do
Andrews Christian, miner,	do do
Abbott James, miner,	do do
Ayer Osborn, miner,	Iowa Hill

Atkinson H. S. miner,	Iowa Hill
Adams Jonathan, miner,	do do
Ackerman J. miner,	do do
Amisk Peter, miner,	do do
Anderson Andrew, miner,	do do
Alex C. miner,	do do
Ashley R. M. miner,	do do
Angle J. D. livery stable keeper,	do do
Arnold L. B .lawyer,	do do
Arrington William, miner,	do do
Archie E. Z. miner,	do do
Andrews N. P. miner,	do do
Allen Easten, miner,	do do
Austin George, miner,	do do
Austin James, miner,	do do
Abrams Frank, miner,	do do
Able William, miner,	do do
Arnold Moses, miner,	do do
Allen L. T. butcher,	do do
Armstrong R. J. miner,	do do
Atkinson Joseph W. miner,	do do
Anderson Nat, miner,	do do
Ault A. J. miner,	do do
Austin Lawrence, miner,	Illinoistown
Ashley J. T. miner,	Forks House
Alexander James, ranching,	Galt House
Able Joseph, merchant,	Texas Flat
Anderson John Z. landlord,	Star House
Abeel Jacob, miner,	Dutch Flat
Annibal Wm. miner,	Mugginsville
Abeel Jno. miner,	Dutch Flat
Abeel Henry, miner,	do do
ARMSTRONG JNO. livery stable	do do
Amburgh R. miner,	do do
Austin Thos. miner,	do do
Austin R. miner,	do do
Antwerp E. lawyer,	do do
Allen Crawford, clerk,	do do
Austin Jno. miner,	do do
Anderson Jno. miner,	do do
Anderson Thos. miner,	do do
Austin E. miner,	do do
Arnstein L. merchant,	do do

B

Browne J. L. clerk,	Hall & Allen's Bank, Main st, Auburn	
BISHOP & CO. Aub. Meat Market,	Main st,	do
Bishop & Long,	res Main st,	do
Broomhead William, carpenter,	res Sacramento st,	do
Beckett J. F. miner,	bds Empire Hotel,	do

Batton S. beer saloon,	Main st,	Auburn
Barny John, Empire Livery Stable,	Washington st,	do
Barrett S. E. carpenter,	bds Empire Hotel,	do
Brown John, teamster,	Gove & Gordon,	do
BROOKS J. P. banker and b'k-st'e,	cor Center Block,	do
Bronson W. S. physician,	County Hospital, Com. st,	do
Barnhart Barnhart, teamster,	Auburn Turnpike Road	
Barckman John, blacksmith,	Baltimore Ravine	
Bullock L. L. Sheriff,	Court House, Auburn	
Banvard E. M. Treasurer,	Court House, do	
Barrett J. S. teamster,	Court st, do	
Butts George C. sawyer,	bds Hogan's Rest, Auburn	
Butler W. S. school teacher,	bds Hogan's do	
Bayard Charles, laborer,	bds Orleans Hotel	
Bigerman M.	Cox's Ranch	
Bird A. B. bar-keeper,	American Hotel, Auburn	
Boggs J. C. Constable,	res Turnp'e R'd, do	
Boyle James, miner,	Millertown	
Bickford D. lawyer,	Ophir,	
Broomley John, miner,	do	
Black R. miner,	bds American Hotel, Gold Hill,	
Blane George, miner,	bds American Hotel, do do	
Bond J. A. physician,	bds Mason's Hotel, Main st, Gold Hill	
Brannon D. H. saloon-keeper,	Main st,	do do
Berk George, butcher,	Main st,	do do
Burton & McCarty, G. H. & L. G. mer,	Main st,	do do
Bell John, teamster,	Main st,	do do
Blankenship J. H. hotel-keeper,	Main st, Virginia,	
Bell A. O. farmer,	do	
Betts G. H. laborer,	do	
Beck Jas. Justice of the Peace,	Fox's Flat	
Bowen M. farmer,	do do	
Barton John, farmer,	on Old Marysville Road	
Bristow Capt. farmer,	Sacramento Road	
Barnhart Charles, farmer,	Fox's Flat	
Bradly, Clark & Co. Magnolia Mill,	Bear River	
Brickell B. prop'r Placer Exchange,	Illinoistown	
Brown Jonathan, Placer Exchange,	do	
Brickell Ed, Illinoistown Hotel,	do	
Beal B. laborer,	do	
Buckley H. bar-keeper,	Blue Wing, Illinoistown	
Baldwin John, butcher,	Illinoistown	
Beals Charles, laborer,	do	
Boles John, miner,	Rock Creek	
Bradley G. lumber merchant,	Magnolia Mills, Bear River	
Baldwin Andrew, lumber merchant,	Magnolia Mills, do do	
Brown G. miner,	Gold Hill	
Bowers D. hotel-keeper,	Turnpike Road	
Banvard B. H. mason,	do do	
Baluss John, laborer,	do do	
Bullard E. C. laborer,	Mountaineer	

Bemis Sam, carpenter,	Whisky Bar Bridge
Beach John H. miner,	Rattlesnake
Beach D. S. Ditch Agent,	do
Bigler C. miner,	do
Becklen C. baker,	do
Beck Sam, clerk,	do
Boles R. miner,	do
Bouillion J. farmer,	do
Bherman — miner,	do
Barkley A. miner,	Auburn Ravine
Barnes John, farmer	Coon Creek
Brouse H. W. farmer,	Doty's Ravine
Black C. S., N. F. Road Sup't,	Auburn
Baker H. W. miner,	Grizzly Bear House
Baldwin E. blacksmith,	Forest Hill
Baglan John D. miner,	do do
Barbour George W. teamster,	do do
Beckman Conrad, merchant,	do do
Baker E. G. tinsmith,	do do
Buckingham W. H. tinsmith,	do do
Brannan John, miner,	do do
Breed Alfred, packer,	do do
Benfeldt Henry, restaurant prop'r,	do do
Burns J. J. miner,	do do
Byrn Robert, miner,	do do
Byrn Patrick, miner,	do do
Borland John, miner.	do do
Borland James, miner,	do do
Bradley J. A. miner,	do do
Bilkey James, miner,	do do
Buchanan William, miner,	do do
Burns D. miner,	do do
Beck Philip, baker,	do do
Besquett Peter, miner,	do do
Ball William C. miner,	do do
Bowen T. D. miner,	Bath
Boyd John, cook,	do
Began William, miner,	do
Burt B. D. merchant,	do
Burt S. B. merchant,	do
Bradford E. W. miner,	do
Banks Joseph, miner,	do
Bruce A. miner,	do
Burt G. A. hotel-keeper,	do
Barrett E. Tax Collector,	do
Backman M. miner,	do
Bartholomew John, miner,	do
Bafman M. miner,	do
Brown John H. miner,	do
Burns James, miner,	do
Brown John, miner,	do

Burns Patrick, miner,	Forest Hill	
Burns Robert, miner,	do	do
Burns Dennis, miner,	do	do
Brewer J. C. miner,	do	do
Bower S. S. miner,	do	do
Brothers A. L. miner,	do	do
Bradley E. S. musician,	do	do
Bissell E. L. miner,	do	do
Blanchard Charles, steward in hotel,	do	do
Burrows G. W. miner,	do	do
Beswick W. G. miner,	do	do
Burdong Henry, miner,	do	do
Baines J. M. miner,	do	do
Baire M. miner,	do	do
Buckman M. miner,	do	do
Babbitt J. J. lumberman,	do	do
Bennett Joshua, lumberman,	Todd's Valley	
Bennett William, lumberman,	do	do
Barnes A. miner,	do	do
Brady M. miner,	do	do
Benninger Lewis, miner,	do	do
Burnell E. S. lumberman,	do	do
Bradley William J. lumberman,	do	do
Bowley William, lumberman,	do	do
Bradley John, butcher,	do	do
Brown J. B. (colored) barber,	do	do
Bradley T. J. butcher,	do	do
Baker P. Z. miner,	do	do
Bunn H. W. Ditch Superintendent,	do	do
Brown A. D. carpenter,	do	do
Blank William H. carpenter,	do	do
Baker Arnold, miner,	do	do
Baker C. O. miner,	do	do
Burtley John, trader,	do	do
Benedict N. merchant,	do	do
Buckner John, miner,	do	do
Ball W. H. miner,	do	do
Blackburn Joseph, miner,	do	do
Bryan H. S. miner,	do	do
Bowers Z. miner,	do	do
Bouty William,	do	do
Brown L. W. miner,	do	do
Burrell T. J. miner,	do	do
Burnham L. blacksmith,	do	do
Barnes W. miner,	do	do
Blanchard T. miner,	do	do
Bullock J. W. miner,	do	do
Brown Dr. William, miner,	do	do
Bishop A. J. miner,	do	do
Bigelow V. G. miner,	do	do
Boyles John M. miner,	do	do

Bachelder Charles. miner,			Todd's Valley	
Brown Pat, miner,			do	do
Bradley G. N. miner,			do	do
Brown Charles, miner,			Forks House	
Belisle E. G. miner,			do	do
Belisle D. G. miner,			do	do
Bullock W. H. lawyer,			Michigan Bluff	
Bowering A. M. miner,			do	do
Black C. T. trader,			do	do
Brady J. W. trader,			do	do
Buck Henry, trader,			do	do
Bullard A. D. trader,			do	do
Barras Thomas, trader,			do	do
Brown Henry, trader,			do	do
Bartlett E. H. trader,			do	do
Burnes Joseph, miner,			do	do
Baldwin M. miner,			do	do
Bell William, miner,			do	do
Bennett Joseph, miner,			do	do
Burg L. A. miner,			do	do
Barnes H. M. ranchman,	Last Chance,		do	do
Bum J. miner,	do	do	do	do
Brooks J. W. miner,	do	do	do	do
Booth Ed. miner,	do	do	do	do
Booth Elijah, miner,	do	do	do	do
Brown Henry, miner,	do	do	do	do
Burns James, miner,	do	do	do	do
Bowers Henry, miner,	do	do	do	do
Brasher Stephen, miner,	do	do	do	do
Brownell William, miner,	do	do	do	do
Bagley Fred. miner,	do	do	do	do
Bartlett J. W. butcher,	do	do	do	do
Brown Robert, miner,	do	do	do	do
Bombay Jacob, miner,	do	do	do	do
Bousley Henry, miner,	do	do	do	do
Brown L. G. miner,	do	do	do	do
Bateo Edward, miner,			do	do
Baldwin Charles, miner,			do	do
Burke Martin, miner,			do	do
Beeman Martin, miner.			do	do
Bullen James, miner,			do	do
Bullen C. J. miner,			do	do
Bullen William, miner,			do	do
Beneman James, miner,			do	do
Bryant James, miner,			do	do
Brown James, miner,			do	do
Brown George, miner,			do	do
Byrd J. W. miner,			do	do
Brodie Robert, miner,			do	do
Benson Charles, miner,			do	do
Brown D. P. miner,			do	do

KEYSTONE STABLES!

MAIN STREET, FOREST HILL, CAL.

Having purchased the entire interest of H. ASH, my former partner, in this well-known LIVERY STABLE, the proprietor would inform his friends and the traveling public, that he is prepared to

FURNISH SADDLE HORSES,

BUGGIES AND HACKS

To all persons desirous of riding for pleasure or on business. Our Saddle and Harness Horses are gentle and well trained. We exchange with the Pioneer Stables, at Auburn; with George Haycock & Co., at Iowa Hill; with Stephens' Stables, at Todd's Valley and Georgetown; with Reed's Stable, at Yankee Jim's, and with George Kimball, at Michigan Bluff.

☞ Horses and Mules Groomed by the day or week, at reduced prices.

JOHH DEWAR.

Braden John, miner,	Michigan	Bluff
Baker H. R. miner,	do	do
Biggs Adam, miner,	do	do
Burke Martin, miner,	do	do
Buzzard L. B. miner,	do	do
Baathe Joseph, miner,	do	do
Bathers Joseph, miner,	do	do
Baker J. H. ranchman,	do	do
Bunker Obe, miner,	do	do
Bleaks John, miner,	do	do
Bleaks Samuel, miner,	do	do
Bardwell John, miner,	do	do
Browning John, miner,	do	do
Benedict Louis, teamster,	Yankee	Jim's
Barstow William, express agent,	do	do
Biteley Robert, dairyman,	do	do
Benjamin John, miner,	do	do
Burns Hugh, miner,	do	do
Burrow A. F. miner,	do	do
Burrow Eli, miner,	do	do
Burrow Aaron, miner,	do	do
Bennett Jo. miner,	do	do
Bowman S. W. miner,	do	do
Baxter N. M. miner,	do	do
Balch George, blacksmith,	do	do
Beilderman Conrad, saloon-keeper,	do	do
Beckford A. miner,	do	do
Burdell George, miner,	do	do
Battman J. W. miner,	do	do
Barnhill Robert, miner,	do	do
Bumgardener J. miner,	Iowa	Hill
Ball J. miner,	do	do
Byers J. miner,	do	do
Bumgardener Jacob, miner,	do	do
Baker J. ranchman,	do	do
Beardsley J. H. miner,	do	do
Bawden H. miner,	do	do
Burnett O. miner,	do	do
Brenneman J. miner,	do	do
Brightmore W. miner,	do	do
Bernadat J. E. miner,	do	do
Benjamin Jacob, miner,	do	do
Bracken John, miner,	Illinoistown	
Barker Jno. miner,	Dutch	Flat
Boke Jno. miner,	do	do
Blanchard N. W. miner,	do	do
Burk F. P. miner,	do	do
Brandy J. miner,	do	do
Boardman J. miner,	do	do
Blackburn B. carpenter,	do	do
Bavin Wm. miner,	do	do

Browning S. M. miner,	Dutch Flat
Boke A. miner,	do do
Boust E. B. editor of *Enquirer*,	do do
Beal G. P. miner,	do do
Baker S. miner,	do do
Bartlett G. F. ditchman,	do do
Barkley J. H. merchant,	do do
Bixbury S. miner,	do do
Barrett E. A. miner,	do do
Brown H. G. miner,	do do
Burns Thos. miner,	do do
Bloom J. S. farmer,	do do
Berdict J. miner,	do do
Barr S. R. miner,	do do
Bradley G. A. ditch-tender,	do do
Belden W. W. miner,	do do
Bock H. miner,	do do
Barker O. C. miner,	do do
Bookstand R. H. miner,	do do
Brown A. milkman,	do do
Bowen H. miner,	do do
Boyd Jno. miner,	do do
Burckhalten F. merchant,	do do
Bennett C. blacksmith,	do do
Brickell I. W. teamster,	do. do
Bower A. J. miner,	do do
Blackmore A. miner,	do do
Bader C. miner,	do do
Brown C. J. miner,	do do
Bentley I. miner,	do do
Bennett J. N. miner,	do do
Barnum S. D. miner,	do do
Blake A. miner,	do do
Bradley Wm. ditchman,	do do
Bresston James, miner,	do do
Beard A. miner,	do do
Budd James, miner,	do do
Brooks Thos. miner,	do do
Boyd C. M. miner,	do do
Briggs E. M. miner,	do do
Bentley A. D. miner,	do do
Bachelor C. D. miner,	Pine Grove
Bolton George, miner,	do do
Beach Julius, ranching,	do do
Bradly S. R. ranching,	Galt House
Blenn James, miner,	Beal's Bar
Bumps Silas, teamster,	do do
Breed J. C. miner,	do do
Bell Robt. miner,	do do
Burk Thos. miner,	Rose Springs
Baldwin D. B. butcher,	Rattlesnake

Blake James, miner,	Rattlesnake		
Bryant Alexander, saloon keeper,	do		
Brown Chas. miner,	do		
Brown L. C. miner,	do		
Behrman Peter, miner,	do		
Boyden A. miner,	Fox's Flat		
Brown Otis, miner,	do do		
Bond Thomas, miner,	Virginia		
Bane Wm. packer,	Illinoistown		
Barrett George, ranchman	do		
Brown L. D. ranchman,	Starbuck's Mill		
Bower David, ranchman,	Wild Cat		
Ball I. C. lawyer,	Galt House		
Borach M. miner,	Dutch Flat		
Broils J. miner,	do do		
Bradley E. L. ditch owner,	do do		
Bailey S. S. clerk,	do do		
Broils Thos. miner,	do do		
Brooks J. W. miner,	do do		
Brown Adam, miner,	do do		
Barker F. miner,	do do		
Browning John, miner,	Michigan Bluffs		
Benedict Louis, teamster,	Yankee Jim's		
Barstow Wm. express agent,	do do		
Bitely Robert, dairyman,	do do		
Benjamin John, miner,	do do		
Burns, Hugh, miner,	do do		
Burrow A. F. miner,	do do		
Burrow Eli, miner,	do do		
Burrow Aaron, miner,	do do		
Bennett Jo. miner,	do do		
Bowman S. W. miner,	do do		
Baxter N. M. miner,	do do		
Balch, Geo. blacksmith,	do do		
Beilderman Conrad, saloon keeper,	do do		
Beckford A. miner,	do do		
Burdell Geo. miner,	do do		
Battman J. W. miner	do do		
Barnhill Robt. miner,	do do		
Booth Arthur, miner,	do do		
Bradley S. R. miner,	do do		
Brown Samuel, miner,	do do		
Barron Fletcher, miner,	do do		
Brown Chas. miner,	do do		
Baker Artemas, miner,	do do		
Baker Artemas jr. miner,	do do		
Brown J. F. merchant,	(Wisconsin Hill)	Iowa Hill	
Brown John, miner,	do do	do do	
Barton, John L. miner,	do do	do do	
Bilden John, miner,	do do	do do	
Brown Alfred, miner,	do do	do do	

Buckhart Fred. miner,	(Wisconsin Hill)		Iowa Hill	
Bird Frank, miner,	do	do	do	do
Brown Philip, miner	do	do	do	do
Brown J. R. ditchowner	do	do	do	do
Bennett Josiah, miner,	Iowa Hill			
Bennett D. C. miner,	do	do		
Bennett Leonard, miner,	do	do		
Bentley T. B. miner,	do	do		
Brensteder Wm. miner,	do	do		
Bowers Dan. miner,	do	do		
Blanchard Wm. miner	do	do		
Bruce Wm. miner,	do	do		
Bradwell Geo. miner,	do	do		
Brown J. B. miner,	do	do		
Brooks Geo. G. miner,	do	do		
Birch J. miner,	do	do		
Barrett A. miner,	do	do		
Barney J. N. merchant,	do	do		
Booth Garrett, miner,	do	do		
Bently Samuel, miner,	do	do		
Blue Gilbert, miner,	do	do		
Blue Wm. miner.	do	do		
Bush Fred, miner,	do	do		
Booth R. J. miner,	do	do		
Blackburn Isaac, miner,	do	do		
Bapp F. miner,	do	do		
Billington Jas. miner,	do	do		
Bounds T. W. clerk,	do	do		
Backus Peter, baker	do	do		
Bumpus E. D. miner,	do	do		
Billington E. miner,	do	do		
Boyden A. L. watchman,	do	do		
Behannen P. M. miner,	do	do		
Bumpus Peter, miner,	do	do		
Bawley J. Q. A. miner,	do	do		
Bisbee John G. blacksmith,	do	do		
Bisbee A. carriagemaker,	do	do		
Breen Patrick, miner,	do	do		
Bisbee D. H. miner,	do	do		
Bisbee H. P. miner,	do	do		
Bisbee A. H. miner,	do	do		
Blake F. miner,	do	do		
Barrenger T. miner,	do	do		

C

CREDIT & BURLINGAM, proprietors Bank Exchange, Main st. Auburn
Cromer, L. W. tinner, Main street, do
Cash Martin, miner, Grizzly Diggings
Cloth Jno. bds. Batton's, Main st. do
Collins M. wood chopper, Empire Hotel, do

AUBURN
DRUG STORE

SIGN OF THE BIG MORTAR,

Corner of Washington and Main Streets,

Where all things pertaining to the trade is constantly kept on hand and for Sale, such as

Drugs, Medicines, Patent Medicines,

HAIR OILS and PERFUMERIES OF ALL KINDS.

PAINTS, OILS,

WINDOW GLASS, BRUSHES OF ALL KINDS, &c.

☞ Orders from the Country promptly attended to. PHYSICIANS' PRESCRIPTIONS prepared with accuracy, by

H. HAZELL, Apothecary.

JO. HAMILTON,
ATTORNEY AT LAW,

(DISTRICT ATTORNEY FOR PLACER COUNTY.)

AUBURN, PLACER COUNTY, CAL.

Will give prompt attention to all CIVIL BUSINESS entrusted to his care.

LOUISIANA RESTAURANT,

JEFFERSON HOGAN, - PROPRIETOR.

BETWEEN WASHINGTON and MAIN STS.

☞ MEALS SERVED UP AT ALL HOURS.

Crandall J. R. Sec'y Bear River Co.	Court st.	Auburn
Conway James, tailor,	bds. Orleans Hotel,	do
Crawford & Openshaw, Temple Saloon,	cor. Com. & Court sts.	do
Credit J. G.	bds. Soda Factory, East st.	do
Caust Jacob, carpenter,	Sacramento st.	do
Crutcher W. M. Deputy Sheriff,	Court House,	do
Curtis, E. J. teamster,	Geo. Willment's store,	do
Conner John, District Collector,	bds. American Hotel,	do
Clancy John, laborer,	bds. Orleans Hotel,	do
Charbonnean John B. clerk,	Orleans Hotel,	do
Coulter Day, miner,	Ill. and Sac. roads,	do
Cross Thos. tinner,	Sacramento st.	do
Clark Jas. H. prop. Yankee Jim's S. L.		do
Christopher B. miner,	Millertown	
Collins James, farmer,	Spanish Flat	
Castello James, miner,	N. Ravine, Millertown,	
Crus A. miner,	Schnable's Quartz Mills, Ophir	
Cunningham M. miner,		do
Choate D. merch't and Dist. Collector,	Main st.	do
Choate M. clerk,	Main st.	do
Choate N. miner,	Main st.	do
Cory Isaac, blacksmith,	Main st.	do
Curtis D. B. miner,	North Ravine,	
Cummings H. farmer,	Ophir	
Curtis George, farmer,	do	
Culleun Geo. prop. El Dorado Saloon,	Main st. Gold Hill	
Campbell Wm. blacksmith,	do do do	
Crocker & Young, merchants,	do do do	
Crocker C. E. of firm C. & Y.	do do do	
Clary S. meat pedler,	Ham & Harford, Gold Hill	
Challioll Geo. miner,	Gold Hill	
Coleman Thos. W. miner,	Virginia	
Colburn Thos. miner,	do	
Cowen J. B. miner,	do	
Carter J. farmer,	Auburn Ravine	
Cadellon W. farmer,	Danesville	
Crosby —. farmer,	do	
Conneyham John, miner,	Fox's Flat	
Cook J. D. B. farmer,	Lincoln	
Conner Patrick, laborer,	Applegate's Ranch, Lisbon	
Curtis Hiram, laborer,	do do do	
Craig John, clerk,	Main st Illinoistown	
Ciouse Jas. blacksmith,	Illinoistown	
Cornelus Wm. laborer,	do	
Collins Dr. D. B. merchant,	Humbug Cañon	
Cole H. farmer,	Spring Ranch	
Clark Ephraim, lumber merchant,	Magnolia Mill, Bear River	
Cummings W. C. cook,	Mountaineer	
Colbreth P. laborer,	do	
Craig C. A. farmer,	Whisky Bar Bridge	
Cordes C. miner,	Rattlesnake	

Casidy A. miner,	Rattlesnake
Cooper D. merchant,	do
Carigener C. blacksmith,	do
Cortez R. miner,	do
Collins J. C. miner,	do
Carpenter C. E. lawyer,	do
Cummings R. P. laborer,	do
Carter —— miner,	do
Campbell H. D. prop. Bloomer Ranch,	
Cox Paul, farmer, Cox's Ranch,	Marysville road
CREDIT I. W. pro. Bank Exchange,	Main st. Auburn
CONKEY W. W. of H. & C.	Sac. st. do
Crious G. laborer,	Coon Creek
Chamberlin S. R. farmer,	do do
Chamberlin T. L. farmer,	do do
Cochrane Thos. hotel keeper,	do do
Carter I. farmer,	Auburn Ravine
Clark Jas. H. farmer,	Newtown Road
Cannaham James, miner,	Pine Grove
Carr George, teamster,	do do
Cousens A. F. blacksmith,	do do
Callender D. S. ranchman,	Galt House
Cromnett T. J. ranchman,	do do
Craft John B. ranchman,	Beal's Bar
Chadwick W. J. miner,	do do
Cornish H. miner,	do do
Cheny John P. saloon keeper,	do do
Coward John, miner,	Rattlesnake
Cobern John, miner,	do
Cowden John, clerk,	do
Conda Patrick, miner,	do
Clemmens Chas.	do
Curtis, W. R. hotel keeper,	Virginia
Combs Chas. laborer,	Illinoistown
Cook Edw. J. P.	Pine Grove
Cartwright George, farmer,	Secret Ravine
Cole A. miner,	Grizzly Bear House
Cameron J. A. miner,	do do do
Cosgrave Michael, toll-gate keeper,	do do do
Cox Frank, miner,	Forest Hill
Copely A. W. carpenter,	do do
Cook Wm. miner,	do do
Cogle John, miner,	do do
Craner A. P. miner,	do do
Creagh Thos. A. saloon keeper,	do do
Collins John, miner,	do do
Carroll G. W. clerk in store,	do do
Crandall Frank, miner,	do do
Chatterson T. D. music teacher,	do do
Clark Henry, miner,	do do
Clark J. H. stage proprietor,	do do

GOLD HILL
LIVERY STABLE

KELLY & ABBOTT,   -   PROPRIETORS.

The undersigned beg leave to inform their former patrons and the public generally, that they have constantly on hand, to let or hire,

HORSES, BUGGIES,
(DOUBLE OR SINGLE.)

BAROUCHES, CONCORD WAGONS, ETC.

HORSES TO DRIVE OR FOR THE SADDLE,

To be had at all times, and of the very best stock. As they design to keep a No. 1 Stable, none but the best Stock will suit them.

TRANSIENT STOCK left at the Stable, will receive every care and attention at Reasonable Prices.

F. H. KELLY.   A. J. ABBOTT.

Conly James, miner,	Forest	Hill
Craig J. W. miner,	do	do
Craig W. P. A. miner,	do	do
Craig R. J. miner,	do	do
Craig M. W. miner,	do	do
Craig F. R. miner,	do	do
Craig P. C. miner,	do	do
Cràig W. H. miner,	do	do
Craig James, miner,	do	do
Covington J. miner,	do	do
Crapsey J. R. miner,	do	do
Curtis C. miner,	do	do
Curtis D. C. miner,	do	do
Creamer A. R. miner,	do	do
Clark Henry J. miner,	do	do
Corcoran John, miner,	do	do
Cullom John, miner,	do	do
Case Charles, miner,	do	do
Cribbs Abraham, miner,	do	do
Carr Joseph, miner,	do	do
Campbell J. A. miner,	do	do
Cawgill Elisha, ditch superintendent,	do	do
Camron John, miner,	do	do
Cox John, miner,	do	do
Caley James, saloon keeper, [H. B.]	do	do
Curran A, miner,	do	do
Cartwell James, miner,	do	do
Cantwell M. miner,	do	do
Cantwell M. Jr. miner,	do	do
Clark Anthony, miner,	do	do
Cassiday John, miner,	do	do
Cox C. miner,	do	do
Calton James, miner,	do	do
Campbell Thomas, ditch owner,	do	do
Crandall H. hotel keeper,	do	do
Caules Wm. miner,	do	do
Crary Joseph, miner,	Todd's Valley	
Casey Edward, miner,	do	do
Casey Thomas, miner,	do	do
Crassman J. S. sawmill proprietor,	do	do
Cawsa John, miner,	do	do
Cadman Thos. miner,	do	do
Crawell Thomas, miner,	do	do
Colquett Henry, miner,	do	do
Carmicle A. miner,	do	do
Carmicle J. S. miner,	do	do
Crane C. A. miner,	do	do
Conner John, miner,	do	do
Carlson John, miner,	do	do
Constable Chas. miner,	do	do
Coburn S. S. lumberman,	Michigan Bluff	

Cunningham W. W. hotel keeper,	Michigan Bluff,	
Craig John, miner,	do	do
Cowden Frank, miner,	do	do
Cory Wm. banker,	do	do
Cory Samuel, banker,	do	do
Cleveland J. J. minister,	do	do
Crosse B. L. miner,	do	do
Chambers Wm. miner,	do	do
Curran Peter, miner,	do	do
Clark L. S. miner,	do	do
Coburn P. F. miner,	do	do
Carpenter, C. H. miner,	do	do
Case H. W. stable keeper,	do	do
Case S. R. carpenter,	do	do
Carter Geo. miner,	do	do
Craig James G. miner,	do	do
Cloudman Thos. H. miner,	do	do
Cally A. miner,	do	do
Curran John, miner,	do	do
Clinting Henry, miner,	do	do
Cusick Geo. miner,	do	do
Crumwalt Frank, miner,	do	do
Collins Thomas, miner,	do	do
Collins Daniel, miner,	do	do
Clark Henry, miner,	do	do
Caana C. J. P. miner, [Last Chance,]	do	do
Cooper James, miner, do do	do	do
Christman P. miner, do do	do	do
Corbett Daniel, miner, do do	do	do
Caldwell C. physician, do do	do	do
Carter, J. miner,	do	do
Conly S. miner,	do	do
Conly F. miner,	do	do
Clark Michael, miner,	do	do
Collins Wm. miner, [Long Cañon,]	do	do
Coffin John, miner,	do	do
Cook Chas. W. miner,	do	do
Clow Edward, ranchman,	do	do
Clark John, miner,	do	do
Cannon John, miner,	do	do
Cheesbrough David, miner,	do	do
Corcoran Wm. miner,	do	do
Carey Joseph, miner,	do	do
Chestnut James, miner,	do	do
Clancy M. miner,	do	do
Clancy O. H. miner,	do	do
Clancy Martin, miner,	do	do
Cahill Patrick, miner,	do	do
Clancy Hugh, miner,	do	do
Calahan Michael, miner,	do	do
Cornett John, miner,	do	do

DUTCH FLAT
LIVERY STABLE,
By THOMAS MORRIS.

The undersigned would inform his friends and the public generally, that he has added extensively to his already large and elegant Establishment of HORSES, BUGGIES, SADDLES, HARNESS, Etc., and is now prepared to afford as fine a Turnout as can be had in the State. ☞ Particular attention paid to Horses on Livery.

THOMAS MORRIS.

A. LIPSETT,
DEALER IN
MENS' AND BOYS' CLOTHING
BOOTS, SHOES, ETC.
STONE BUILDING, CORNER OF MAIN AND COURT STS.
AUBURN, CAL.

T. LAUTENSHLAGER,
MERCHANT TAILOR,
COMMERCIAL STREET, AUBURN.

Keeps constantly on hand a carefully selected assortment of GERMAN and FRENCH CLOTHS, CASSIMERES and VESTINGS, which he is now prepared to cut and make up in the latest style, at moderate charges. ☞ Give me a Call.

Caffyn Stephen, miner,	Michigan Bluff	
Cooney John, miner,	Yankee Jim's,	
Crane H. F. miner,	do	do
Crane R. W. miner,	do	do
Coffin Wm. L. soda factory,	do	do
Copenhagen G. merchant,	do	do
Christian James, miner,	do	do
Condon Joseph, miner,	do	do
Condon Henry, miner,	do	do
Cravens R. O. miner,	do	do
Carlisle C. W. miner,	do	do
Cranage Wm. miner,	do	do
Campbell A. miner,	do	do
Champion L. miner,	do	do
Crary Wm. miner,	do	do
Castrum J. B. miner,	do	do
Cross W. T. miner,	Iowa Hill	
Chittenden, W. S. miner,	do	do
Conner Wm. miner,	do	do
Christie W. F. miner,	do	do
Campbell Thos. miner,	do	do
Caval Benj. miner,	do	do
Carr John, miner,	do	do
Capen Ed. miner,	do	do
Culp David, miner,	do	do
Cail Patrick, miner,	do	do
Cook John, cabinet maker,	do	do
Cook J. M. miner,	do	do
Currier J. B. hotel proprietor,	do	do
Currier J. B. Jr. hotel clerk,	do	do
Currier J. M. hotel clerk,	do	do
Colgan J. merchant,	do	do
Calvin S. N. express agent,	do	do
Chubb A. R. miner,	do	do
Carder J. B. hotel clerk,	do	do
Cullen Hugh, miner,	do	do
Cucarr Louis, miner,	do	do
Carse John, miner,	do	do
Coleman Fred. boardinghouse keeper,	do	do
Coleman J. C. miner,	do	do
Cavanaugh P. miner,	do	do
Conley J. J. miner,	do	do
Curtis Byron, miner,	do	do
Cummings J. F. ranchman,	do	do
Clark Wm. miner,	do	do
Cross Wm. T. miner,	do	do
Caywood A. W. cook,	do	do
Crowley Henry, miner,	do	do
Cosgrove J. miner,	do	do
Carter S. miner,	do	do
Cooper, S. H. miner,	do	do

Conner T. miner,	Iowa Hill
Clark J. H. blacksmith,	do do
Caststeel F. L. miner,	do do
Cosgrove M. miner,	do do
Camboy T. miner,	do do
Conner L. T. miner,	do do
Crary W. miner,	do do
Claugh E. miner,	do do
Cole A. P. constable,	do do
Colgrove J. S. miner,	Dutch Flat
Cortilyou W. K. miner,	do do
Cook Jacob, miner,	do do
Currier E. C. miner,	do do
Cassiday Owen, miner,	do do
Caldwell W. R. miner,	do do
Colvin A. J. miner,	do do
Chapmin F. B. miner,	do do
Casidy C. C. miner,	do do
Childs H. F. tinner,	do do
Cassidy G. W. miner,	do do
Clark C. S. miner,	do do
Combs W. G. miner,	do do
Clark Paul, miner,	do do
Caldawood J. F. miner,	do do
Currier C. C. clerk,	do do
Cole J. miner,	do do
Caldawood M. H. hose-maker,	do do
Cooper B. saloon keeper,	do do
Chamberlin Geo. W. miner,	do do
Curtis Henry, miner,	do do
Conald C. miner,	do do
Cox John, miner,	do do
Churchill J. miner,	do do
Cummings J. miner,	do do
Copp L. D. butcher,	do do
Cohen G. merchant,	do do
Clark S. H. saloon-keeper,	Iowa Hill
Canoboy M. miner,	do do
Clark Charles, miner,	do do
Cunningham S. miner,	Forks House
Caker A. M.	do do
Caker William,	do do
Carm J. D. miner,	do do

D

Dallman Joseph, clerk,	Commer'l st, Auburn	
DODSWORTH M. butcher,	Main st.	do
Durst F. bds Batton,	Main st.	do
Davidson A. merchant,	Main st.	do
Donner Charles, blacksmith,	Main st.	do

JAMES NOLAN,
MERCHANT TAILOR,
MAIN STREET.

Next door to
NORCROSS' JEWELRY STORE, }   AUBURN, CAL.

Has always on hand a fresh assortment of CLOTHS, CASSIMERES, DOESKINS, and SILK VELVETS.   ☞ Suits furnished at the shortest notice.

R. C. POLAND.   C. W. C. ROWELL.

POLAND & ROWELL,
ATTORNEYS AT LAW,
OFFICE, IN GIBSON'S STONE BUILDING,

Under Recorder's Office,   AUBURN, CAL.

M. O'REILLY.   J. O'NEILL.

HEAD QUARTERS SALOON,
O'REILLY & O'NEILL, PROPRIETORS.

THE BEST OF
WINES, LIQUORS & CIGARS,
Always to be had at this Establishment.

☞ Please Call and See for yourselves.   **O'REILLY & O'NEILL.**

REED & FRENCH,
BUILDERS AND CARPENTERS
AND DEALERS IN DOORS, SASH, ETC.,

Take this method of informing the public that they are at all times prepared to take Contracts for Building, or doing all kinds of Carpenter or Joiner's Work, in a workman-like manner and at Low Rates. ☞Shop, on AUBURN RAVINE, where those wanting anything in the above line, can be promptly accommodated.

REED & FRENCH.

Duncan William,	Sacramento st. Auburn
Drew H. L. stage driver,	Sacramento road, Auburn
Doig Thomas, miner,	Ophir
Day N. L. speculator,	Main st. Gold Hill
Dark Jas. O. bar kp. El Dorado Sal'n.	Main st. do
Dickinson N. barkeeper,	Pine Grove
Deadman William, saloon keeper, bds	Mason's hotel, Main st. Gold Hill
Duvall A. J. ditch agent, boards at	Mason's hotel, Main st. Gold Hill
Decker Jo. prop. bakery,	Main st. Gold Hill
Duchstein F. shoemaker,	Main st do do
Dake H. H. miner,	Virginia
Dowles James, farmer,	Antelope Ravine,
Darlington William, miner,	Fox's Flat
Darlington Daniel, miner,	do do
Davidson Jno. miner,	do do
Dodd Sam. farmer,	Auburn Ravine
Dodd Jno. farmer,	do do
Dodd Sam. jr. farmer,	do do
Deady Edward, gardener and vintner,	Lisbon
Dunning W. A. farmer,	do
Dyer, Charles, farmer,	Illinoistown
Densmore G. P. miner,	Gold Hill
Douglas Jno. prop. Traveler's Rest,	Horse Shoe Bar
Dyer C. miner,	Rattlesnake
Duncan Jo. miner,	do
Dicky J. G. clerk,	do
Droge D. miner,	do
Duncan Jack, miner,	do
Dugan H. stage driver,	do
DAGUERREAN ROOMS, entrance	Norcross' store, Main st. Auburn
Duncan H. miner,	Dutch Flat
Dorenbach C. F. miner,	do do
Davis M. miner,	do do
Drouthman —, miner,	do do
Daniel R. miner,	do do
Dykes T. J. miner,	do do
Davidson B. miner,	do do
Dickerson William, miner,	do do
Drum P. D. miner,	do do
Davis Charles, miner,	do do
Davis H. millman	do do
Davis P. F. miner,	do do
Darmen Thomas, miner,	do do
Daniels N. miner,	do do
Dorenbach J. miner,	do do
Downs J. miner,	do do
Denning W. S. miner,	do do
Davis W. D. miner,	do do
Denoyer Frank, miner,	do do
Dolstown Peter, miner,	do do
Dulang Jas. miner,	do do

Doolittle U. E. miner,	Griz. Bear House
Davis John L. miner,	Forest Hill
Denton Benjamin, carpenter,	do do
Dempwolff —, merchant,	Forest Hill
Dickinson John, miner,	do do
Durien John, boot-maker,	do do
Dempy Jo. miner,	do do
Dewar John, livery stable prop'r,	do do
Dunlap John, miner,	do do
Durkee F. D. watchmaker,	do do
Dodd James, merchant,	do do
Dunn E. P. miner,	do do
Davis D. W. saloon keeper,	do do
Dean James C. miner,	do do
Days Oliver, miner,	do do
Dupey Hugh, miner,	do do
Driskell M. miner,	do do
Dodds David, miner,	do do
Dunn A. engineer,	do do
Dore Robert, miner.	do do
Dow C. W. miner,	do do
Dagan Frank, miner,	do do
Davis G. S. miner,	do do
Davis J. L. miner,	do do
Davis H. R. miner,	do do
Davison A. N. surveyor,	do do
Dewy Charles H. miner,	do do
Dunlap John, miner,	do do
Davis J. W. miner,	do do
Davis William E. miner,	do do
Davis Benjamin, miner,	do do
Davis Daniel, miner,	do do
Dyer W. S. miner,	do do
Dasey Tim. miner,	do do
Duffee John, miner,	do do
Dignum John, miner,	do do
Dunn Thomas, miner,	do do
Dixon George, miner,	do do
Driskell T. miner,	do do
Douglas John, miner,	do do
Dunn Joseph, miner,	do do
Daggett Charles, miner,	do do
Dubuque P. miner,	do do
Deeds William M. miner,	do do
Dickerson —, ranchman,	Todd's Valley
Donley M. livery stable proprietor,	do do
Dodds Thomas, saloon-keeper,	do do
Decker George W. shoemaker,	do do
Dorr Henry, miner,	do do
Dorr C. miner,	do do
Donley Patrick, miner,	do do

Downs George, hotel keeper,	Todd's Valley	
Dilts Joseph, blacksmith,	Michigan Bluff	
Dierden Ralph, miner,	do	do
Dunham B. D. butcher,	do	do
Dooley E. L. butcher,	do	do
Davis W. J. miner,	do	do
Davis George O. miner,	do	do
Davis L. W. miner,	do	do
Davis C. C. miner,	do	do
Davis Matthew, miner,	do	do
Davis William, miner, [Last Chance]	do	do
Davis Amos, miner,	do	do
Davis Robert, miner,	do	do
Davis J. W. miner,	do	do
Davis William, miner,	do	do
Davis John, miner,	do	do
Davis William, miner,	do	do
Darling E. F. miner,	do	do
Dawd Edwin, miner,	do	do
Densmere J. N. miner,	do	do
Duffee T. miner,	do	do
Devern John, miner,	do	do
Dean John, miner,	do	do
Dunlap H. miner,	do	do
Dye Daniel, miner,	do	do
Danforth A. C. miner,	do	do
Davidson J. P. miner,	do	do
Dewitt David, miner,	do	do
Dewitt William, miner,	do	do
Denny John, miner,	do	do
Dunn James, miner,	Iowa	Hill
Davenport William, miner,	do	do
Dunn William, miner,	do	do
Dick John C. miner,	do	do
Dabney W. E. miner,	do	do
Davy P. miner,	do	do
Davidson G. H. miner,	do	do
Daw J. C. P. clerk in store,	do	do
Douglas Jesse, miner,	Illinoistown	
Devely W. R. miner,	Forks House	
Devely J. R. miner,	do	do
Dixon N. miner,	Iowa	Hill
Donaldson E. M. miner,	do	do
Dobey Madison, miner,	do	do
Date Thos. ditchowner,	do	do
Date Geo. ditchowner,	do	do
Davis W. H. miner,	do	do
Dodds James, merchant,	do	do
Day Zeb. miner,	do	do
Dugan Patrick, miner,	do	do
Dunswiler J. miner,	do	do

Douglas Wm. N. miner,	Iowa Hill
Defindiner F. miner,	do do
Devinport J. A. stablekeeper,	do do
Dunnagan F. miner,	do do
Dudley C. C. lawyer,	do do
Davis Z. J. carpenter,	do do
Duck Wm. merchant,	Yankee Jim's
Duncan Adam, miner,	do do
Devine John, miner,	do do
Drinkhouse Robt. miner,	do do
Davis Fletcher, miner,	do do
Doyle Wm. H.	do do
Denny Michael, miner,	do do
Dotry Francisco, miner,	do do
Dewarto Francisco, miner,	do do
Desoisa Manuel, miner,	do do
Dunn Edward, miner,	do do
Doty H. miner,	Pine Grove Secret Ravine P. O.
Devlin Hugh, miner,	do do do do
Dempsey Edward, ranchman,	Secret Ravine
Dana Dennis, miner,	do do
Davis J. T. miner,	do do
Day Dorrence, miner,	Rattlesnake
Drew Frank, miner,	Fox's Flat
Drew James, miner,	do do
Dows Wm. workman,	Starbuck's Mill
Drape Samuel, miner,	Star House

E

Evans E. teamster, Gove & Gordon, Auburn	
Elliott S. G. County Surveyor, bds Empire Hotel, Auburn	
Enix Jno. laborer, Sac. and Ill. roads, Auburn	
Eams J. miner,	Ophir
Eastman Stephen, miner,	do
Evertt P. merchant,	Virginia
Evertt G. merchant,	do
Evans Ben.	do
Elder C. farmer,	Fox's Flat
Enry Jno. ditch agent,	Lisbon
EGBERT ROBERT, merchant,	Illinoistown
Esterbrooks Sam. blacksmith,	Rattlesnake
Eatman M. H. miner,	Dutch Flat,
Ebeet G. miner,	do do
Eckels S. A. J. miner,	do do
Elm Casper, miner,	do do
Easten Stephen, miner,	do do
Elliott L. M. miner,	do do
Emmon Peter, miner,	do do
Eddy W. miner,	do do
Egan James, miner,	do do

Pine Grove Hotel

— BY —

WM. DANA PERKINS,

SECRET RAVINE, PLACER CO.

THE PINE GROVE HOTEL

CONTAINS A SPACIOUS AND MAGNIFICENT

DANCING HALL,

The same being 32 by 80 Feet,

And is fitted up in a most magnificent style.   The Public will receive superior accommodations, as usual; the rooms being nice and airy, and the bedding clean and comfortable.

The Proprietor will use his best endeavors to please his patrons.   His Bar will be

SUPPLIED WITH GOOD LIQUORS,

And his TABLE THE BEST THE MARKET AFFORDS.

There is also connected with the Pine Grove Hotel, a

SPLENDID RACE TRACK,

And EXTENSIVE STABLING for the Accommodation of Horses, &c., &c.

Erwin Robert, miner,	Dutch Flat
Eres William, miner,	do do
Ellis L. M. miner,	do do
Ewing Titus, farmer,	Coon Creek
Edgington, Geo. miner,	Grizzly Bear House
Engel John F. blacksmith,	do do
Empty B. miner,	do do
Elliott G. W. miner,	do do
EIDENGER E. merchant tailor,	Forest Hill
Eddy J. N. miner,	do do
Edgington A. M. clerk in store,	do do
Emerson L. H. teamster,	do do
Evans John, miner,	do do
Evers Martin, miner,	do do
Eddy Geo. miner,	do do
Ewert Chas. miner,	do do
Elfendahl Ernst, miner,	do do
Elsey John, miner,	do do
Elsey Wash. miner,	do do
Ellenwood D. lumberman,	do do
Edmundson J. W. miner,	do do
Eddy John, miner,	Todd's Valley
Elser John, stableman,	do do
Ely Andrew, musician,	Michigan Bluff
Engler Matthias, merchant,	do do
Elliott Robt. miner,	do do
Ebbert Louis, miner,	do do
Ebbert Louis. Jr., miner,	do do
Ebbert Wm. miner,	do do
Eppler John, saloon keeper,	do do
Edinger J. butcher, (Last Chance)	do do
Evans Wm. S. miner,	do do
Edwards R. miner,	do do
Early Edward, miner,	do do
Enwright Burt, miner,	do do
Eckle, Lawrence, miner,	Yankee Jim's
Emmens F. M. miner,	do do
Elton Samuel,	do do
Evans Philip, miner,	Iowa Hill
Eigenson Peter, miner,	do do
Engleman Chas. miner,	do do
Evans P. miner,	do do
Eizler John, bootmaker,	do do
Esselberg Louis, miner,	do do
Eddings G. F. miner,	do do
Evans Philip, miner,	do do
Edwards Elias, miner,	do do
Evans W. P. ranchman,	do do
Engles E. teamster,	do do
Erving Robert, miner,	do do
Esselman Geo. miner,	do do

Eaton T. J. miner,	Pine Grove
Easton Jno. miner,	Taylor's Ravine
Ellis C. P. laborer,	Beal's Bar,
Evans B. H. merchant,	Fox's Flat
Ebert M. E. teamster,	Illinoistown
Elgin Wm. laborer,	Illinoistown

F

FURNISS MILES, pr. Star Bakery and Restaurant Commercial st. Auburn	
FELDBERG I. clothing merchant, Commercial street,	Auburn
Foster Geo. (W. F. & Co.'s messenger) bds Star Bak'y & Res. Com. st. do	
FISHER R. J. carpenter,	bds Empire Hotel, do
Faigle Charles, saddler's shop,	Main street, Auburn
Fleming Jos. steward,	Empire Hotel, Auburn
Furniss Chas. laborer,	Turnpike Road, do
Finley C. W. surveyor,	Auburn
Foch C. miner,	Schnable's Quartz Mill, Ophir
Franks F. J. lawyer,	N. Ravine, near Ophir,
Flure E. prop. ball-alley,	Main street, Gold Hill
Finley D. J. L. physician and surgeon, Virginia	
Franklin W. M. farmer,	Fox's Flat
Fletcher Charles, miner,	Auburn Ravine
Fox Thomas, miner,	Quartz Flat
Ferguson Wm. C. farmer,	Doty's Ravine
Francis Hiram, musician,	Gold Hill
Fawcett George, butcher,	Rattlesnake
Fairchilds Thomas, farmer,	Coon Creek
Foust Benjamin, miner,	Dutch Flat
Fogle Lewis, milkman,	do do
Fowler A. C. miner,	do do
Foster Jno. miner,	do do
Fry W. A. miner,	do do
Fredrick D. miner,	do do
Fiddler W. K. miner,	do do
Fuller J. N. miner,	do do
Forner Jno. miner,	do do
Fitz Patrick Barney, miner,	do do
Ford W. miner,	do do
Farber J. miner,	do do
Fulmer N. miner,	do do
Farr Philip, miner,	do do
Furman Otto, miner,	do do
Fridle Andrew, miner,	do do
Fairchilds H. R. miner,	do do
Fritz Michael, butcher,	do do
Farr Adam miner,	do do
Fillmore A. B. miner,	do do
Freedman A. merchant,	do do
Fake D. A. miner,	do do
Flinn Larry, miner,	Forest Hill

EMPIRE HOTEL

AUBURN, CAL.

CHAS. J. SWAN, - PROPRIETOR.

HAVING TAKEN CHARGE OF THIS

WELL KNOWN STAND,

The Proprietor hopes by a strict attention to business, to make this HOTEL worthy of the patronage of his friends and the traveling community generally.

The House is Large and Well Ventilated!

THE PROPRIETOR HAS RECENTLY MADE A

LARGE ADDITION OF ROOM,

AND ADDED A

LARGE STOCK OF FURNITURE!

Which makes it one of the most desirable Hotels in the Mountains.

☞ The TABLE will be furnished with the VERY BEST viands in the Market, and the BAR will contain the BEST of

LIQUORS AND CIGARS.

CHAS. J. SWAN.

DEMOCRATIC SIGNAL

NEWSPAPER AND JOB

PRINTING OFFICE,

COMMERCIAL STREET, AUBURN.

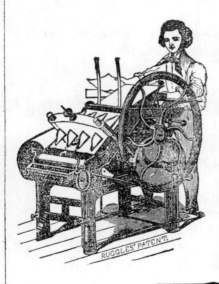

RUGGLES' PATENT.

THIS Establishment has now as good facilities for doing

JOB WORK

AS ANY OTHER

COUNTRY PRINTING OFFICE

IN THE STATE,

And NEW MATERIAL is being constantly received.

PRINTING,

Of all descriptions, executed with neatness and dispatch; such as

BUSINESS CARDS, CIRCULARS, HANDBILLS, BILL HEADS, POSTERS, LAW BLANKS BALL TICKETS, PROGRAMMES, ETC., ETC.

PRINTING OF EVERY KIND,

BOTH PLAIN AND FANCY,

DONE AT SACRAMENTO PRICES.

Felt Charles, merchant,	Forest	Hill
Forest William, machinist,	do	do
Forest William jr. machinist,	do	do
Fitch, J. Ives, lawyer,	do	do
Fisher J. W. carpenter,	do	do
Follensbee Fisher, miner,	do	do
Follensbee J. S. miner,	do	do
Farry Daniel, saloon keeper,	do	do
Fagan William M. ditch owner,	do	do
Fillbrown Charles, miner,	do	do
Fitzpatrick P. miner,	do	do
Fitzpatrick W. miner,	do	do
Fletcher Edward, miner,	do	do
Farrell Patrick, miner,	do	do
Fannon M. millman,	do	do
Fannon Dan. miner,	do	do
Fike Samuel, miner,	do	do
Flinn Thomas, miner,	do	do
Ford Henry, miner,	do	do
Faler A. lumberman,	do	do
Field William, miner,	do	do
Field Peter, miner,	do	do
Field Anson, miner,	do	do
Fast William D. miner,	do	do
Fast Adolph, miner,	do	do
Fich Frank, miner,	do	do
Foster C. miner,	do	do
Fox Thomas, miner,	do	do
Fox James, miner,	do	do
Fisher J. E. miner,	do	do
Fisher S. H. miner,	do	do
French John, miner,	do	do
FRIEDLANDER H. merchant,	do	do
Frosberg John, miner,	do	do
Fowles Thomas, miner,	do	do
Ferris William, miner,	do	do
Faylor William, miner,	do	do
Foskett E. D. C. prop.	Grizzly Bear h.	
Foskett William, miner,	do	do
Flinn Patrick, miner,	Todd's Valley	
Fox James, miner,	do	do
Fitz Simmons H. lawyer,	do	do
Fitz Gerald E. dairyman.	do	do
French John, miner,	do	do
Frasier S. miner,	do	do
Frank E. packer,	Michigan Bluff	
Franz William, brewer,	do	do
Favor Kimball, physician,	do	do
Fuller H. H. miner,	do	do
Fugeron A. tinsmith,	do	do
Flood M. C. miner,	do	do

Fairfield William, miner,	Michigan Bluff	
Fleming C. B. miner,	do	do
Fryer Charles, miner,	do	do
Frazier James, miner,	do	do
Felch A. J. miner (Deadwood)	do	do
Fescher Chas. miner do	do	do
Farnsworth J. C. miner (Last Chance),	do	do
Frasier James, miner, do do	do	do
Frasier Hugh, miner, do do	do	do
Freely Patrick, miner,	do	do
Finly Eb. miner,	do	do
Fords Samuel, miner,	do	do
Flinn Lawrence, miner,	do	do
Frisbie S. J. merchant (Stony Bar),	do	do
Ferguson John, miner,	do	do
Fitz Gerald Pat. miner,	do	do
Flinn Patrick, miner,	do	do
Fowler H. B. miner,	do	do
Farthing T. miner,	Yankee Jim's	
FRIEDLANDER S. merchant,	do	do
Fullwiler A. miner,	do	do
Fitz Gerald James, miner,	do	do
Frasier J. C. miner,	do	do
Fife B. F. miner,	do	do
Forward S. R, lumberman,	do	do
Farrell Jonathan, miner,	do	do
Furg W. miner,	do	do
Findlin John, miner,	do	do
Fish Louis, miner,	do	do
Ford D. M. miner,	Iowa Hill,	
Findley John, miner,	do	do
Ferguson S. C. miner,	do	do
Francis Geo. miner,	do	do
Francis William, miner,	do	do
Findley William, miner,	do	do
Freeman J. G. miner,	do	do
Fuller H. H. miner,	do	do
Foster Walter, miner,	do	do
Flinn David, miner,	do	do
Fitzer S. C. miner,	do	do
Flick M. miner,	do	do
Flick C. miner,	do	do
Ferrier G. W. miner,	do	do
Farrell J. O. miner,	do	do
Fieldman J. miner,	do	do
Flint Levi, miner,	do	do
Fields V. T. miner,	do	do
Fuller Edward, miner,	Pine Grove	
French Samuel, ranchman,	Secret R. P. F.	
Friend Charles, ranchman,	do	do
French Hosea, ranchman,	Beal's Bar	

Finemore Thomas, blacksmith,   Rattlesnake
French M. G. miner,   Virginia

G

Grant A. S. Justice of the Peace,   Main st.   Auburn
Greenaway R. cook,   Star Bak'y Res't Com. st.   do
Gaunt Jas. M. miner,   bds in Auburn,   do
GUIOU, TOWLE & Co., proprietors livery stable,   do
GOVE & GORDON, merchants,   Center block,   do
Gambell A. N. clerk,   cor. Center block,   do
Gibson Jacob, prop'r Orleans Hotel, Washington st.   do
Gibson Robert, teamster,   Gibson's Saloon,   do
GWYNN JOHN R. variety store,   Main st.   do
Gibson Wm. prop'r Gibson's Saloon,   Main st.   do
Gibson M. stone-mason,   Gibson's Saloon,   do
Gwynn B. F. printer,   Placer Herald,   do
GORDON R. merchant,   cor. Main and Com. sts.   do
Gordon James, teamster,   cor. Main and Com. sts.   do
Gordon Thos. clerk,   cor. Main and Com. sts.   do
Gooding Henry, Co. clerk,   bds at Horn's, Com. st.   do
Gove Amos F. merchant, firm G. & G. Union Store,   do
Gordon A. C. merchant,   Sac. G. & G. Union Store,   do
Garoin Edward, shoemaker,   Main st.   do
Gibson H. miner,   Millertown,
Gains John P. water agent,   Spanish Flat
Gatshet F. miner,   Placer Quartz Mill, Ophir
Grop F. miner,   Schnable's Quartz Mill, Ophir
Grove Rev. P. minister,   Ophir
Groesbach John, saloon keeper,   Main st. Ophir
Gillson H. A. painter,   Gold Hill
GUGGENHEIM Sam. variety store,   Main st. Gold Hill
Gold Hill Store and Lumber Yard,   Main st. Gold Hill
Greer W. B. lawyer,   Gold Hill
Goodhall J. E. butcher,   Main street, Virginia
Goodwyn T. W. saloon keeper,   Main street, Virginia
Glass Thos. stock raising,   Virginia
Goodrich A. F. mining,   Virginia
Glass Geo. shoemaker,   Main street, Virginia
Gray G. livery stable,   Main street, Virginia
Green H. wagon maker,   Main street, Virginia
Gordon A. D. herder,   Mt. Pleasant House, Turnpike Road
Gooding Geo. laborer,   Turnpike Road
Genal L. farmer,   Rattlesnake
Gilman M. B. miner,   Rattlesnake
Greenwood S. S. Supt. Com. Schools, Big Hill Turnpike Road
Gardner —,   Nevada and Sacramento Road
Gibbons L. G. butcher,   bds at Orleans Hotel, Auburn
Green John, prop'r Crescent City,   Sacramento street,   do
Gazley G. W. miner,   North Fork American
Goode D. B. farmer,   Coon Creek
Grable Paul, farmer,   Dutch Flat

Grigsby John, miner,	Dutch Flat
Gilbreath Austin, miner,	do do
Gay W. C. miner,	do do
Gise J. H. miner,	do do
Gross Louis, merchant,	do do
Gale W. A. miner,	do do
Gillman A. S. miner,	do do
Gooding A. J. miner,	do do
Gay E. miner,	do do
Gross F. butcher,	do do
Gafiney John, miner,	do do
Grischott M. miner,	do do
Graves John J. turner,	do do
Gallinton A. B. miner,	do do
Gillman Wm. miner,	do do
Georges, J. miner,	do do
Gleason J. H. miner,	do do
Gibson J. J. miner,	do do
Gardner E. L. clerk,	Pine Grove
Green Joseph L. miner,	Pine Grove
Greer J. M. Justice of the Peace,	Galt House
Gorden John C. workman,	Galt House
Gorden Given B. workman	Galt House
Gallagher G. B. miner,	do do
Greely G. L. miner,	Rattlesnake
Gehagen Wm. miner,	Rattlesnake
Geisendorfer Geo. miner,	Wild Cat
Gassaway Upton S.	Golden Gate Hotel
Goodrich A. H. teacher,	Rattlesnake
Gallagher Thomas, miner,	Forest Hill
Gover Frank, blacksmith,	do do
Gehrmann J. C. C. carpenter,	do do
Grant Daniel, teamster,	do do
Goff A. W. miner,	do do
Glisson Wm. merchant,	do do
Garrett James, miner,	do do
Gillespie S. miner,	do do
Gillespie A. miner,	do do
Green Gilbert, miner,	do do
Goble Hugh, miner,	do do
Grover J. miner,	do do
Goller John, miner,	do do
Green Michael, miner,	do do
Greeley John, miner,	do do
George Thomas, miner,	do do
Gould George, miner,	do do
Grant Richard, miner,	do do
Green M. miner,	do do
Gorman Patrick, miner,	do do
Glover J. J. miner,	do do
Genther A. miner,	do do

SULLIVAN'S

PREMIUM PICKS,

MADE OF THE BEST NORWAY IRON, WARRANTED TO LAST FOR YEARS, AT

GREATLY REDUCED PRICES.

ALL KINDS OF

HEAVY AND LIGHT BLACKSMITH'S WORK

DONE ON THE MOST REASONABLE TERMS, BY

C. J. SULLIVAN,

Shop on Center St., opposite Forest House,

FOREST HILL.

HORSE SHOEING

DONE BY AN EXPERIENCED MECHANIC.

ALL WORK GUARANTEED OF THE BEST AND ON THE MOST REASONABLE TERMS.

Gray G. W. miner,	Forest Hill
Gallaway Robert,	do do
Gage R. W. miner,	do do
Ganson T. miner,	do do
Goldie Marcus, miner,	do do
Garrison J. C. miner,	do do
Grogan Thomas, miner,	do do
Grant J. A. lumberman,	do do
Getchell G. W. lumberman,	do do
Goodrich Charles, miner,	Grizzly Bear House
Gates D. V. druggist,	Michigan Bluff
Gould James, clerk,	do do
Greeley John, miner,	do do
Gray John, packer,	do do
Grant S. L. miner,	do do
Greenwood Wm. miner,	do do
Green Horace, miner,	do do
Grinell H. J. butcher,	do do
Gilman George, watchmaker,	do do
Green Fred. miner,	do do
Griffith David, miner,	do do
Gillespie Simon, miner,	do do
Griffith Syrus, miner,	do do
Grants Conrad, miner,	do do
Gibbons F. miner, [Last Chance]	do do
Gilchrist J. L. miner, do do	do do
Grisham William, carpenter,	do do
Getson Dr. miner, [Long Cañon]	do do
Gerry Ambrose, miner,	do do
Glann D. miner,	do do
Glann V. miner,	do do
Glann Peter, miner,	do do
Gorman D. L. miner,	do do
Greeley J. S. miner,	do do
Greeley H. H. miner,	do do
Griffin Martin, miner,	do do
Garrison J. J. merchant, [H. S. Bar]	do do
Grant James, miner,	do do
Gilchrist John, miner,	do do
Grammar Joseph, miner,	do do
Gifferd Thomas, miner,	do do
Gahan Michael, miner,	Illinoistown
Gunsel Capt. J. H. miner,	Todd's Valley
Gaferth M. P. miner,	do do
Gearheart C. D. miner,	do do
Gray G. W. miner,	do do
Gilmore John, miner,	do do
Gilbert N. T. miner,	Yankee Jim's
Gilbert B. F. miner,	do do
Gilbert G. W. miner,	do do
Gunsell J. H. miner,	do do

Goodwin Henry, miner,	Yankee Jim's
Gardner Charles B. miner,	do do
Gregg John, miner,	do do
Games J. M. miner,	do do
Gillespie James, miner,	Iowa Hill
Gamble J. C. miner,	do do
Gregory David, miner,	do do
Gilbert A. T. miner,	do do
Goos N. miner,	do do
Gormerly —, miner,	do do
Gets Jerome, miner,	do do
Gleason M. ranchman,	do do
Glasscock A. B. musician,	do do
Gatins Barny, miner,	do do
Garrity Owen, liquor merchant,	do do
Garrity Thomas, liquor merchant,	do do
Gleason Patrick, miner,	do do
Gamble A. miner,	do do
Greenward G. miner,	do do
Gray D. M. lawyer,	do do
Garlach Henry, miner,	do do
Garvey J. S. miner,	do do
Gilbert Luke, miner,	do do
Green J. M. miner,	do do
Gottschalk C. miner,	do do
Gwins W. miner,	do do
Goodin W. E. miner,	do do

H

Hillyer C. J. attorney at law,	Commercial street, Auburn
Hillyer E. W. attorney at law,	Commercial street, do
Halley E. baker,	Star Bak'y & Rest. Com. st, Auburn
HALL E. M. banker,	Main st, do
HENSON, W. T. City B. & S. Store,	Main st, do
Hoin P. P. Lafayette Saloon,	Main st, do
HIGGINS F. B. lawyer,	bds Empire Hotel, do
HIGGINS A. S. lawyer,	bds Empire Hotel, do
Hammond John, turner,	bds Empire Hotel, do
HOTCHKISS T. B.	Centre Block, Main st, do
HAWKINS HIRAM R. druggist,	cor. Centre Block, do
Hastings James, butcher,	Main st, do
HAZELL H. druggist,	cor. Main and Washington sts, do
Holmes Dr. George,	cor. Main and Washington sts, do
Harrison & White, blacksmith shop,	Washington st, do
Hildreth L. G. wagon maker,	Turnpike road, do
Harty R. printer,	Herald office, do
HAMILTON JO. lawyer,	Court st, do
HUBBARD HENRY, physician,	Court st, do
Hyneman Sam.	bds at American Hotel, do
HARWOOD & CONKEY, mercht's,	Sacramento st, do

W. B. WILSON'S STORE.

ALL KINDS OF

GROCERIES, PROVISIONS,

Paints, Oils, Burning Fluids, Window Glass, and all kinds of Miners' Supplies.

☞ GOODS DELIVERED FREE OF CHARGE.   W. B. WILSON.

GOLD DUST

ASSAYED AT FOREST HILL

GOLD DUST MELTED AND ASSAYED.

RETURNS MADE IN FROM 6 to 12 HOURS WHEN DESIRED.

COIN PAID FOR BARS AT SAN FRANCISCO RATES AND FREIGHTS. Coin advances made on Gold Dust. Assays guaranteed to be correct. Melting done in the presence of the Depositor.

RATES:

GOLD BARS OVER $1,200.............. ....1-4 PER CENT.
GOLD BARS LESS THAN $1,200.................................$3 00.

☞ **GOLD DUST BOUGHT AT THE HIGHEST LIVING PRICES.**

Office at WELLS, FARGO & CO'S, FOREST HILL.

GEORGE G. WEBSTER.

GEO. G. WEBSTER,

ATTORNEY AND COUNSELOR AT LAW, AND NOTARY PUBLIC,

Naturalization Papers issued to Foreign Miners.

OFFICE AT WELLS, FARGO & CO'S, FOREST HILL.

DENTISTRY!

DR. LIBBE

ATTENDS TO ALL OPERATIONS PERTAINING TO THE

TEETH and MOUTH.

OFFICE—AT HIS COTTAGE, FOREST HILL,

PLACER COUNTY, CAL.

HALE, JAS. E. lawyer,	Commercial st,	Auburn
Higgins C. B. Deputy Recorder,	bds at Empire Hotel,	do
Holdrige D. carpenter,	Sacramento st,	do
Hoin P. P. Jr. printer,	Signal office,	do
Horan John, miner,	North Ravine, Millertown	
Horan M. miner,	North Ravine, Millertown	
Hani C. miner,	Schnable's Quartz Mill, Ophir	
Hill J. K. laborer,	North Ravine, Millertown	
Hussey Capt. John, hotel keeper,	Ophir	
Hathaway W. watchmaker,	Main st, Ophir	
Hilton Ed. miner,	North Ravine	
Hilton Robert, miner,	do	do
Hilton Albert, miner,	do	do
Hendon A. P. preacher,	Ophir	
Harsh George, miner,	do	
Heath A. water agent,	do	
Holden Thomas, miner,	do	
Horn William, watchman,	Virginia	
Henn F. W. butcher,	Main st, Gold Hill	
Harford P. F. butcher,	Main st,	do do
Hess F. miner,		do do
Hall R. B. physician and surgeon,	Main st,	do do
Hill Dr. J. A. agent W. F. & Co.	Main st,	do do
Harrington John, miner,	Virginia	
Hart E. miner,	do	
Haggert M. miner,	do	
Hirst O. W. blacksmith,	Main st, Virginia	
Harris G. farmer,	Doty's Ravine	
Hilton William, miner,	Auburn Ravine	
Howard Sam. miner,	Fox's Flat	
Hill George, miner,	do do	
Heaton W. prop'r People's Mill,	Lisbon	
Hawkins B. B. farmer,	do	
Hill John, farmer,	do	
Hawkins John, farmer,	do	
Hightower William, miner,	Illinoistown	
Haggard Martin, miner,	Virginia	
Henson Andrew, miner,	Rattlesnake	
Harned S. K. miner,	do	
Hill Wm. miner,	do	
Higgins B. S. miner,	Baltimore Ravine	
HARWOOD J. Harwood & Conkey,	Sacramento st, Auburn	
Howard Amos,	American Hotel do	
HOGAN JEFFERSON, (colored)	Louisiana Rest. do	
Hetrin Wm. laborer,	Coon Creek	
Hubbard A. miner,	Dutch Flat	
Holcomb James, miner,	Mugginsville, Virginia	
Hathaway D. F. miner,	Dutch Flat	
Hawkins W. L. miner,	do do	
Hudepohl H. merchant,	do do	
Harriman S, B. miner,	do do	

Hightower W. miner,	Dutch Flat	
Hose Stephen, miner,	do	do
Hooper W. miner,	do	do
Hyslop John, miner,	do	do
Homan Frank, miner,	do	do
Hayne S. A. miner,	do	do
Hall T. miner,	do	do
Hughs J. miner,	do	do
Hemphill A. miner,	do	do
Hoover C. miner,	do	do
Heath M. miner,	do	do
Hurbergen M. miner,	do	do
Higgins Sam. miner,	do	do
Higby J. O. miner,	do	do
Hansen F. miner,	do	do
Hilton C. miner,	do	do
Hansen J. miner,	do	do
Hunt C. miner,	do	do
Hodges S. C. miner,	do	do
Holmes P. B. blacksmith,	do	do
Hall W. W. miner,	do	do
Hogon E. miner,	do	do
Hurn William, miner,	do	do
Harding D. M. miner,	do	do
Hudepohl R. merchant,	do	do
Hedrich Andrew, miner,	do	do
Hildreth H. miner,	do	do
Harriman W. D. miner,	do	do
Herron E. C. merchant,	do	do
Hunter Samuel, miner,	do	do
Huff R. miner,	do	do
Harvey Geo. A. turner,	do	do
Hillyer H. miner,	do	do
Haynes Z. M. miner,	do	do
Hamel William, miner,	do	do
Heyman S. saloon keeper,	do	do
Hobbs G. B. miner,	do	do
Howard Joseph, miner,	do	do
Hamilton A. H. miner,	do	do
Huyck Aaron, miner,	do	do
Harding A. miner,	do	do
Hoffman William, miner,	do	do
Hill James, ranching,	Secret Ravine	
Henly Thomas, miner,	do	do
Henderson A. B. ranchman,	Galt House	
Hall James, miner,	Beal's Bar	
Haskill William, miner,	do	do
Hill C. B. miner,	do	do
Haskill William H. miner,	do	do
Hovey James, ranchman,	do	do
Hovey Perkins, ranchman,	do	do

HERMAN KRAUSE'S
PREMIUM
STEREOSCOPIC
AMBROTYPE GALLERY!

In HARDY & KENNEDY'S New Fire-Proof Block.

Next door to the Post Office,   **FOREST HILL.**

The undersigned would inform the public that he will take Ambrotypes, Melaineotypes, Lockets, Lamprotypes, and Patent Leather Pictures, superior to any ever taken in this place, and at prices within the reach of everybody.

Copies of Machinery, Paintings, Drawings, and all other Pictures taken, of any kind or size. All Pictures warranted to stand heat or any damp climate. None but perfect work passed. ☞ Perfect instructions given in all branches of the Art, in a very short time. CHARGES MODERATE.

☞ Ladies will please take notice that the Daguerrean Rooms at the new place have no connexion with any other business. Entrance at the stairs leading to the

ODD FELLOWS' HALL.

H. KRAUSE,
WHOLESALE AND RETAIL DEALER IN
WINES AND LIQUORS,
CIGARS,
VIRGINIA CHEWING AND SMOKING TOBACCO,

PERFUMERY, CUTLERY, CONFECTIONERY, STATIONERY, FRESH AND DRIED FRUITS, CARDS, PIPES, YANKEE NOTIONS, Etc.

At Hardy & Kennedy's Fire-Proof Block, next door to the Post Office,
BROADWAY STREET, FOREST HILL.

Thankful for the Liberal patronage within the last seven years, that we are dealing on this Divide, we will assure the public that we keep nothing but the very best in our line, and in prices defy competition. Our new establishment is wanting in nothing for the comfort of all who may please to pay us a visit.

A GERMAN AND ENGLISH LIBRARY KEPT.

Also, Agency for the German Benevolent Society, of San Francisco. ☞ Best Phelan's Cushion slate bed Billiard Tables kept for the lovers of the game.

☞ CELEBRATED SAN FRANCISCO LAGER BEER. ☜

☞ Orders promptly attended to, and Goods packed at the Lowest Market Prices.

Hovey Isaac, ranchman,	Beal's Bar		
Holmes Victor, teamster,	Carrolton		
Hill James, miner,	Rattlesnake		
Hillman George, miner,	do		
Hawks William, miner,	do		
Hale D. H. miner,	do		
Honeycut —, saloon keeper,	Fox's Flat		
Hoffman J. J. saloon keeper,	do	do	
Henderson Austin, clerk,	do	do	
Harris James, miner,	do	do	
Harris Lewis A. stock dealer,	do	do	
Hines W. A. packer,	Illinoistown		
Howell H. B. ranchman,	Starbuck's Mill		
Hall Josiah, laborer,	do	do	
Huse C. B. prop'r of Liberty Hotel,	Grizzly Bear House		
Huse J. J. prop'r of Liberty Hotel,	do	do	do
Hills Benj. J. miner,	do	do	do
Haupt Victor, miner,	do	do	do
Hackley G. W. barkeep'r, [Mile Hill]	do	do	do
Hines John L. miner,	do	do	do
Howard Charles, butcher,	Forest	Hill	
Homier Max, saloon-keeper,	do	do	
Hawkett A. W. brick-mason,	do	do	
Hause Lucien, miner,	do	do	
Herold Philip, shoe-maker,	do	do	
Hules Arnold, packer,	do	do	
Holland H. R. (colored) barber,	do	do	
Harrington J. H. butcher,	do	do	
Hamilton R. J. tinsmith,	do	do	
Haskell A. C. constable,	do	do	
Haskell W. L. miner,	do	do	
Howard James, miner,	do	do	
Hardy William H. merchant,	do	do	
Huntly A. clerk,	do	do	
Horine John, miner,	do	do	
Howatt James, miner,	do	do	
Howatt James, jr. miner,	do	do	
Hannan John, miner,	do	do	
Hawell Fred. miner,	do	do	
Hawell Morgan, miner,	do	do	
Hawell M. P. miner,	do	do	
Hurtzig Nathaniel, miner,	do	do	
Hyland Dennis, hotel keeper,	do	do	
Hummel Benedict, miner,	do	do	
Hatch J. A. miner,	do	do	
Hatch John, miner,	do	do	
Herrick J. E. miner,	do	do	
Hurd W. T. miner,	do	do	
Houlton C. A. miner,	do	do	
Herbert J. B. merchant [H. S. Bar],	do	do	
Hicks Joseph, miner,	do	do	

Hoburn F. miner,	Forest	Hill
Henry William, miner,	do	do
Hews Evan, miner,	do	do
Hall George, miner,	do	do
Henning Paul, miner,	do	do
Herphy Henry, miner,	do	do
Huffman Henry, miner,	do	do
Hanson George, miner,	do	do
Hull George, miner,	do	do
Hewes Joshua, miner,	do	do
Hill J. A. miner,	do	do
Herchberger Jacob, miner,	do	do
Hemsley John, miner,	do	do
Hersey W. G. miner,	do	do
Haskell Edward, miner,	do	do
Hamilton E. miner,	do	do
Hoffner Samuel, ranchman,	do	do
Hayward James, miner,	do	do
Hodgdon John, miner,	do	do
Hiser Joseph, miner,	do	do
Hoyt E. F. clerk of mill,	do	do
House L. M. lumberman,	do	do
Horn G. W. lumberman,	do	do
Haworth J. T. miner,	do	do
Hani John A. miner,	Todd's Valley,	
Hoag Jacob, ranchman,	do	do
Hoag Justin, ranchman,	do	do
Hackett C. miner,	do	do
Hanley Philip, saloon keeper,	do	do
Hosmer Thomas N. miner,	do	do
Hosmer D. M. miner,	do	do
Hall H. R. miner,	do	do
Harville J. W. miner,	do	do
Hamilton E. trader,	do	do
Hicks Daniel, miner,	do	do
Hall R. B. miner,	do	do
Hill S. G. sport,	do	do
Huber H. miner,	do	do
Hill J. P. miner,	do	do
Heuston William, miner,	do	do
Henry William, miner,	do	do
Henly R. S. carpenter,	do	do
Hubland Thomas, miner,	do	do
Huff L. miner,	do	do
Halleck W. G. ranchman,	do	do
Humphrey L. E. ranchman,	do	do
Hause J. T. miner,	do	do
Hamilan Jacob, miner,	do	do
Hueston S. T. miner,	do	do
Howell S. A. carpenter,	Michigan Bluff,	
Haugh Noah, teamster,	do	do

Haugh John, teamster,	Michigan	Bluff
Hefter N. merchant,	do	do
Haven G. H. miner,	do	do
Helm James, butcher,	do	do
Houlton Samuel, miner,	do	do
Hill James, painter,	do	do
Hurd E. D. miner,	do	do
Huffman Frank, miner,	do	do
Higbee J. T. druggist,	do	do
Haligan D. M. livery stable keeper,	do	do
Halliday A. toll-gate keeper,	do	do
Hews John, miner [Deadwood]	do	do
Hornbay H. miner, do	do	do
Howe Joseph, miner do	do	do
Hayden Luellen, miner, do	do	do
Harnett A. miner, do	do	do
Hyland P. G. miner [Last Chance],	do	do
Hyland Jack, miner, do do	do	oo
Hendershott W. D. miner,do do	do	do
Hackstaff E. K. miner, do do	do	do
Hank Andrew, miner, do do	do	do
Harrison P. Y. miner, do do	do	do
Harrison W. J. miner, do do	do	do
Heal Charles, miner, do do	do	do
Howell Fred. miner,	do	do
Hunt N. P. miner,	do	do
Hughes R. R. miner,	do	do
Holden Samuel, miner,	do	do
Holt Henry, miner,	do	do
Hill J. miner,	do	do
Humphrey G. H. miner,	do	do
Hart Jas. A. miner,	do	do
Higgins Jonathan, miner,	do	do
Hill John, miner,	do	do
Hill Robert, miner,	do	do
Hoffman M. ranchman,	do	do
Hancock Charles H. miner,	do	do
Hopkins Samuel, miner,	do	do
Harwood Abner, miner,	do	do
Houser Samuel, miner,	do	do
Hassett M. W. miner,	do	do
House H. C. saloon keeper,	do	do
Hazlett M. miner,	do	do
Haley Michael, miner,	do	do
Humphrey Jerry, miner,	do	do
Hill James, miner,	do	do
Huntsly Martin, miner,	do	do
Hammond John, miner,	do	do
Haven George, miner,	do	do
Hanson Charles, miner,	do	do
Haworth J. T. miner,	Forks	House

Herrick G. W. miner,	Yankee Jim's	
Herrick James, miner,	do	do
Hani John, bootmaker,	do	do
Houser C. B. miner,	do	do
Hermann Otto, miner,	do	do
Hermann John, saloon keeper,	do	do
Hughes G. miner,	do	do
Hall R. M. miner,	do	do
Histed D. E. miner,	do	do
Haley J. miner,	do	do
Henderson Oliver, miner,	do	do
Hamby A. M. miner,	do	do
Hissington Reuben, miner,	do	do
Harris Nathan, miner,	do	do
Hattan John, miner,	do	do
Hoofman Fred. miner,	do	do
Hews Evan, miner,	do	do
Hull Isaac A. miner,	Iowa Hill	
Higgee William, miner,	do	do
Hall Marshall, miner,	do	do
Heskett A. H. expressman,	do	do
Huff A. J. miner,	do	do
Harvill J. C. miner,	do	do
Hausell W. A. merchant,	do	do
Hall R. B. miner,	do	do
Hopkins Seth, miner,	do	do
Hopkins E. L. miner,	do	do
Hoppert Chris. miner,	do	do
Harrman ——. miner,	do	do
Hawley Chris. miner,	do	do
Hungerford Charles, miner,	do	do
Hanse William, miner,	do	do
Hall T. A. miner,	do	do
Hall I. A. miner,	do	do
Hoffman J. miner,	do	do
Hubbell William, miner,	do	do
Huvas Daniel, miner,	do	do
Heald Israel, miner,	do	do
Hackett C. miner,	do	do
Hackett G. W. miner,	do	do
Halloway P. miner,	do	do
Huston David, miner,	do	do
Hoppert John, collecting agent,	do	do
Henson J. P. carpenter,	do	do
Harvey J. C. miner,	do	do
Hatch George, clerk in store,	do	do
Hight John, miner,	do	do
Hart James, dairyman,	do	do
Hall S. A. miner,	do	do
Harper John, miner,	do	do
Haycock George, livery stable prop.	do	do

Harrington N. miner,   Iowa Hill
Hinneman E. saloon keeper,   do   do
Hammon H. butcher,   do   do
Hays J. miner,   do   do
Hogan J. miner,   do   do
Haden M. miner,   do   do
Hemmegan R. miner,   do   do
Hopkins T. C. miner,   do   do
Hebbard G. W. painter,   do   do
Hill Mrs. Adelia, ditch proprietress,   do   do
Heaney Daniel, Mineral Bar road sup. Illinoistown

I

Isaacs Henry M. cigar and fruit store, Empire Saloon, Main st, Auburn
Irwin David, miner,   Dutch Flat
Irvion Henson, miner,   do   do
Isaacs F. M. packer,   Illinoistown
Ives Wm. H. miner,   Forest Hill
Inefeldt Joseph, miner,   do   do
Isle John, miner,   Michigan Bluff
Irwin James, miner,   do   do
Ike John, miner,   do   do
Irish S. L. miner,   Iowa Hill
Ingersoll D. miner,   do   do
Irwin Robt. miner,   do   do
Iserman Lewis, hotel keeper,   do   do
Iserman Fritz, miner,   do   do
Isler Andrew, shoemaker,   do   do
Inman H. miner,   do   do

J

JACKSON J. Q. (W. F. & Co's agent) Main street, Auburn
Johnson W. P. clerk,   Main st,   do
Johnson F. prop'r Eagle Bakery,   Main st,   do
Johnson Jno. cook,   Empire Hotel, do
JAMISON THOS. cabinet maker,   Auburn Turnpike
Johnson Geo. under sheriff,   Court House, Auburn
Jamison Stephen, miner,   Ophir
James Jno. clerk,   Main st, Gold Hill
Janson Chas. clerk,   Main st, do   do
Jones Jno. miner,   Virginia
Jackson L. clerk,   Main st, Virginia
Johnson Julius, farmer,   Auburn Ravine
Jones M. miner,   Fox's Flat
Jones Geo. W. miner,   Mountaineer
Johnson N. miner,   Dutch Flat
Johnson J. J. miner,   do   do
Jackson Andrew, miner,   do   do
Jones J. milkman,   do   do

Johnston E. E. miner,	Dutch Flat
Jones T. L. miner,	do do
Jones S. D. miner,	do do
Jamison Frank, carpenter,	do do
Jones Moses W. miner,	do do
Jackson Andrew, miner,	do do
Janchins B. miner,	do do
James Isaac, miner,	Beal's Bar
Johnston M. ranchman,	do do
Jenkins James, painter,	Rattlesnake
Jackman A. miner,	Iowa Hill
Just T. P. miner,	do do
Johnston J. R. miner,	do do
Joseph W. miner,	do do
James James, miner,	do do
James John, miner,	do do
Jefferds Benj. miner,	do do
Jamison James, barber,	do do
Jase Benjamin, miner,	do do
Jackson W. H. miner,	do do
Jessup Wilson, miner,	do do
Johnson John, miner,	do do
Julian Nicholas, miner,	do do
Johnson J. miner,	Forks House
Jewett H. lumberman,	Forest Hill
Julius John, teamster,	do do
Johnson Otto, saloon keeper,	do do
Jase Benjamin, miner,	do do
James Wm. miner,	do do
Jessen Henry, miner,	do do
Jackson J. J. miner,	do do
Jenkins E. miner,	do do
Jones John E. miner,	do do
Jones John D.	do do
Jones C. F. miner,	do do
Jones John N. miner,	do do
Jones John, miner,	do do
Jones Wm. miner,	do do
Johnson Samuel, miner,	do do
Johnson J. miner,	Forks House
Johnson C. A. miner,	Grizzly Bear House
Johnson S. D. miner,	Todd's Valley
Johnson A. miner,	do do
Johnson G. M. painter,	do do
Journick Martin, miner,	do do
Jones J. B. miner,	Michigan Bluff
Jones Josephus, miner,	do do
Jones Nat. miner,	do do
Jones Robert, boardinghouse keeper,	do do
Jones John, miner,	do do
Jones James, miner,	do do

GEORGE WILLMENT,

Cor. of Commercial and Court Sts. Auburn,

WHOLESALE AND RETAIL DEALER IN

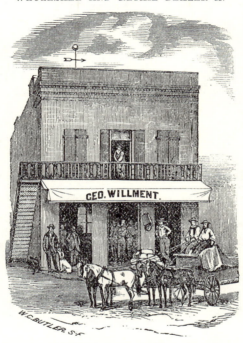

HARDWARE **GROCERIES,**

PROVISIONS

WINES, LIQUORS,

Crockery, Flour, Grain, Feed, Oils, Cutlery,

MINING IMPLEMENTS, ETC.

Large additions are being constantly received to this already large and
and extensive stock of Goods.

☞ Purchasers' Goods Delivered Free of Charge. ↩

9

LIGHT FOR THE MILLION.

J. B. OWENS & CO.

No. 102 J Street,

SACRAMENTO.

The Only Legitimate

KEROSENE

—AND—

Coal Oil Dealer !

IN CALIFORNIA.

We wish the Public to understand that our Oils are free from adulterations with CAMPHENE or any other FLUIDS.   We keep no other Burning Material for sale but the pure Kerosene, and in all cases WARRANTED as represented.

The largest supply of Kerosene Lamps to be found in the State.

We are the only importers of

HALE'S Improved PATENT BURNER !

We can refer to THOUSANDS in California who have tried the HALE'S BURNER, and give it the preference above all others, it being the only Burner that is perfect in its combinations and durable in its operations.

Lamp Wick, Chimnies, Etc., Wholesale and Retail.

Jones Benjamin, miner, [Deadwood,] Michigan Bluff
Jones H. miner, [Last Chance,]   do   do
Jones Benjamin, miner,   do   do
Jones Hugh, miner,   do   do
Jones Wm. miner,   do   do
Jones Thomas, miner,   do   do
Jones Thos. R. miner,   do   do
Jones W. miner,   do   do
Jones R. miner,   do   do
Jones M. miner,   do   do
Johnson W. H. lawyer,   do   do
Jarvis A. blacksmith,   do   do
Jordan C. S. miner,   do   do
Johnson Wm. miner,   do   do
Johnson J. miner, [Deadwood,]   do   do
Johnson J. M. miner, [Last Chance,]   do   do
Johnson J. miner,   do   do
Johnson James, miner,   do   do
Jordan Chas. miner,   do   do
Jergeson Peter, miner, [Last Chance,]   do   do
Janson Matthew, hotel keeper, do   do   do
James Joseph, miner,   do   do
Jackson W. H. miner,   do   do
Jamison S. M. merchant,   Yankee Jim's
Johnson W. G. hotel keeper,   do   do
Johnson Thomas, miner,   do   do
Jarvis Augustus, teamster,   do   do
Jennings R. S. miner,   do   do
Johnson Christopher, saloon keeper,   do   do

K

Kohn & Steinhert, clothing mercht's, Main street,   Auburn
Kimball M.   bds Empire Hotel, do
Keadle Geo. teamster,   Court street,   do
Kaiser John, cooper,   Placer Quartz Mill, Ophir
Kaiser F. miner,   do   do   do   do
Kirk Frank, miner,   Ophir
Knight Geo. farmer,   do
Kirk John F. milkman,   do
KELLY F. H. prop'r livery stable,   Gold Hill
Kennedy H. miner,   do   do
Keener E. miner,   Virginia
Kelly W. J. miner,   do
Kier —, farmer,   Danesville
Kier W. farmer,   do
Kile —, miner,   Fox's Flat
Kelly Wm. miner.   Quartz Flat
Keck Jacob, prop'r Blue Wing,   Illinoistown
Keller John, blacksmith,   do
Kelly M. miner,   Rattlesnake

Kelly J. miner,	Rattlesnake
Kerny D. miner,	do
Kurger W. H. clerk,	Dutch Flat
Kyle Thos. miner,	do do
Koppmanan John, miner,	do do
King A. M. carpenter,	do do
Keener Geo.	Sacramento street, **Auburn**
Kimble H. baker,	Dutch Flat
Knight A. miner,	do do
Kitcher A. B. miner,	do do
Kopp Chas. M. saloon keeper,	do do
Kane Thos. miner,	do do
Kessler Julius, miner,	do do
Kipp A. miner,	do do
Keller H. D. miner,	do do
Kinsley Jacob, miner,	do do
Kinsley Henry, miner,	do do
Klink Peter, miner,	Grizzly Bear House.
Keys James, miner,	Forest Hill
Knight Wm. C. miner,	do do
Krysher J. barkeeper,	do do
Kilmar John, baker,	do do
Kibard Jacob, miner,	do do
Kurne Chas. saloon keeper,	do do
Krause H. daguerreotypist,	do do
Krause Davis, saloon keeper,	do do
Kennedy Sam'l S. merchant,	do do
Kinman Levi, miner,	do do
Kelly Edward, miner,	do do
Kinney Wm. miner,	do do
Klener Henry, miner,	do do
Knowles Robt. miner,	do do
Koch Adam, miner,	do do
Kidd A. U. miner,	do do
Kidd L. W. miner,	do do
Kirby John, miner,	do do
Keenan M. miner,	do do
Kenna Wm. miner,	do do
Kay Wm. miner,	do do
Kay Joseph, miner,	do do
Kent Wm. L. miner,	do do
Kelly Michael, miner,	do do
Kate James, miner,	do do
Kelly Ed. lumberman,	do do
Keely James, lumberman,	Todd's Valley
Knott Jo. clerk,	do do
Keck Geo. miner,	do do
Keegler B. miner,	do do
King Wm. miner,	do do
Killpatrick D. M. trader,	do do
Key Wm. miner,	do do

BAKER & HAMILTON,

AGRICULTURAL WAREHOUSE
HARDWARE AND SEED STORE,
J Street, Between Front and Second,   SACRAMENTO.

MANUFACTURERS, AGENTS AND DEALERS IN

John A. Pitt's, Buffalo, N. Y., C. M. Russell & Co.'s, Massillon, Ohio,
And other popular **THRESHING MACHINES.**

Also the following **REAPERS AND MOWERS,** improved for the Harvest of 1861:

New York Combined Machine,	*Manny's Improved Machine*
Burt's Eagle " "	*Esterly's* " "
McCormick's " "	*Rugg's Combined* "
Heath's Eagle "	*Vermont Moving* "
Kentucky Harvester "	*Buckeye* " "

AND SOLE AGENTS FOR THE CELEBRATED NOURSE, MASON & CO.'S

KETCHUM'S IMPROVED MOWERS,
With or without Reaper Attachments, the best Mowing Machine in use.

☞Also, all kinds of FARMING IMPLEMENTS, HARDWARE and SEEDS.☜

JUSTIN GATES & BROS.

No. 72 K St., and 218 J St., Sacramento, Cal.

IMPORTERS, WHOLESALE AND RETAIL DEALERS IN

DRUGS, MEDICINES

AND CHEMICALS,

Atlantic Lead Paints, Oils, Varnish, Brushes,

LARD, SPERM, POLAR, KEROSENE, COAL, NEATSFOOT
AND LINSEED OILS,

ALCOHOL, CAMPHENE, BURNING FLUID

TARTARIC ACID, SODA, CREAM TARTAR,

Trusses, Surgical and Dental Instruments,

HOPS, SEIDLITZ POWDERS, CASTILE SOAP,

FINE TOOTH AND HAIR BRUSHES,

BAY WATER, SHAKERS' HERBS AND ROOTS,

Tilden's Extracts, Botanic Medicines, Eclectic Concentrated Preparations, Toilet Articles, Fancy Soaps, Perfumery,

ALL PATENT MEDICINES

OF THE DAY,

And all other Articles kept in a well furnished Drug Store.

Our arrangements for purchasing in the Atlantic States and Europe are not surpassed by any Drug House in California, and being in constant receipt of Fresh Drugs by Express and every Clipper, we can offer to buyers superior inducements as to quality and prices. . . COUNTRY ORDERS SOLICITED, and promptly executed at the Lowest Prices.

BRANCH STORE AT MICHIGAN BLUFFS. }   **JUSTIN GATES & BROS.**
                                                     72 K and 218 J Streets.

Kelly R. D. watchmaker,	Todd's Valley	
Kimball G. M. livery stable keeper,	Michigan Bluff	
Kinney Geo. M. boot maker,	do	do
Kennedy Robt. Deputy Sheriff,	do	do
Kloppenberg D. W. merchant,	do	do
Katszenberg B. merchant,	do	do
Keiser A. B. musician,	do	do
Kairns Chas. D. miner,	do	do
Kingsberry Geo. boot maker,	do	do
Kline Wm. miner,	do	do
Kinney S. miner,	do	do
Kelly Matthias, hotel keeper, [D'dw'd,]	do	do
Kaler Thomas, miner, do	do	do
Kroffoth Jacob, miner, do	do	do
Keller Godfrey, miner, do	do	do
Kline Henry, miner, do	do	do
Kelly Henry, miner, do	do	do
Kilburn W. L. barkeep'r, [Last Chance]	do	do
Kuder Geo. miner, do do	do	do
Knott E. miner,	do	do
King Anthony, miner,	do	do
Knowles Robert, miner, [Long Cañon]	do	do
Keiser John F. miner,	do	do
Kelly Michael, miner,	do	do
Kimberly M. C. miner,	do	do
Keeler O. ranchman,	Yankee	Jim's
Keeler Chas. ranchman,	do	do
Keeler Aaron, ranchman,	do	do
Keiser John, hotel keeper,	do	do
Keiser Sam'l, miner,	do	do
Kirk Theodore, miner,	do	do
Kates Pat. miner,	do	do
Kerr Wm. miner,	do	do
King Manuel, merch't, [Yorkville,]	do	do
Katurn Francisco, miner,	do	do
Knox J. W. miner,	Iowa	Hill
Kilgore Andrew, miner,	do	do
Kelly Frank, miner,	do	do
Kline Conrad, shoemaker,	do	do
Keene James, miner,	do	do
Kilgo Wm. blacksmith,	do	do
King J. N. butcher,	do	do
Kingston Thos. miner,	do	do
King Morris, miner,	do	do
Kiho Pat. miner,	do	do

L

Lauterbach Edward, shoemaker,	Main st,	Auburn
Levy B. clothing merchant,	Sacramento st,	do
Lancaster William, carpenter,	bds. Empire Hotel,	do

Lockhart J. turner,   bds Empire Hotel,   Auburn
Livergood D. W. teamster,   do
Langdon Joseph B. clerk for Gove & Gordon, Centre Block,   do
Leach I. B. road agent, Toll House   do
LIPSETT A. cl thing merchant,   Gibson's stone build. Main st, do
LAUTENSHLAGER, T. mer. tailor, Commercial st,   do
Love M. P. H. farmer [Ill. and Sac. roads,   do
Loving E. T. merchant,   Millertown,
Luchsingen F. miner,   Schnable's Quartz Mill, Ophir,
Lopez Jno. miner,   do   do   do   do
Leaigh Jno. prop. Exchange Saloon, Main st,   do
Lamphere J. miner,   Ophir
Lawhorn G. W. miner,   Mason's Hotel, Gold Hill,
Lahsl H. prop. ball alley,   Main st,   do   do
Love Jno. miner.   do   do
Lahsl N. clothing,   Main st,   do   do
Lyons R. W. miner,   Virginia,
Lankford W. P. miner,   Fox's Flat
Laschelle, miner,   do   do
Levy Thomas S. farmer,   Lincoln
Leach Jno. miner,   Rattlesnake,
Lovenfeld William, saloon and bakery   do
Lobner L. merchant,   do
LUBECK D. W. drygoods merchant, cor. Main and Commercial st, Auburn
LEIGHTON & HOWARD, prop. American Hotel, Main st,   do
Leighton Geo. C. prop.   do   do   do   do   do
Leginbine Jno. merchant,   Danesville
Lakamp J. H. shoemaker.   Dutch Flat
Lewis T. M. miner,   do   do
Lewis Sam. P. miner,   do   do
Lyons Charles, miner,   do   do
Leeman James, miner,   do   do
Lyons C. miner,   do   do
Lee W. N. miner,   do   do
Long D. miner,   do   do
Logan Robert, miner,   do   do
Law James S. ditch tender,   do   do
Lee O. H. miner,   do   do
Lowry Sam. miner,   do   do
Lawer William, prop. of U. S. House, Grizzly Bear House
LIBBEE Dr. M. L. dentist,   Forest Hill
Langdon George, saloon keeper,   do   do
Larrabee Samuel A. miner,   do   do
Lunbacher Peter, barber,   do   do
Luitz M. H. bootmaker,   do   do
Lander John, miner,   do   do
Lyons Michael, miner,   do   do
Landman L. miner,   do   do
Lowell N. T. ranchman,   do   do
Lynch Philip, editor,   do   do
Lawrence J. A. miner,   do   do

QUARTZ MINERS, ATTENTION!

DR. BEERS

Would call particular attention to his improved

AMALGAMATORS,

FOR GOLD OR SILVER ORES,

Which are claimed to possess the following advantages over all others now in use, viz:

1st. They are equally adapted to the amalgamation of Ores, either wet or dry crushed.

2d. Being Self-feeding and Self-discharging, they require but little attention; one man being sufficient to attend thirty or more.

3d. During the process of amalgamation, they reduce the ore to an almost impalpable powder, in close contact with a large surface of mercury, but do not grind the mercury.

4th. It is also claimed for them, and demonstrated, that they will save from 25 to 100 per cent. more gold, than any other amalgamators now in use.

The Amalgamating Pans are put up in sets of three, discharging into each other; three of which sets are capable of thoroughly amalgamating at least ten tons of Gold Ore per day, and, with a slight addition, are equally adapted to the amalgamation of Silver Ores by any of the old or new processes.

The pans are about four feet in diameter, and supplied with a false, perforated, or grate bottom, upon which the grinding is done, and which allows the gold, as soon as united with the mercury, to settle beneath the grate, and remain as safe as if under lock and key.

In cleaning up the pans and separating the amalgam, but about one-tenth the usual labor is required.

The parts most exposed to wear are made of hard iron, and easily replaced, at trifling cost.

☞ All orders for these Amalgamators can be sent to PETER DONAHUE, on First Street, San Francisco, at whose Foundry they can also be seen in operation.

For further particulars, inquire of the Patentee.

J. B. BEERS, 165 Clay Street.

 DENTISTRY!

CHEAPEST AND AS GOOD AS THE BEST,

At 185 Clay Street, - San Francisco.

WM. C. KELLUM, after eighteen years' constant practice in the profession, was awarded Four Premiums, at the late Mechanics' Fair, for superior Dentistry; and will operate at the following Low Prices. Terms—Invariably Cash before work leaves the office:

For a Full Set of Teeth above, on fine Gold plate, in the best manner,	**$70**
On Silver,	**30**
On Rubber or Amber,	from $30 to 40
Continuous Gums on Platina,	**75**

Less number of Teeth in the same ratio. Teeth filled with Pure Gold, and the decay thoroughly arrested, from one to two dollars a cavity Toothache cured and nerves killed, one dollar. Extracting, $1, or gratis for the poor. All work warranted, and that which does not please need not be taken.

☞ **CALL AND EXAMINE SPECIMENS OF WORK.**

Lowden Thomas, miner,	Forest Hill
Laird William, miner,	do do
Libo H. miner,	do do
Lynn Robert, miner,	do do
Long John, miner,	do do
Loller Patrick, miner,	do do
Leat Jack, miner,	do do
Linck Henry, miner,	do do
Lowe George, miner,	do do
Lunn George, shoemaker,	do do
Lyons Thomas, miner,	do do
Love W. W. P. miner,	do do
Lewis Robert, miner,	do do
Lofrath Henry, miner,	do do
Longley W. R. miner,	do do
Longley A. S. miner,	do do
Lawdon William, miner,	do do
Lawselle L. miner,	do do
Larratt L. E. miner,	do do
Lee D. H. clerk in hotel,	do do
Lyman J. P. miner,	do do
Lampman Charles, ranchman,	do do
Lyons M. R. miner,	do do
Lum George, miner,	do do
Lanier J. P. miner,	Todd's Valley
Lennen James, miner,	do do
Luce John, ranchman,	do do
Lambright J. S. mill-man,	do do
Linn James, miner,	do do
Layton Jordan S. hotel proprietor,	do do
Leet William N. merchant,	Michigan Bluff
Leet Samuel, merchant,	do do
Long Henry, miner,	do do
Lloy John, blacksmith,	do do
Lowd Thomas, miner,	do do
Lumbacher Charles, barber,	do do
Labaree Seth, miner,	do do
Loring L. G. miner,	do do
Livzig Henry, miner,	do do
Lattier Louis, miner,	do do
Levin Jacob, merchant,	do do
Levin Louis, merchant, Deadwood,	do do
Lewis Alfred, miner, Last Chance,	do do
Lewis Robert, miner, do do	do do
Linstram E. miner, do do	do do
Link H. C. miner, do do	do do
Ludwig E. B. miner, do do	do do
Lane Abraham, miner,	do do
Labrie Lanie, miner,	do do
Leddy J. miner,	do do
Lewis John, miner, Long Canon,	do do

Lewis Wm. miner, [Long Canon,]	Michigan Bluff
Lemmon R. J. miner,	do do
Louison Andrew, miner,	do do
Lowry Michael, miner,	do do
Legler J. P. miner,	do do
Lee Patrick, miner,	do do
Lamont Isaac, miner,	do do
Lovell Rev. J. W. Methodist minister,	Yankee Jim's
Linenberg A. R. miner,	do do
Livingston Henry, miner,	do do
Libert Frank, miner,	do do
Lindsey William, lumberman,	Forest Hill
Lewis W. L. lumberman,	do do
Luitzheizer — miner,	Iowa Hill
Love Charles T. miner,	do do
Lermond George, miner,	do do
Little William, miner,	do do
Loomis H. miner,	do do
Lipp W. P. miner,	do do
Leddill William, miner,	do do
Lodge Thomas, miner,	do do
Lyons W. B. druggist,	do do
Luce George H. butcher,	do do
Laughlin Thomas, miner,	do do
Lacky William A. miner,	do do
Leonard John G. miner,	do do
Luce J. B. miner,	do do
Leighton A. miner,	do do
Lawrence E. miner,	do do
Lingard Samuel, miner,	do do
Lawrence William D. miner,	do do
Lovejoy E. P. miner,	do do
Lack L. lumberman,	do do
Lyman C. D. miner,	Forks House
Lussaye A. miner,	• do do
Lombard J. N. miner,	do do
Libbee — merchant,	do do
Levit Daniel, ranchman,	Wild Cat
Little John, miner,	Pine Grove, S. R. P. O.
Lamer John H. ranchman	Galt House
Lack Jonathan, ranchman	Beal's Bar,
Lind C. T. miner,	do do
Lane John, miner,	do do
Lee John, miner,	do do
Lesslie Nelson, clerk,	Dotan's Bar
Lester Garrett, miner,	do do
Logan Archy, miner,	Rattlesnake
Lockerich John, miner,	Star House

M

MILLS M. E. attorney at law,	cor. Commercial and Court sts, Auburn	
Maguire Joseph, clerk,	cor. Commercial and Court sts,	do
McBurney & Higgins, Magnolia Sal'n,	Commercial street,	do
McDaniel Wm. merchant,	Sacramento street,	do
Marsh D. clerk,	Sacramento street,	do
McColm R. C. bar-keeper,	Empire Hotel,	do
McGuire John, steward,	Empire Hotel,	do
McGinley James, mason,	bds at American Hotel,	do
MITCHELL, T. & C. H. pro's Herald,	Main street,	do
MARKS DR. J. physician,	Gibson's stone building, M'n st,	do
MYERS DR. J. M. dentist,	do do do do	do
Merriam E. D. photographic artist,	Main street, Auburn	
McDermitt P. teamster.	bds Orleans Hotel, Auburn	
McCreedy George W. soda factory,	East street,	do
Moore Wm. jobber,	Court street,	do
McDonald —. miner,	bds Hogan's Rest.	do
Miller Frank, speculator,	bds Horn's,	do
McGinnis W. F. miner,	bds Orleans Hotel,	do
Mullin E. laborer,	Ill. & Sac. roads,	do
Mullin B. laborer,	Turnpike road,	do
Morris Sam. steward,	American Hotel,	do
Myers B. F. District Judge,	residence, Sac. st,	do
Mouse Chas. miner,	Millertown	
Murphy J. R. farmer,	Spanish Flat	
McKelvy L. clerk,	Main street, Ophir	
Moore James, merchant,	do do do	
McNeal John, miner,	Ophir	
McCurday John, farmer,	do	
MORRISON C. prop'r U. S. Stand,	Turnpike road	
Mason D. O. prop'r Mason's Hotel,	Main st, Gold Hill	
Malsh Julius, dry goods merchant,	Gold Hill	
Mahoney D. prop'r American Hotel,	Main street, Gold Hill	
Mahoney Thos. miner,	do do do do	
Moore Sam. H. prop'r stage line,	Gold Hill	
Maude C. dry goods merchant,	bds Mason's Hotel, Main st, Gold Hill	
McClure G. W. laborer,	Gold Hill	
McClure Sam. laborer,	do do	
MERRICK S. D. saloon keeper,	do do	
Millett Peter, miner,	do do	
Miller Zelous, miner,	do do	
Means W. C. bar-keeper,	Virginia	
McCray J. G. farmer,	do	
Mankiney P. butcher,	do	
Magly P. butcher,	do	
Morris J. miner,	Fox's Flat	
Marks M. merchant,	Main st, Virginia	
Miller R. H. miner,	Virginia	
McGinnis G. miner,	do	
Mayo U. blacksmith,	do	

Munsell James, wagon maker,	Mt. Pleasant House, Turnpike road
Munsell Alvin E. painter,	Auburn
Murphy John, miner,	Quartz Flat
Mitchell John, miner,	do do
Montgomery —, miner,	Fox's Flat
Miller Wm. E. prop'r People's Mill,	Lisbon
Miller Jas. E. miller,	Garland's Hill, Forest Hill
Miller & Heaton, prop'rs People's Mill,	Lisbon
Marsh H. J. saloon keeper,	do
Moore Wm. teamster,	do
Mendenhall E. T.	Mendenhall's Mill
Madden D. Wash. prop'r Madden's Toll Road, 6 miles in length	
McMahon —, miner,	Georgia Ravine
Marriner J. miner,	do do
McCuler Geo. miner,	do do
Morris S. G. hotel keeper,	Rattlesnake
Martino T. S. B. miner,	do
Merrill G. H. saloon keeper,	do
McDonald W. C. miner,	do
Maher P. miner,	do
Mead P. shoe maker,	do
Martin N. S. carpenter,	do
Martin H. teamster,	do
Miller L. E. farmer,	do
Martino T. S. miner,	do
Moffatt W. miner,	do
Miller —. farmer,	do
Moore H. miner,	do
Martin R. miner,	do
Morgans Francis, miner,	do
Morgans Isaac, miner,	do
Morgans Morgan, miner,	do
Mabuks —. farmer,	Danesville
Miles C. R. farmer,	do
Murphy John, miner,	Dutch Flat
Mushrush J. blacksmith,	do do
Murphy James T. miner,	do do
Myers H. L. miner,	do do
Myer John B. miner,	do do
McDonald J. B. miner,	do do
McVay W. miner,	do do
Morris Thos. miner,	do do
McDonald L. W. miner,	do do
Myers E. G. miner,	do do
Miller G. W. miner,	do do
Matoon J. S. blacksmith,	do do
McMichal John, miner,	do do
McKinney Willis, miner,	do do
Mansfield M. F. miner,	do do
Mahns Chas. miner,	do do
Mooney Thos. miner,	do do

TESTIMONIALS.

NEVADA, Nov. 19, 1860.

Mr. S. D. Staats—Sir: I hereby certify that we have been using Hose sewed on Rice's newly invented Hydraulic Sewing Machines. We have had them in use since the first of May last, and we are perfectly satisfied with the Hose, and find them tighter in the seam than hand sewing, and do not leak. The duck is 4–0 Lawrence's treble Hose, and our pressure is 132 feet. We have no hesitation in recommending them to the Miners at large.   T. D. GRIMES,
Superintendent of Manzanita Claims.

OWNERS—MALTMAN, MERSELUS & Co.

NEVADA, Nov. 23, 1860.

Mr. S. D. Staats—Sir: I take pleasure in stating to you that I have used Hose sewed by Rice on his newly invented Hydraulic Hose Sewing Machines, since April last, and I have no hesitation in saying that I believe them to be better than hand sewing, and the sewing will last as long as the duck, and they do not leak in the seam. My Hose was Double Hose, and under a pressure of 130 feet, and have had them in constant use, and I am confident that they will supersede hand sewing altogether, and I will recommend your hose to the Miners at large.   Respectfully yours, etc.,   C. K. HOTALING.
Witness, V. H. HELM.

CHIMNEY HILL, Nov. 16, 1860.

Mr. S. D. Staats—Sir: We are perfectly satisfied with your Hose. We find them tighter in the seam than hand sewing, and we do not hesitate to recommend them to the Mining community.

M. A. CLARK,   J. B. ROBINSON,   W. J. CLARK,
THOS. W. MOORE,   J. M. DEAVON.

SEBASTOPOL HILL, Nov. 14, 1860.

Mr. S. D. Staats—Sir: I take pleasure in stating to you, as the Agent of Rice's Hydraulic Hose Sewing Machines, that I have at this time fifty odd yards of Hose sewed by you on Rice's Machine, and I have no hesitation in saying that I prefer them to hand sewing, so far as I have used them. I have had them in actual use for the last five weeks, and I find them tighter in the seam than hand sewing, and will recommend your Hose to the miners.   A. M. STROBRIDGE & CO.

QUAKER HILL, Nov. 28, 1860.

S. D. Staats—Sir: The Hose made by you on Rice's Machine, of last March, are perfectly good, and in constant use to this day.
W. N. JACOBS & CO.

QUAKER HILL, Nov. 28, 1860.

Mr. Staats—Sir: I take pleasure in stating to you that the Hose made by you on Rice's Machine, is, in our opinion, superior to any in use.   C. B. AULT & CO.

NORTH SAN JUAN, Dec. 16, 1860.

Mr. Staats—Sir: Your Hose that we have in use stands well. Please send me one hundred yards more of the same quality of duck as that we have now in use.
A. M. STROBRIDGE & CO.

February 9, 1861. Mr. Staats—Sir: Send me one hundred yards of your Hose immediately; the same as you sent before.   A. M. STROBRIDGE & CO.

Meek Abram, miner,	Dutch	Flat
Mitchell Wm. miner,	do	do
Mason Joseph, miner,	do	do
McCamish David, miner,	do	do
Mushrush J. B. miner,	do	do
Moore B. F. agent W. F. & Co.	do	do
Mahoney Michael, miner,	do	do
Mattoon E. blacksmith,	do	do
McGrew F. A. miner,	do	do
Moody John F. miner,	do	do
Murrah J. miner,	do	do
Marr Benj. A. miner	do	do
McMullen R. miner,	do	do
Mackin Geo. miner,	do	do
Miller C. W. clerk & gold dust buyer,	do	do
McCulloch Geo. W. farmer,	do	do
McKee W. S. farmer,	do	do
Moses Felix, miner,	do	do
Mathewson Jas. T. constable,	do	do
Mayn J. A. miner,	do	do
McHally F. N. miner,	do	do
Mathews J. B. miner,	do	do
Melzner G. W. saloon keeper,	do	do
Milney Jas. miner,	do	do
Maloney Thomas, boot & shoemaker,	Pine	Grove
Martin Daniel, miner,	do	do
Moore Thomas, miner,	do	do
Michael George, ranchman,	Galt	House
Morse Frank, miner,	do	do
Mayo Albion, miner,	do	do
Moody Hopkin, miner,	Beal's	Bar
Murry James, miner,	do	do
Marble Frank, carpenter,	Rattlesnake	
Mills Alexander, speculator,	Fox's Flat	
Marshall S. W. miner,	Virginia	
Meating N. J. laborer,	Illinoistown	
McCauly T. laborer,	Starbuck's Mill	
Murphy —. ranchman,	do	do
McGoldrich Thomas, miner,	Rattlesnake	
Mills J. miner,	Iowa	Hill
Morse M. miner,	do	do
McLaughlin E. G. miner,	do	do
McDonald J. D. miner,	do	do
Mulligan Philip, miner,	Illinoistown	
Miller Joseph, miner,	Iowa	Hill
Makins Wm. S. miner,	do	do
Makins J. N. miner,	do	do
Mundy Felix, miner,	do	do
Mink Elijah, miner,	do	do
McKee Thos. miner,	do	do
Maddy F. M. miner,	do	do

McLain Daniel, minister,	Iowa Hill
Merritt J. T. miner,	do do
Murphy B. miner,	do do
Morgan T. miner,	do do
Mulligan J. miner,	do do
McCrellen O. miner,	do do
Mattison Louis, saloon keeper,	do do
Maxly Caleb, miner,	do do
Melbourne A. miner,	do do
Mercer J. W. miner,	do do
McKinnan Daniel, miner,	do do
McGowan Chas. miner,	do do
Morrison G. R. miner,	do do
McGanele B. miner,	do do
McLaughlin J. miner,	do do
Marshall C. R. miner,	do do
McCumber J. B. miner,	do do
McCullough Wm. miner,	do do
McCormick James, miner,	do do
Morrison Geo. miner,	do do
McKinzie Christian, miner,	do do
McKinnan Wm. miner,	do do
Mills Wm. miner,	do do
May Richard, miner,	do do
Mill William, miner,	do do
McDaniel F. miner,	do do
McCaul Pat. miner,	do do
McDaniel R. J. carpenter,	do do
Meyers W. H. miner,	do do
Myrick J. W. miner,	do do
Marksley Caleb, miner,	do do
Mattox H. A. miner,	do do
Metcalf E. miner,	do do
McGaw Owen, miner,	do do
Mullen J. miner,	do do
McGowan Wm. miner,	do do
Mott M. miner,	do do
Mack John, miner,	do do
McDaniel F. M. miner,	do do
Mundy Pat. miner,	do do
Mooney H. Z. miner,	do do
Munse Jonathan, miner,	do do
McGinnis Pat. miner,	do do
McDonald Frank, miner,	do do
McDowell Geo. miner,	Forks House
Morgan A. V. miner,	do do
Moreland Thos. merchant,	do do
Moran Michael, miner, [N. F. bridge,]	Auburn
Morris David, prop. of N. F. House,	Grizzly Bear House
McCabe Geo. lumberman,	Forest Hill

B. R. SWEETLAND,

DRUGGIST,

WHOLESALE AND RETAIL DEALER IN

PATENT

Botanic and Family Medicines,

PERFUMERY AND FANCY ARTICLES.

CORNER OF K AND SIXTH STS.

SACRAMENTO.

Maurice Jos. porter in Forest House, Forest Hill		
Mills John S. teamster,	do	do
Miller Alfred, miner,	do	do
Miller Abraham, miner,	do	do
Miller Henry, miner,	do	do
McClanahan Wm. miner,	do	do
McRae Geo. miner,	do	do
Means Robt. miner,	do	do
McIntire Benj. miner,	do	do
McGill James, miner,	do	do
Monroe J. M. K. saloon keeper,	do	do
McInnerny Pat. miner,	do	do
McManus Thos. miner,	do	do
McCullin Michael, miner,	do	do
Maye Hermann, miner,	do	do
McRitchie —. miner,	do	do
McCullough A. miner,	do	do
McCullough L. J. miner,	do	do
McClary Carr, blacksmith,	do	do
McKinnan Daniel, miner,	do	do
McLean James, painter,	do	do
Mewer James, miner,	do	do
Mewer Wm. miner,	do	do
Mewer Thos. miner,	do	do
Manix John, saloon keeper,	do	do
McGlin Daniel, miner,	do	do
Mills John L. miner,	do	do
Mundell John, printer,	do	do
Marshall D. P. miner,	do	do
Moore John, miner,	do	do
Morrison John, watchman,	do	do
McKean John, miner,	do	do
McKean Wm. miner,	do	do
McCorcle S. miner,	do	do
McComb Wm. miner,	do	do
Morehead A. miner,	do	do
McDougle D. miner,	do	do
McDougle Wm. miner,	do	do
McFee C. miner,	do	do
McDermott John, miner,	do	do
McAvoy Joseph, miner,	do	do
Myers Mark H. miner,	do	do
McMannery Thos. miner,	do	do
Maus Matthew, miner,	do	do
Moore Samuel, miner,	do	do
Melton Wm. J. miner,	do	do
Moore Alex. miner,	do	do
May Martin, miner,	do	do
McGlenn Daniel, miner,	do	do
McQuade James P. miner,	do	do

May Martin, miner,	Forest Hill
May Henry, miner,	do do
May Hermann, miner,	do do
May George, miner,	do do
Maler Henry, miner,	do do
Manplasure J. B. carpenter,	do do
Mullen Edward, miner,	do do
Murray John, miner,	do do
Moffatt L. S. miner,	do do
Moore John, miner,	do do
M'Dole —, miner,	dd do
Manhan J. L. miner,	do do
Mason R. T. miner,	do do
Mattason Jas. A. road prop'r,	do do
Melcherson John, miner,	do do
Moorehead John, miner,	do do
Murphy Matthew, miner,	do do
Matthew Frank M. miner,	do do
Morehead Andrew, miner,	do do
McGoey Thos. miner,	do do
McGoey James, miner,	do do
McEnerney —, miner,	do do
McManus Thos. miner,	do do
McGlin D. miner,	do do
McGlin Bartlett, miner,	do do
McDonald Adam, miner,	do do
Mooney James, miner,	do do
McDermott Henry, miner,	do do
Mayfield P. miner,	do do
McCoon Chas. miner,	Michigan Bluff
Mitchell Frank, miner,	do do
Matteson Alphe, miner,	do do
Maxwell Wm. miner,	do do
Manser H. C. miner,	do do
McDonald E. miner,	do do
McLaughlin Hugh, miner,	do do
Mellus H. J. miner,	do do
Morse B. miner,	do do
May J. S. miner,	do do
McKensie John, blacksmith,	do do
McDonald Duncan, blacksmith,	do do
Miden John, saloon keeper,	do do
Mitchell A. G. restaurater,	do do
Mitchell J. W. merchant,	do do
McDonald E. butcher,	do do
Miller Fred. butcher,	do do
McCoy D. butcher,	do do
McGuire Wm. B. saloon keeper,	do do
Montmorquet P. C. saloon keeper,	do do
Miller Mrs. H. F. lodging house,	do do

Miller Chas. A. trader,	Michigan	Bluff
Matcenback Wm. board'ghouse keeper,	do	do
McComb Geo. saloon keeper,	do	do
McKinney Geo. boot store,	do	do
Milks E. miner,	do	do
Miller John, miner,	do	do
Martin Chas. miner,	do	do
McPherson Wm. miner,	do	do
McHale Patrick, miner,	do	do
McCollum Archie, miner,	do	do
McCollum John, miner,	do	do
Milligan John, miner,	do	do
Moore Nelson, miner,	do	do
McCauly Mat. miner,	do	do
McCauly James, miner,	do	do
McClure Thos. miner,	do	do
Mallenux J. G. miner,	do	do
McBride John, miner,	do	do
Morton G. W. saloon keeper, [D'w'd,]	do	do
McCannell M. E. miner, do	do	do
Mosier John, miner, do	do	do
Michaels Geo. miner, [Last Chance,]	do	do
Merriman T. E. miner, do	do	do
McQuavry Alex. miner, do	do	do
Mellenburg A. O. miner, do	do	do
McColm Nat. miner, do	do	do
McGrady Hugh, miner, do	do	do
Meinhardt Fred. miner, do	do	do
Mulferd John, miner, do	do	do
Morgan Bart. saloon keeper, do	do	do
McCarte P. A. miner, do	do	do
McIntosh —, miner, do	do	do
McBride M. miner,	do	do
McDonald Thos. miner,	do	do
McBride P. miner,	do	do
Mansfield Wm. miner,	do	do
Moss James, miner,	do	do
Moss Wm. miner,	do	do
McGary A. miner,	do	do
Murphey Wm. miner,	do	do
McNamara —. miner,	do	do
McDonald R. A. miner,	do	do
Mattock J. miner, [Long Cañon,]	do	do
Morris John, miner, do	do	do
Mayo John, miner,	do	do
Morgan John, miner.	do	do
Morse Benjamin, miner,	do	do
Moss John, miner,	do	do
Muhlin Gibson, miner,	do	do
Muhlin J. H. miner,	do	do
McCarty Wm. miner,	do	do

Marshall Wm. miner,	Michigan Bluff	
Myers C. G. miner,	do	do
Masters Frank, miner,	do	do
McLean Alex. miner,	do	do
McKee I. J. miner,	do	do
Maloney Seth, miner,	do	do
Mowen Patrick, miner,	do	do
Means David, miner,	do	do
McIntire Wm. miner,	do	do
McCarty John, miner,	do	do
McGrew John, miner,	Todd's Valley	
Miller Chauncy, saloon keeper,	do	do
McGinn Larry, miner,	do	do
Marks Chas. merchant,	do	do
McBurney Geo. miner,	do	do
McBurney H. miner,	do	do
Myers H. L. miner,	do	do
McMahill G. B. miner,	do	do
Miner Frank, ranchman,	do	do
Mayfield E. miner,	do	do
McKinzie Alex. miner,	do	do
Murray J. W. ranchman,	do	do
Miller J. miner,	do	do
Moore E. B. miner,	do	do
Manser Jo. miner,	do	do
Miner John, express agent,	do	do
McDonald Isaac, miner,	do	do
Montgomery M. miner,	do	do
McDougle G. W. miner,	do	do
Mayward Simon, miner,	do	do
Manly J. M. miner,	Yankee Jim's	
McClure Col. Wm. ditch proprietor,	do	do
McClure Samuel, teamster,	do	do
McClure Jas. C. clerk,	do	do
McClure Wm. H. miner,	do	do
Michaels G. A. butcher,	do	do
Martin B. B. miner,	do	do
McKinna J. C. miner,	do	do
Manning A. H. merchant,	do	do
Morrill H. C. millman,	do	do
Morrill E. B. millman,	do	do
Mannion Larra, miner,	do	do
Miller Fred. miner,	do	do
Moore E. W. miner,	do	do
McDougle Alex. miner,	do	do
Moulton J. M. tinsmith,	do	do
Morse B. T. carpenter,	do	do
McIntosh Joseph, miner,	do	do
Martin B. B. miner,	do	do
McCauley A. miner,	do	do
Mora Manuel, miner,	do	do

THE ONE PRICE DRY GOODS HOUSE
OF SACRAMENTO.

HARDY BRO'S & HALL,
IMPORTERS AND DEALERS IN

Fancy and Staple Dry Goods,

Removed to their NEW and Spacious Store,

189 J STREET, ONE DOOR BELOW SEVENTH STREET,
SACRAMENTO.

☞ Rich SILKS, LACES, SHAWLS, MANTLES, EMBROIDERIES, HOSIERY, Etc., Etc.   The choicest and most desirable styles of Dress Goods, received by every Steamer.

DANIEL HARDY.   WM. HARDY.   G. C. HALL.

L. WELLS,
HORSE SHOER,

Two doors from the Golden Eagle Hotel, K St., bet. 6th and 7th,
SACRAMENTO.

☞ Fancy and Race Stock Shod with skill and taste, and work executed with dispatch.   Wild Stock shod on short notice, and to the satisfaction of all customers.   ☞ TERMS REASONABLE.

Mosslander Thos. miner,   Yankee Jim's
McGlinn B. miner,   do   do
McDonald John, miner,   do   do
Martin H. B. miner,   do   do
Maines John, miner,   do   do
McGraw Dennis, miner,   do   do

N

Nosler Thos. M.   bds American Hotel, Auburn,
NOLAN JAS. merchant tailor,   Main st, Auburn
NORCROSS W. F. jeweler,   sign mammoth watch, Main st, Auburn
Neall James, sup't Bear River ditch, bds Star Bakery and Rest. Auburn
Nelson G. farmer,   Spanish Flat
Naeler E. miner,   Ophir,
NUNNALLY T. C. El Dorado saloon, Main st, Gold Hill
NAGEL JAS. M. saloon keeper,   Main st, Gold Hill
Nickerson R. M. saloon keeper,   Main st, Virginia
Newell Asa, farmer,   Danesville
Ninns N. hotel keeper,   Turnpike Road
Nagle M. miner,   Rattlesnake Bar
Nodin F. miner,   Dutch Flat
Nichols Wallace, miner,   do
Nelson H. W. physician and surgeon,   do
Nighthart P. miner,   do
Nichols T. J. clerk,   do
Noyes C. A. miner,   do
Norris J. W. miner,   do
Norton Harry, miner,   do
Nayor F. miner,   do
Nichols J. H. miner,   do
Nasman A. miner,   do
Nichol S. miner,   do
Neff B. F. blacksmith,   Secret Ravine
Nickson —, ranching   Rattlesnake
Nichols —, laborer   Star House
Nithart George, laborer,   Forest Hill
Nelson Thomas, laborer,   do   do
Newth Robert, laborer,   do   do
Norres P. laborer,   do   do
Nelson T. miner,   do   do
Nisson Earnst, miner,   do   do
Northcut M. miner,   do   do
Northwood William, miner,   do   do
Nightingale James, miner,   Todd's Valley
Neavy Pat, miner,   do   do
Nelson Charles, miner, Deadwood,   Michigan Bluff
Newell P. W. miner,   do   do   do
Norman James, miner, Last Chance,   do   do
Newton George, miner, do   do   do   do
Newstream Andrew, miner,   do   do
Noel John, miner,   do   do

Nede James, miner,	Michigan Bluff
Nede Michael, miner,	do do
Nash E. H. miner,	do do
Nadger Fred. miner,	Iowa Hill
Noble David, miner,	do do
Noble David, Jr., miner,	do do
Noble Robt. miner,	do do
Neff J. H. miner,	do do
Newbegin Chas. miner,	do do
Newbegin Jerry, miner,	do do

O

O'NEIL JNO. Headquarters Saloon,	Centre Block, Auburn
O'REILLY M. Headquarters Saloon,	do do do
Osburn G. residence Turnpike road,	Auburn
Openshaw Jno. bar-keeper,	Temple Saloon, Auburn
Osburn Wm. night watchman,	residence Ill. and Sac. roads, Auburn
Ogden Geo. prop'r stage line,	Gold Hill
Ohje Jno. miner,	do do
Owens J. W. constable,	Virginia
Ollaway —, miner,	Quartz Flat
O'Conner Jno. laborer,	Lisbon
Owens M. S. wood-sawyer,	Gold Hill
Ovare Jno. miner,	Millertown
Ormsby Oliver, miner,	Dutch Flat
O'Niel R. C. tinner and merchant,	do do
O'Connel John, miner,	Pine Grove
Osbroom Wm. miner,	do do
Ogden James, miner,	Rattlesnake
Orr David, livery-stable keeper,	Forest Hill
Owen W. W. packer,	do do
Ott H. miner,	do do
O'Rourke James, miner,	do do
O'Neil F. miner,	do do
Osborne Henry, miner,	do do
O'Conner J. miner,	do do
O'Conner C. miner,	do do
O'Conner J. C. miner,	Forks House
O'Connell Pat. miner,	Todd's Valley
Oxendine A. M. millman,	do do
Olsen John, miner,	do do
Otis Geo. musician,	Michigan Bluff
O'Bryan Wm. miner,	do do
O'Bryan Ned. miner,	do do
O'Toole Peter, miner,	do do
Ott V. G. expressman, [Last Chance,]	do do
O'Riley Barney, miner,	Iowa Hill
Odgers Thos. miner,	do do
Osborne Thos. miner,	do do

CALIFORNIA
STEAM NAVIGATION CO.

THE FAST AND SPLENDID STEAMERS

CHRYSOPOLIS,......**E. C. M. Chadwick, Master**
ANTELOPE,................**E. A. Poole, Master**
ECLIPSE, and QUEEN CITY,

WILL LEAVE FOR

SAN FRANCISCO, DAILY,

SUNDAYS EXCEPTED, AT 2 O'CLOCK, P. M.

FROM THE FOOT OF K STREET.

— FROM —

MARYSVILLE AND INTERMEDIATE LANDINGS,
EVERY DAY.

YOUNG AMERICA,..........**Littleton, Master**
— AND —
SWALLOW,................**Summers, Master**

Will Leave on Alternate Days, at 6 A. M.

FOR COLUSA, RED BLUFFS

AND INTERMEDIATE LANDINGS,

SAM SOULE,...........**Wm. Pierce, Master**
SWAN,................**J. C. Rogers, Master**
GEM,.................**A. Foster, Master**
VICTOR,.............——— **Master**

Will leave for the above named Places, on TUESDAYS, THURSDAYS and SATURDAYS, at 6 A. M. from Storeship, foot of J Street.

For Freight or Passage by any of the above Boats, apply on board, or at the Office of the California Steam Navigation Co., on board Brig Globe.

REDINGTON, }
W. H. TAYLOR, } **Agents.**

11

SACRAMENTO VALLEY

THE CARS LEAVE SACRAMENTO

At 6½ A. M., 2¼ and 5 P. M. }
   LEAVE FOLSOM.   } Summer Arrangement.
At 6½ A. M., 12 M., and 5¼ P. M. }

LEAVE SACRAMENTO
At 6½ A. M., 1½ and 4¼ P. M. }
   LEAVE FOLSOM   } WINTER ARRANGEMENT.
At 7 A. M., 12 M., and 4½ P. M. }

6½ A. M. from Sacramento, and 12 M. Train from Folsom, connect with stages to and from all Mountain Towns.

FREIGHT TAKEN BY EVERY UPWARD TRAIN.

☞ Arrangements are being made to run the Cars over the C. C. R. R., as far as the Half-Way House, on the Sacramento and Auburn Road, of which due notice will be given.

J. P. ROBINSON,

MAY 1st, 1861.   *Superintendent.*

Overbaugh Joseph miner,   Iowa Hill
Otto L. miner,   do   do
Odges Jack, miner   do   do

P

Patton R. R. attorney at law,   cor. Commercial and Court sts, Auburn
Palmer C. T. clerk, W. F. & Co.   Main st, Auburn
PARKINSON WM. K. merchant,   cor. Main and East sts, Auburn
Palmer Geo. wagon maker,   bds at Empire Hotel, Auburn
POLAND & ROWELL, lawyers,   Gibson's stone build'g, Main st, Auburn
Peterson Henry, milkman,   Baltimore Ravine
Pitcher Wm. miner,   bds at Orleans Hotel, Auburn
Perry Greenleaf, merchant,   Main st, Ophir
Perry Dr. W. physician,   Ophir
Pickens James, miner,   North Ravine
Pugh C. D. miner,   Ophir
Price W. W. miner,   Gold Hill
Peterson James, turner,   bds Mason's Hotel, Gold Hill
Powers L. miner,   residence Main st, Gold Hill
Peterson Chas. miner,   Gold Hill
Peterson Christian, miner,   do   do
Purdy J. E. merchant,   Main st, Virginia
Porter J. miner,   Fox's Flat
Prescot John,   Mendenhall's Mill
Porter T. A. engineer,   Illinoistown
Peterson A. laborer,   do
Peterson Chas. miner,   Auburn Ravine
Price Wm. gardener,   Mountaineer
Poland J. C. laborer,   do
Perkins F. L. farmer,   Rattlesnake
Plank A. saloon keeper,   do
Popper C. butcher,   do
Patterson J. miner,   do
Praigg J. G. miner,   Auburn Ravine
Peterson Howard, miner,   do   do
Perry John, miner,   Donix Hill
Philips Thos. butcher,   Virginia
Philips Theo. butcher,   do
Porter A. miner,   Dutch Flat
Pollard W. miner,   do   do
Parsons Wm. biggest liver in town, do   do
Plumber C. B. clerk,   do   do
Pollard B. miner,   do   do
Platceck Wm. miner,   do   do
Phillips W. W. miner,   do   do
Priest James, miner,   do   do
Palmer W. C. miner,   do   do
Painter M. B. miner,   do   do
Pratt H. A. miner,   do   do
Paine F. A. miner,   do   do

Peterson E. miner,	Dutch Flat
Parker Thos. D. miner,	do do
Pinney R. H. miner,	do do
Palrick E. B. miner,	do do
Pottle J. W. miner,	do do
Phillips Geo. miner,	do do
Pisenti Jno. miner,	do do
Pisenti Martin, miner,	do do
Powers O. P. miner,	do do
Palridge A. S. miner,	do do
Perry T. miner,	do do
Page N. S. physician,	Antelope Ravine
Patten A. miner,	Taylor's Ravine
Parker Albert, miner,	Beal's Bar
Pebble Alfred, miner,	Rattlesnake Bar
Peterson John, miner,	do do
Prebble Frank, miner,	do do
Porter A. J. miner,	Fox's Flat
Pritchard N. prop'r of toll road,	Grizzly Bear House
Pansetter Louis, miner,	do do do
Phelan M. restaurateur,	Forest Hill
Parkhurst R. druggist,	do do
Prescott —, saloon keeper,	do do
Prescott J. merchant,	do do
Prescott A. merchant,	do do
Preston Ed. miner,	do do
Page J. H. miner,	do do
Paff Chas. miner,	do do
Paff Anthony, miner,	do do
Platt James, miner,	do do
Porter C. miner,	do do
Peas John, miner,	do do
Peas Geo. miner,	do do
Perada John, miner,	do do
Peters Wm. miner,	do do
Peterson Wm. miner,	do do
Peterson Peter, miner,	do do
Parker Wm. miner,	do do
Parker E. bar keeper,	do do
Pierson John, miner,	do do
Pape Samuel, ranchman,	Todd's Valley
Perkins P. H. teamster,	do do
Powell P. ditch superintendent,	do do
Philbrook A. miner,	do do
Pond A. A. merchant,	do do
Pierce Franklin, road superintendent,	Michigan Bluff
Powers Geo. millman,	do do
Powers Robt. millman,	do do
Pierson E. butcher,	do do
Prout Geo. (colored,) barber,	do do
Pierson Richard, miner,	do do

DR. C. Y. GIRARD'S
GINGER BRANDY

W. B. CROWELL, Jr., NEW YORK,
AGENT FOR THE UNITED STATES AND CANADA.

This Celebrated Preparation was discovered and extensively used during the progress of the CHOLERA in London, 1832, and since then in the United States. In 1849–50, while the disease was spreading over the Southern and Western States, it was found to be a reliable and certain cure.

As only the very best articles are used, and from its peculiar combination, it possesses in a high degree the properties of a stomachic stimulant,

☞ IT IS RECOMMENDED FOR ☜

Colic, Cramps, Diarrhœa, Flatulency,

SPASMS OF THE STOMACH AND BOWELS, (AFFORDING IMMEDI-
ATE RELIEF,) DYSPEPSIA, ATONIC GOUT,

PROMOTES DIGESTION, CHECKS AND PREVENTS NAUSEA,
And is a Certain Cure for Sea Sickness,

☞ As a BITTERS it is unequalled in the world.

C. Y. GIRARD, 110 Piccadilly, London.

☞ For Sale by all the principal Grocers and Druggists.

S. C. SHAW, San Francisco,

Agent for California.

Peck Chas. miner,	Michigan	Bluff
Park James, miner,	do	do
Percival Joseph, miner,	do	do
Perry J. H. miner,	do	do
Pierson, E. V. miner,	do	do
Parker E. T. miner,	do	do
Philman John, miner,	do	do
Parker E. miner,	do	do
Parker Alonzo, miner,	do	do
Parker James, miner,	do	do
Prockett Enoch, miner, [Deadwood,]	do	do
Perkins Jotham, miner, [Last Chance,]	do	do
Parkinson W. H. millman, do do	do	do
Pulliam W. M. miner, do do	do	do
Park Samuel, miner, do do	do	do
Peterson C. miner, do do	do	do
Penman W. A. miner, do do	do	do
Penman Dave, miner, do do	do	do
Porter, E. J. miner, do do	do	do
Perry H. J. miner,	do	do
Parkham Sam'l, miner,	do	do
Page Geo. W. miner,	do	do
Prichard David, miner,	do	do
Poland J. miner, [Long Cañon,]	do	do
Proctor Wm. B. miner,	do	do
Prior John B. miner,	do	do
Pryor Wm. (colored,) miner,	do	do
Pease H. L. miner,	do	do
Pratt Frank, miner,	do	do
Parker E. miner,	do	do
Pettigrew W. J. miner,	do	do
Parmelee Walter, miner,	do	do
Puntney N. S. miner,	do	do
Perkins R. N. miner,	do	do
Phelps E. A. surveyor,	do	do
Power M. H. miner,	Forks	House
Parrier G. miner,	do	do
Poole A. W. miner,	do	do
Peterson Wm. miner,	do	do
Perry W. B. miner,	Iowa	Hill
Parish C. H. miner,	do	do
Perry Chas. miner,	do	do
Peiner Julius, miner,	do	do
Priest J. L. miner,	do	do
Priest D. Q. miner,	do	do
Pursely Jas. miner,	do	do
Patterson Thos. miner,	do	do
Peterson O. H. physician,	do	do
Perkins J. miner,	do	do
Paine Jerry, musician,	do	do

Peoples J. J. miner,   Iowa Hill
Pool W. W. miner,   do   do

Q

Quinn D. B. teamster,   Illinoistown
Quinn C. farmer,   Marysville Road, Coon Creek
Quinn M. miner,   Dutch Flat
Quillin O. S. M. miner,   do   do
Quinn Duncan, miner,   Forest Hill

R

Russo Jno.   bds Star Bak'y Rest. Com. st, Auburn
Russell Jno.   dwelling house, Main st, Auburn
REED & FRENCH, carpenters,   cor. Turnpike and Main sts, Auburn
Richardson A. bar-keeper,   Temple saloon, Auburn
Russell Geo. district assessor,   bds Orleans Hotel, Auburn
Rackliff A. carpenter,   Ill. and Sac. Roads,   do
Reno Stephen, Justice of Peace,   Ophir
Robinson S. miner,   do
Ritche Frank, miner,   do
Ritche Wm. miner,   do
Ross Edward, miner,   do
Rogers Sam. saloon keeper,   Main st, Gold Hill
Ross Thatcher, merchant,   do do   do   do
Renoer Wm. carpenter,   Commercial st, Auburn
Rodick Thos. meat-pedler,   Henn & Harford, Gold Hill
Reamer E. miner,   Auburn Ravine, Virginia
Rosenbohm Jno. miner,   Gold Hill
Rogers Thos. miner,   do   do
Rattle Jno. S. miner,   Virginia
Rainbean Chas. miner,   do
Robinson J. M. farmer,   Pleasant Grove Creek
Robinson W. B. saloon-keeper,   Main st, Virginia
Richards H. R. miner,   Virginia
Robinson W. miner,   Fox's Flat
Rice Chas. farmer,   Auburn Ravine
Rielly G. machinist,   Lincoln
Ragsdale & Smothers, butchers,   Illinoistown
Rogers Augustus, miner,   Gold Hill
Robinson C. W. miner,   Auburn Ravine
Roberts Henry, miner,   Virginia
Riche J. L. miner,   Auburn
Rice D. A., W. F. & Co's agent,   Rattlesnake
Riche Jas. carpenter,   do
Rackliff Jas. miner,   do
Richmond W. C. merchant,   Dutch Flat
Racklin B. miner,   do   do
Rhodes A. J. miner,   do   do
Rhodes A. miner,   do   do

COLUMBUS
BREWERY,

CORNER OF K AND SIXTEENTH STREETS,
SACRAMENTO.

E. & C. GRUHLER, - PROPRIETORS.

ORDERS FROM THE MOUNTAIN COUNTIES
FILLED with PROMPTNESS and DISPATCH.

DEPOT IN SACRAMENTO,

AT J. GRUHLER'S SALOON,

SIXTH STREET, BETWEEN J and K.

☞ Orders addressed to either of the above parties, will be
promptly responded to.

PRICES REASONABLE.

Read G. miner,	Dutch Flat		
Russell R. H. miner,	do	do	
Rathborn L. C. miner,	do	do	
Ruperight John, miner,	do	do	
Rorve Wm. miner,	do	do	
Rathborn A. A. miner,	do	do	
Rodewald Chas. miner,	do	do	
Richards J. miner,	do	do	
Roberly John, miner,	do	do	
Roservean J. W. miner,	do	do	
Reynolds Chas. miner,	do	do	
Richer R. A. school-teacher,	do	do	
Rodgers W. A. miner,	do	do	
Raywood W. A. miner,	Grizzly Bear House		
Rice Harvey, miner,	do	do	do
Rolf H. merchant, [B. R.]	do	do	do
Richt Michael, ranchman,	do	do	do
Record Chas. carpenter,	Forest Hill		
Rustler John, miner,	do	do	
Reno H. B. miner,	do	do	
Rassoe Eugene, livery-stable keeper,	do	do	
Rannison James, miner,	do	do	
Richards Wm. miner,	do	do	
Richardson R. engineer,	do	do	
Russell James, miner,	do	do	
Randlett John, miner,	do	do	
Rowell John W. miner,	do	do	
Redmond James, miner,	do	do	
Redmond Wm. miner,	do	do	
Ratwan Chas. miner,	do	do	
Randolph —, blacksmith, [H. S. Bar,]	do	do	
Rafty Pat. miner,	do	do	
Reamer G. W. miner,	do	do	
Ruckenberger Lewis, blacksmith,	do	do	
Regles August, miner,	do	do	
Rarey Martin, miner,	do	do	
Rulafs A. miner,	do	do	
Roach Geo. miner,	do	do	
Richards Wm. miner,	do	do	
Robertson J. S. miner,	do	do	
Roland Willis, miner,	do	do	
Reason John, miner,	do	do	
Randlett Chas. ranchman	do	do	
Ray T. lumberman,	do	do	
Ray Wm. lumberman,	do	do	
Rice H. lumberman,	do	do	
Robinson John, miner,	Todd's Valley		
Reed A. G. merchant,	do	do	
Ring Clay, miner,	do	do	
Russell J. B. miner,	do	do	
Randolph S. blacksmith,	do	do	

Randall A. miner,	Todd's Valley	
Remler L. miner,	do	do
Rogers Chas. millman,	Michigan Bluff	
Reed F. S. miner,	do	do
Reinstein S. merchant,	do	do
Raabe Chas. brewer,	do	do
Rice Jerome D. miner,	do	do
Roberts John, bowling saloon keeper,	do	do
Rankin Cullen miner,	do	do
Rausso S. saloon keeper,	do	do
Rasiere Chas. saloon keeper,	do	do
Rowley John M. carpenter,	do	do
Rosenan H. miner,	do	do
Ritchie Wm. miner,	do	do
Robertson J. L. miner, [Deadwood,]	do	do
Randolph John, miner, do	do	do
Reed Henry, miner, [Last Chance,]	do	do
Rabbitt Patrick, miner, do do	do	do
Richards J. W. miner,	do	do
Robins Thos. miner,	do	do
Ressler Jacob, miner,	do	do
Ryan James, miner, [Long Cañon,]	do	do
Robinson —, daguerrean artist,	do	do
Russell —, miner,	do	do
Rice Wm. miner,	do	do
Rains Jacob, miner,	do	do
Reed James, miner,	do	do
Rowland James, miner,	Yankee Jim's	
Rood D. miner,	do	do
Raselle John, miner,	do	do
Record John, miner,	do	do
Riley Philip, miner,	do	do
Rouarke Barney, miner,	do	do
Robinson M. M. road proprietor,	Iowa Hill	
Robertson James, miner,	do	do
Richardson E. H. miner,	do	do
Richardson S. W. miner,	do	do
Ryan John, miner,	do	do
Richards Matthew, miner,	do	do
Richards I. W. miner,	do	do
Rady Lewis, miner,	do	do
Rutherford J. W. miner,	do	do
Rathburn J. miner,	do	do
Ricer J. miner,	do	do
Rich W. C. miner,	do	do
Reno C. P. merchant, [Ind. Hill,]	do	do
Rand Thos. B. ranchman,	do	do
Ryan Michael, ranchman,	do	do
Riley John, miner,	do	do
Riley B. A. miner,	do	do
Roberts R. L. miner,	do	do

SMITH'S
GARDENS AND NURSERY,
SACRAMENTO,

On the American River 2½ miles from the Steamboat Levee and Stage Office.

A LARGE AND FULL STOCK OF

FRUIT, SHADE AND ORNAMENTAL TREES,
SHRUBS AND PLANTS,

The most extensive variety in the State; Also,

200,000 FOREIGN GRAPE VINES
OF THE CHOICEST VARIETIES,
FOR MARKET, TABLE AND WINE PURPOSES.

—— ALSO, ——

CALIFORNIA GROWN GARDEN SEEDS,

Of our own raising, at wholesale or retail, at LOWER prices than any other Establishment in the State.

SEED AND TREE DEPOT, 40 J STREET, BETWEEN 2d and 3d,
SACRAMENTO.

☞ Catalogues Mailed to all applicants } Free of Charge.   **A. P. SMITH, Proprietor.**

INDEPENDENT.

THE ELEGANT

STEAMER NEVADA

W. L. PHILLIPS, MASTER,

Will make Regular Trips from foot of L Street, leaving SACRAMENTO every MONDAY, WEDNESDAY and FRIDAY, at TWO P. M., and returning from SAN FRANCISCO, on TUESDAY, THURSDAY and SATURDAY, at FOUR P. M.

CABIN FARE, - - **$1 00 DECK,** - - **25 CTS.**
FREIGHT, - - - - - - - **$1 PER TON.**

The NEVADA will run on alternate days with the JOHN T. WRIGHT.

WHITNEY & CO., 54 Front Street, Agents.

CHOICE DRUGS, Chemicals EXTRACTS, ECLECTIC PREPARATIONS PERFUMERY, Fancy Goods, PAINTS AND OILS, LAMP OIL, SODA CORKS, HOPS, ETC., ETC.

R. H. McDONALD & CO WHOLESALE IMPORTING DRUGGISTS SACRAMENTO CAL.

Dental Goods, GOLD FOIL, GUM TEETH, CHEVALIERS, FORCEPS, SURGICAL Instruments, TRUSSES, SUPPORTERS, PATENT MEDICINES, ETC., ETC.

For Sale at Reduced Prices. ☞ Orders respectfully solicited.   **R. H. McDONALD & Co., Sacramento.**

Rosenberg M. merchant,	Iowa Hill
Rich J. J. miner,	do do
Roberts H. W. hotel keeper,	do do
Riley F. miner,	do do
Ray M. miner,	do do
Reagan J. miner,	do do
Reed Thomas, miner,	do do
Reagan T. miner,	do do
Reagan Dennis, miner,	do do
Ruthardt V. saloon keeper,	do do
Ryan T. miner,	do do
Roach P. E. miner,	do do
Riley E. miner,	do do
Rutherford J. tanner,	do do
Rice Chas. road proprietor,	Illinoistown
Rodgers P. R. blacksmith,	Pine Grove
Rean John, miner,	Rattlesnake
Rogers James H. ditch agent,	Secret Ravine

S

Siefert Alex. butcher,	Main st, Auburn
Sherman M. liquor dealer,	do do do
Sherman Thos. plumber,	dwelling house, Sac. st, Auburn
Samtir H. clothing merchant,	Main street, Auburn
Samtir L. clothing merchant,	do do do
Sanders L. merchant,	do do do
STERNFELS M. cigar store,	do do do
Shepard John, hostler,	Empire Stable, Main street, Auburn
Sleach R. hostler,	do do do do
SWAN CHAS. J. prop.Empire Hotel,	Washington st, Auburn
Sullivan W. H. bar-keeper,	Union Saloon, Centre Block, Auburn
Stewart James, teamster,	Gove & Gordon, Auburn
Sopher John, blacksmith,	cor. Cal. and Washington sts, do
Stewart John, blacksmith,	do do do
Stone & Freedman, blacksmiths,	Turnpike Road, Auburn
Stevens Thos. E. clerk,	Commercial st, do
Scott D. C. deputy county clerk,	bds American Hotel, Auburn
Smith E. G. machinist,	Ill. and Sac. sts, do
Steele S. R. laborer,	bds Orleans Hotel, do
Shanon John, cook,	American Hotel, do
Stanton John, stage driver,	bds American Hotel, do
Strong John L. stage driver,	Marysville road
Shroutz Jas. miner,	Millertown
Smock Chester, laborer,	Spanish Flat
Shids Philip, miner,	Placer Quartz Mill, Ophir
Schnable John, miner,	Schnable's Quartz Mill, Ophir
Smith Wm. miner,	Ophir
Sanderson H. A. clerk,	Main st, Ophir
Scobey J. W. lawyer,	Ophir
Smith John, miner,	do
Shimer M. miner,	do

Smith Frank, miner,	Ophir
Soufrane Frank, miner,	do
Stinson Benoni, daguerrean artist,	Gold Hill
Stinson L. J. daguerrean artist,	do do
Smith Rufus, public administrator,	bds American Hotel, Gold Hill
Starr H. W. carpenter,	bds Mason's Hotel, Main st, Gold Hill
Smith John, blacksmith,	Main st, Gold Hill
Schultz Chas. miner,	Gold Hill
Stechler John, miner,	do do
Sanders C. C. hotel keeper,	Main street, Virginia
STUART C. H. physician & surgeon,	do do do
Smith C. barber,	do do do
Sherman Ed. W. butcher,	Fox's Flat
Salsbury Sam. meat-pedler,	do do
Steadman W. water agent,	Danesville
Salsbury E. farmer,	Auburn Ravine
Strealer Chas. gardener,	do do
Stricker —, miner,	Quartz Flat
Simpson Geo. miner,	do do
Stewart W. W. farmer,	Auburn Ravine
Simpson J. E. farmer,	Sac. and Ill. roads
Stuart Wm. cabinet maker,	Illinoistown
Salsig Sam. farmer and miner,	Aub'n Turnpike road
Stonecipher Isaac, miner,	Gold Hill
Smith Jesse, miner,	Auburn Ravine
Stockton S. laborer,	Mountaineer
Smith B. F. toll-keeper,	Whisky Bar Bridge
Stancliffe Wm. miner,	Rattlesnake
Stiner & Cohn, merchants,	do
Sexton Wm., Justice of Peace,	do
Silva C. M. merchant,	do
Sears Jack, miner,	do
Smith Adam, miner,	do
Sosten P. miner,	do
Swines J. miner,	do
Schulthciss G. gun-smith,	Auburn Turnpike
Stephens Geo. H. speculator,	bds American Hotel
St. Clair L. turner,	Gold Hill
Slocumb Geo. L. clerk,	Dutch Flat
Shuts Daniel, miner,	do do
Sanks F. miner,	do do
Spencer E. miner,	do do
Shoup Jacob, miner,	do do
Suensen A. C. miner,	do do
Shultz John, miner,	do do
Speak Richard, tailor,	do do
Smith A. miner,	do do
Smith Nathan, miner,	do do
Stone J. B. miner,	do do
STRONG DR. D. W. druggist,	do do
Shering Jas. miner,	do do

GRIMES & FELTON,

SUCCESSORS TO JONAS G. CLARK & CO.

IMPORTERS, MANUFACTURERS,

WHOLESALE AND RETAIL DEALERS IN

EVERY DESCRIPTION OF

FURNITURE,

— AND —

BEDDING,

49 and 51 Fourth Street,

BETWEEN J AND K,

SACRAMENTO.

12   GRIMES & FELTON.

Smith W. H. miner,	Dutch	Flat	
Smith William, miner,	do	do	
Sendy D. M. miner,	do	do	
Smith J. C. miner,	do	do	
Scull A. C. miner,	do	do	
Snyder J. E. miner,	do	do	
Slade Thos. P. lawyer,	do	do	
Shaw Andrew, miner,	do	do	
Smith T. R. miner,	do	do	
Salon T. F. miner,	do	do	
Shafer Silas, miner,	do	do	
Stein Wm. miner,	do	do	
Shaw Wm. miner,	do	do	
Snider, W. H. miner,	do	do	
Spiden M. miner,	do	do	
Stroben Chas. miner,	do	do	
Shirley Peter, miner,	do	do	
Seffens Chas. hotel keeper,	do	do	
Smith Joseph, miner,	do	do	
Seabert Chas. miner,	do	do	
Squire Geo. miner,	do	do	
Strickland M. L. engineer,	do	do	
Staples J. P. miner,	do	do	
Stratton W. C. State Librarian,	do	do	
Sprague Chas. miner,	Pine Grove		
Shirly A. K. miner,	do	do	
Smith Edwin, carpenter,	Galt House		
Snow Frank, miner,	Beal's Bar		
Sullivan A. miner,	do	do	
Strand Wm. miner,	do	do	
Small Isaac, miner,	do	do	
Shelden W. W. water agent,	do	do	
Samus Moses P. miner,	do	do	
Seals D. S. miner,	Dotan's Bar		
Stancliff S. B. miner,	do	do	
Stancliff R. J. miner,	do	do	
Sylva Manwell, miner,	do	do	
Sprague Samuel,	do	do	
Sheppard Nathaniel, shoe-maker,	Rattlesnake		
Suinsen Samuel, miner,	do		
Snyder Peter, miner,	do		
Sylvester Docter, miner	do		
Stewart James, miner,	do		
Stephens Hyram, miner,	do		
Spain A. A. miner,	do		
Shoemaker James, laborer,	Illinoistown		
Stephens John, cook,	Starbuck's Mill		
Savery Hiram N. miner,	Grizzly Bear House		
Schot John, prop'r toll road,	do	do	do
Stiner, Jacob, miner,	do	do	do
Smith J. J. ranchman,	do	do	do

Stephenson G. C. carpenter,	Forest	Hill
Steele Chas. H. miner,	do	do
Slaughbauer Robt. teamster,	do	do
St. John M. miner,	do	do
Smith Daniel, miner,	do	do
Smith Stephen C. saloon keeper,	do	do
Sherridan Dr. G. M. physician,	do	do
Smith Wm. C. wagon maker,	do	do
Sutton N. B. miner,	do	do
Spear S. N. miner,	do	do
Scott J. C. merchant,	do	do
Stratton J. N. clerk,	do	do
Schmitt Jacob, merchant,	do	do
Scott A. B. prop'r of water works,	do	do
Sack L. musician,	do	do
Spencer Dr. C. G. physician,	do	do
Sullivan C. J. blacksmith,	do	do
Shaw J. W. miner,	do	do
Sheaver Jo. miner,	do	do
Steele Wm. miner,	do	do
Steward John, miner,	do	do
Steele S. G. miner,	do	do
Stanwood A. K. P. miner,	do	do
Stanwood Robt. miner,	do	do
Sears John, miner,	do	do
Sears Louis, miner,	do	do
Sheller Chas. miner,	do	do
Schmutzler Chas. miner,	do	do
Stick Philip, saloon keeper,	do	do
Shelden Chas. miner,	do	do
Snodgrass A. miner.	do	do
Strasburg John, miner,	do	do
Sawyers S. T. miner,	do	do
Sherridan Felix, miner,	do	do
Senate Thos. miner,	do	do
Sullivan Dennis, miner,	do	do
Sullivan Case, miner,	do	do
Sullivan Jerry, miner,	do	do
Sherror Wm. miner,	dc	do
Singleton Willis, miner,	do	do
Steele John, miner,	do	do
Shaw J. W. miner,	do	do
Simpson Robt. miner,	do	do
Silverthorn Wm. T. cook,	do	do
Seer Oliver, steward,	do	do
Spear S. miner,	do	do
Sutton James, miner,	do	do
Sherman James, miner,	do	do
Stone O. J. miner,	do	do
Spaulding G. K. miner,	do	do
Scott L. W. miner,	do	do

Stevens D. P. miner,	Forest	Hill
Sherridan B. K. miner,	do	do
Streeter B. lumberman,	do	do
Smith James, miner,	Forks House	
Saunders Geo. ranchman,	Todd's Valley	
Schmidt Morris, miner,	do	do
Smith Chas. lumberman,	do	do
Seaman M. miner,	do	do
Smith J. F. dentist,	do	do
Searls Hiram, miner,	do	do
Seaman Wm. H. hotel keeper,	do	do
Staker C. miner,	do	do
Spangler Dan. miner,	do	do
Staatt Fred. miner,	do	do
Seibert John, miner,	do	do
Searing Thos. miner,	do	do
Searing S. J. miner,	do	do
Shields Wm. S. miner,	do	do
Smith A. B. miner,	do	do
Sternples John, miner,	do	do
Story Matthew, miner,	do	do
Sleighter Wm. miner,	do	do
Shearer Fred. brewer,	do	do
Schmidt Casper, brewer,	do	do
Swearinger Geo. livery stable keeper,	Michigan Bluff	
Spaulding O. G. tinsmith,	do	do
Steele James, miner,	do	do
Sims Thomas, miner,	do	do
Stangroom M. L. surveyor,	do	do
Swartwaut M. T. druggist,	do	do
Schweer John, miner,	do	do
Sweeney James, butcher,	do	do
Seibert Fred. brewer,	do	do
Spangler J. H. miner,	do	do
Scott Philip, miner,	do	do
Strabel Chas. miner,	do	do
Smeile Chas. miner,	do	do
Stuart J. Kennedy, miner,	do	do
Straus D. merchant,	do	do
Shawl Mark, merchant,	do	do
Steen Geo. tinsmith,	do	do
Sisley John, miner,	do	do
Shanly C. G. miner,	do	do
Streem Fred. miner,	do	do
Schnaffer Wm. miner,	do	do
Sawyer Andrew, miner,	do	do
Spillman James, miner,	do	do
Smith Wm. miner,	do	do
Smith A. J. miner,	do	do
Smith John, miner,	do	do
Smith J. miner,	do	do

Smith A. miner,	Michigan	Bluff
Spraul James, miner,	do	do
Steely James, miner,	do	do
Spear Wm. miner,	do	do
Sharrack Thomas, miner,	do	do
Simmons Peleg, miner,	do	do
Smith Wm. miner, [Last Chance,]	do	do
Snyder E. H. miner, do do	do	do
Sherd W. miner, do do	do	do
Sperry G. F. miner, do do	do	do
Shelback A. miner, do do	do	do
Streete Solon, miner, do do	do	do
Sykes N. miner, do do	do	do
Seely I. miner,	do	do
Smily Chas. miner,	do	do
Shain W. C. miner,	do	do
Strobridge R. miner,	do	do
Swinson Chris. miner,	do	do
Stackhouse J. S. miner,	do	do
Sibley E. miner,	do	do
Seely Wm. miner,	do	do
Sayles Louis, miner,	do	do
Slifer Adam, ranchman,	do	do
Smith Wm. ranchman,	do	do
Stewart J. C. ditch superintendent,	do	do
Smith H. C. miner,	do	do
Starkweather, J. M. miner,	do	do
Sprinkles Wm. miner,	do	do
Starkweather E. M. miner,	do	do
Steele P. L. miner,	do	do
Stanford Lyman, merchant,	do	do
Sherman —, blacksmith,	do	do
Smith A. B. miner,	do	do
Spear David, miner,	do	do
Smith W. miner,	do	do
Stammer, C. miner,	do	do
Sanburn J. L. tax collector,	Yankee	Jim's
Speedy Samuel, butcher,	do	do
Simpson Wm. millman,	do	do
Stander Henry, miner,	do	do
Sherwood John, miner,	do	do
Smith A. miner,	do	do
Smith A. T. miner,	do	do
Simpson E. B. miner,	do	do
Sheehe Pat. miner,	do	do
Sheehe Tim. miner,	do	do
Swett M. miner,	do	do
Sevey Eli, miner,	do	do
Shirly E. P. miner,	do	do
Sanborn D. S. dairyman,	do	do
Smith John N. miner,	do	do

JOHN BREUNER & CO.,

IMPORTERS AND DEALERS IN HOUSEHOLD

FURNITURE,

MATTRESSES,

SPRING BEDS,

Etc., Etc.

No. 170 K Street,

BETWEEN SIXTH AND SEVENTH

SACRAMENTO.

All kinds of FURNITURE made to order.

Sawyer M. ditch tender,	Yankee	Jim's
Snyder John, miner,	do	do
Simon John, miner,	do	do
Schaffer M. miner,	do	do
Schall Jacob, miner,	do	do
Silva Manuel, miner,	do	do
Scott John, miner,	do	do
Stewart Wm. miner,	do	do
Shepherd J. G. butcher,	Iowa	Hill
Stephens J. P. miner,	do	do
Simpson Sam'l, miner,	do	do
Smith H. C. miner,	do	do
Swallenberg J. miner,	do	do
Shaw Wm. miner,	do	do
Sherman V. miner,	do	do
Spinney John, miner,	do	do
Schlachter John, miner,	do	do
Stephens J. W. blacksmith,	do	do
Smith Nicholas, miner,	do	do
Spencer E. miner,	do	do
Steele John, miner,	do	do
Steele John, jr. miner,	do	do
Solomon L. merchant,	do	do
Saunders J. miner,	do	do
Schwabacher L. merchant,	do	do
Sibley P. H. lawyer,	do	do
Sterling J. miner,	do	do
Stone A. J. musician,	do	do
Stone Levi, miner,	do	do
Stone James, toll-road prop'	do	do
Stratton Chas. miner,	do	do
Stines W. R. miner,	do	do
Schmitt John, miner,	do	do
Stephens F. A. miner,	do	do
Simms Wm. miner,	do	do
Smith L. F. miner,	do	do
Sprague C. L. miner,	do	do
Sparrowhawk J. S. miner,	do	do
Sherrett W. C. miner,	do	do
Stone G. D. miner,	do	do
Semmons C. W. miner,	do	do
Strassman Chas. merchant,	do	do
Smith N. T. merchant,	do	do
Skellen H. F. miner,	do	do
Shepperd J. G. miner,	do	do
Sherridan Jas. miner,	do	do
Snitzer Louis, brewer,	do	do
Saul Andrew, miner,	do	do
Smith A. miner,	do	do
Sullivan F. miner,	do	do
Scott P. W. miner,	do	do

Sullivan J. miner,	Iowa Hill
Sylvester H. miner,	do do
Sayer L. miner,	do do
Smith N. miner,	do do
Strong T. miner,	do do
Stummel H. miner,	do do
Swoob N. miner,	do do
Simole T. M. miner,	do do
Shemble T. miner,	do do
Shields W. miner,	do do
Sullivan J. miner,	do do
Sparks R. miner,	do do
Sparks Jo. miner,	do do
Sheehon Pat. miner,	do do
Sullivan J. S. miner,	do do
Shearer P. miner,	do do
Smitzer H. miner,	do do
Smitzer J. miner,	do do
Smitzer M. miner,	do do
Smith J. M. miner,	do do
Shaw D. miner,	do do
Sibley E. miner,	do do
Schauer S. miner,	do do
Scott John, lumberman,	do do

T

Tuttle C. A. lawyer,	Commercial st, Auburn
Towle Wm.	Empire and Pioneer stables, Auburn
Turner W. A. J.	bds Brooks', Auburn
Thompson John, blacksmith,	bds Orleans Hotel, Auburn
Tuttle E. D. laborer,	Ill. and Sac. roads, do
Tuttle James, laborer,	American Hotel, do
Thompson Geo. miner,	Millertown
Templer Thos. farmer,	do
Tize M. miner,	Schnable's Quartz Mill, Ophir
Taylor G. W. carpenter,	Main st, Ophir
Till Geo. miner,	Ophir
Throp Thos. miner,	do
Tramell J. miner,	bds Mason's Hotel, Main st, Gold Hill
Trummel Albert, carpenter,	Gold Hill
Taturn S. C. miner,	Fox's Flat
Teeter E. miner,	Virginia
Toole Jas. H. miner,	Rattlesnake
Turner Wm.	Elephant House, A. and N. roads
Thomas Chas. E. bar-keeper,	Auburn
Tamrer O. miner, ·	Dutch Flat
Trim Robt. M. ditchman,	do do
Thomas E. M. miner,	do do
Thomas J. G. miner,	do do
Thompson W. miner,	do do

Tower Gideon, miner,	Dutch Flat
Teal J. W. miner,	do do
Thomas Edward, miner,	do do
Turk David, miner,	do do
Thompson Alex. miner,	do do
Terry J. L. tailor,	do do
Thorndike D. W. miner,	do do
Tomlinson S. miner,	do do
Taylor Cornelius, miner,	Pine Grove
Taylor James M. miner,	do do
Taylor J. M. miner,	do do
Thompson A. V. miner,	Galt House
Thompson H. N. miner,	Beal's Bar
Thomas John, miner,	do do
Thompson Cyrus, miner,	do do
Tailor Geo D. miner,	do do
Townsend E. miner,	do do
Towns Robt. miner,	do do
Tomilson Geo. miner,	Rattlesnake
Turner John, miner,	Illinoistown
Thayer F. M. carpenter,	Forest Hill
Tritton Thos. carpenter,	do do
Tannehill A. miner,	do do
Trask E. F. painter,	do do
Tipton Robt. teamster,	do do
Thomas R. M. miner,	do do
Trumbull L. ranchman,	do do
Thomas Richard, miner,	do do
Thomas W. G. miner,	do do
Thomas John, miner,	do do
Thomas Wm. miner,	do do
Twahchman Fred. miner,	do do
Trumbull John, miner,	do do
Taylor Wm. miner,	do do
Taylor A. lumberman,	do do
Taylor S. lumberman,	do do
Thomas F. miner,	Forks House
Thomas A. miner,	do do
Tracy P. S. merchant,	do do
Turley John, pedler,	Todd's Valley
Turley John, jr. miner	do do
Turley Peter, miner,	do do
Trask Dr. J. H. physician,	do do
Truworthy Frank, miner,	do do
Terry C. F. miner,	do no
Tway John, miner,	do do
Todd Dr. F. W. physician,	do do
Taylor T. J. miner,	do do
Truworthy Chas. miner,	do do
Thompson Fred. miner,	do do
Tennent W. R. miner,	Michigan Bluff

Tyler Edwin, expressman,	Michigan	Bluff
Taylor Joseph, miner,	do	do
Traphagan N. R. D. dentist,	do	do
Tripp Geo. F. miner,	do	do
Thompson Stephen, miner,	do	do
Thompson John, miner,	do	do
Thomas John, miner,	do	do
Torrence Milton, miner,	do	do
Torrence Hugh, miner,	do	do
Thompson Wm. miner,	do	do
Tripp Nat. miner, [Last Chance,]	do	do
Thomas Wm. miner, do do	do	do
Taylor Harvey, miner, do do	do	do
Thomas David, miner,	do	do
Trazier Joseph, miner,	do	do
Thomas E. miner,	do	do
Thompson J. miner,	do	do
Towle Wm. miner,	do	do
Thomas Samuel, miner,	Yankee	Jim's
Trask R. H. millman,	do	do
Tubbs M. B. saloon keeper,	do	do
Tyler C. miner,	do	do
Tracy John, miner,	do	do
Trapton Chas. miner,	do	do
Theal Peter, miner,	Iowa	Hill
Ten Eyck Geo. miner,	do	do
Ten Eyck Ed. miner,	do	do
Teasland Geo. miner,	do	do
Taylor G. M. miner,	do	do
Tedd J. M. miner,	do	do
Travino Wm. miner,	do	do
Tallman R. J. miner,	do	do
Thompson M. miner,	do	do
Thorp David, miner,	do	do
Tillman John, miner,	do	do
Thompson M. saloon keeper,	do	do
Taylor John, miner,	do	do
Tibbetts J. P. physician,	do	do
Thomas H. M. miner,	do	do
Thompson Jacob, miner,	do	do
Trask L. miner,	do	do
Tucker W. miner,	do	do
Tracy E. expressman,	do	do
Tigler M. miner,	do	do
Tobin Wm. miner,	do	do
Trask W. millman,	do	do
Trasure J. millman,	do	do
Trasure Jo. millman,	do	do
Taylor O. miner,	do	do
Trask C. O. merch't, [Monona Flat,]	do	do

U

Uwmon Wm. miner,	Schnable's Quartz Mill, Ophir,
Underwood J. miner,	Doty's Ravine
Uren Wm. blacksmith,	Dutch Flat
Undry Wm. miner,	do do
Utz Adam, miner,	Grizzly Bear House
Udell C. P. miner,	Michigan Bluff
Utter Wm. miner,	do do
Utter Joseph, miner,	do do
Urmy Peter, miner,	do do
Ulcan D. miner,	do do

V

Vanmater J. M. hardware merchant,	Main street, Auburn,
Vandecar E. H. county judge,	bds Hoin's, do
Vincent Chas. miner,	Virginia
Vance James, miner,	do
Voidt Chas. miner,	do
Vanitta Isaac, miner,	do
Vant John, miner,	Secret Ravine
Vail A. E. ranchman,	do do
Vantrees Daniel, ranchman,	Galt House
Vice David, saloon keeper,	Rattlesnake
Vance John, miner,	do
Vookarick Geo. miner,	Star House
Varuld H. C. boot maker,	Forest Hill
Vanderwalker J. lumberman,	do do
Van Vankin B. carpenter,	do do
Van Ahnden Johannes, miner,	do do
Vandiver J. F. miner,	Iowa Hill
Vaughn D. J. miner,	do do
Vagley C. C. miner,	do do
Vagley John, miner,	do do
Van Vacter Wm. miner,	do do
Varnum J. B. teacher,	do do
Voorhees W. miner,	do do
Verney V. R. miner,	do do
Volny W. D. miner,	do do
Voland E. miner,	do do
Vincent John, miner,	Michigan Bluff
Van Zandt J. B. miner, [Deadwood,]	do do
Van Dusen Thos. miner, [Last Chance]	do do
Van Emmon James, miner,	do do
Vore Ed. miner,	Yankee Jim's
Vance Wm. M. miner,	do do
Vail John, miner,	do do
Viar McCage, miner,	do do
Vanberger Richard, miner,	do do

W

WILLMENT GEO. merchant,	cor. Court and Com. sts, Auburn
WEIL S. S. fruit store,	Goodkind & Co. Main st, do
Woods & Angell, butchers,	Main st, do
Walsh Edward, merchant tailor,	Main st, do
Walkup Joseph,	bds Empire Hotel, do
Waterman Wm. carpenter,	bds Empire Hotel, do
Whitmarsh Sam. H., C. S. Co's agent,	bds Empire Hotel, do
Walker John, butcher,	bds Empire Hotel, do
WILSON W. B. merchant,	Main st, do
Worsley John, shoemaker,	Main st, do
Wells R. B. carpenter,	bds Orleans Hotel, do
WELSH JAMES F. lawyer,	Court st, do
Woods Owen, hostler,	Pioneer stable, do
Woods Thos. hostler,	Pioneer stable, do
Wadleigh B. P. clerk,	Pioneer stable, do
Woodin S. B. supervisor,	bds Mrs. Roussin, do
Williams Thos. wood-sawyer,	Willments, do
Weld Wm. painter,	Sacramento st, do
Wilson D. W. miner,	Baltimore Ravine, do
Walker M. G. steward,	county hospital, Com. st, do
Wilson John A. farmer,	Millertown
Wright Thos. constable,	Ophir
Winters —, farmer,	do
Waldren M. ditch agent,	residence Gold Hill
Waldren Thos. meat pedler,	Henn & Harford, Gold Hill
Whipple H. teamster,	Main st, do do
Webber Chas. wagon maker,	Main st, do do
Wolford C. L. miner,	Virginia
Wharton —, farmer,	Auburn Ravine
Wharton —, farmer,	do do
Wharton —, farmer,	do do
Wallace W. H. merchant,	Illinoistown
Wooly —, miner,	Bear River
Williard Daniel, miner,	Georgia Ravine
Wilson Chas. miner,	Rattlesnake
Wyman S. B. farmer,	Virginia, residence Auburn Ravine
Weddle A. T. miner,	Dutch Flat
Williams John T. miner,	do do
Whiting Leonard, miner,	do do
Waters Wm. miner,	do do
Whiteup T. C. miner,	do do
Wisgasper H. miner,	do do
Williams S. miner,	do do
Warner C. miner,	do do
Williams L. miner,	do do
Wilkinson S. A. miner,	do do
Williams T. J. miner,	do do
White Samuel, miner,	do do
Wanmington Joseph, miner,	do do
Warner E. miner,	do do

Wyruns A. C. miner,	Dutch Flat
Williams S. miner,	do do
Welkey Wm. miner,	do do
Wodworth Isaac, miner,	do do
Williams H. miner,	do do
Willis A. miner,	do do
Waters Abram, miner,	do do
Wallace Chas. miner,	do do
Warner Thos. miner,	do do
Weeks W. miner,	do do
Warren O. F. miner,	do do
Walker B. F. clerk,	do do
Wagoner J. N. miner,	do do
Washburn C. miner,	do do
Wright W. saloon keeper & carpenter,	do do
Wick C. miner,	do do
Wick Philip, miner,	do do
Weeks C. S. miner,	do do
Walton G. S. miner,	do do
Wallhizer Wm. saloon keeper,	do do
Wheeland M. miner,	do do
Waters H. miner,	do do
Willits Jas. H. merchant,	do do
Walker David M. miner,	Secret Ravine
Williams Augustus, miner,	Halfway House
Whitcher Abner, miner,	Beal's Bar
Wells C. C. blacksmith,	Dotan's Bar
Wilbert Seth, miner,	do do
Wardell John T. miner,	Rattlesnake
Wickson John, hotel keeper,	Franklin House
Welson W. J. miner,	Rattlesnake
Willard Geo. miner,	Michigan Bluff
Wentworth Nathan, mill owner,	do do
Wentworth A. J. blacksmith,	do do
Wentworth Thomas, miner,	do do
Wentworth T. miner,	do do
Wallace W. miner,	do do
Woodruff H. tinsmith,	do do
Witcer James, miner,	do do
Westfall A. butcher,	do do
Warren E. R. miner,	do do
Whiting D. L. miner,	do do
Wallou W. R. cook,	do do
Wing Abraham, merchant,	do do
Wyatt Louis, bar-keeper,	do do
Woodruff H. R. tinsmith,	do do
Washeim Chas. miner,	do do
Washeim F. S.	do do
Whitcomb A. L. miner,	do do
Williams John, miner,	do do
Walker John, miner,	do do

Webster D. B. miner,	Michigan Bluff	
Whitfield John, miner,	do	do
Winters Henry, miner,	do	do
Webley Wm. miner,	do	do
Waters Joseph, miner,	do	do
Wilson Thos. miner,	do	do
Wilkerson James, miner,	do	do
Wilkerson Wm. miner,	do	do
Ward Geo. miner, [Last Chance,]	do	do
Welsh J. miner,	do	do
Whitlock J. miner,	do	do
Waters Jo. miner, [Long Cañon,]	do	do
Wills James, miner,	do	do
Watkins Thos. miner,	do	do
Walker J. O. miner,	do	do
Walker O. miner,	do	do
Waymouth John, miner,	do	do
Waters Jo. miner,	do	do
Washburn Geo. miner,	do	do
Waite W. H. miner,	do	do
Wright O. F. miner,	do	do
Weber C. miner,	do	do
Williamson J. R. merchant,	do	do
Wilson James, merchant,	do	do
Weskill Adolphus, miner,	do	do
Webber Chas. miner,	do	do
Williams Peter, miner,	do	do
Wilson J. miner,	Forks House	
Wright W. H. miner,	do	do
Westervelt J. H. miner,	Grizzly Bear House	
Wentworth T. miner,	Forest Hill	
Welsh Thos. miner,	do	do
Welsh Pat. miner,	do	do
Wright Chas. miner,	do	do
Whitton D. M. blacksmith,	do	do
White Walter R. ditch superintendent,	do	do
Williams Richard, butcher,	do	dd
Wilson S. S. saloon keeper,	do	do
Wright Chas. S. lumberman,	do	do
Westenfeldt H. J. clerk,	do	do
Westenfeldt John O. miner,	do	do
Webster, G. G. express agent,	do	do
Wright J. B. miner,	do	do
Weed Wm. miner,	do	do
Welsh Thos. miner,	do	do
Wier Geo. miner,	do	do
Wier Wm. miner,	do	do
Willets P. miner,	do	do
Williams Evan, miner,	do	do
Williams Wm. miner,	do	do
Wilson James, miner,	do	do

13

Won John, miner,	Forest	Hill
Willett Edward, miner,	do	do
Willett Sefoid, miner,	do	do
Williams D. R. miner,	do	do
Woolney Joseph, miner,	do	do
Watkins —, miner,	do	do
White P. C. miner,	do	do
Whitney W. M. miner,	do	do
Willis Wm. miner,	do	do
Wilson Chas. miner,	do	do
Ward Mrs. B. saloon keeper,	do	do
Williams Wm. miner,	do	do
Williams R. J. miner,	do	do
Welsh Thos. miner,	do	do
Welsh Pat. miner,	do	do
Waddell David, miner,	do	do
Whitton Chas. miner,	do	do
Winspear Robt. teacher,	do	do
Welsh H. miner,	do	do
Weed A. miner,	do	do
Wiggins Ambrose, miner,	do	do
Wilson Edward, miner,	do	do
White Tim. miner,	do	do
Willis M. miner,	do	do
Wilson J. B. lumberman,	do	do
Werley A. ranchman,	Yankee	Jim's
Woodburn A. miner,	do	do
Werley Antoin, miner,	do	do
Watkins W. miner,	do	do
Woodward P. E. miner,	do	do
Woodward E. P. miner,	do	do
Welden Wm. miner,	do	do
Welden Allen, miner,	do	do
Wade Lem. miner,	do	do
Wetherbee J. B. miner,	do	do
Winchester Wm. miner,	do	do
Wassen Wm. miner,	do	do
Ward Wm. miner,	do	do
Wright John, miner,	Todd's	Valley
White Wm. miner,	do	do
Ware Hiram, prop'r of toll-road	do	do
Wier —, lumberman,	do	do
Wallace Matthew, livery stable,	do	do
Walker J. blacksmith,	do	do
Watson E. L. trader,	do	do
Willard S. S. ditch superintendent,	do	do
Whithurst H. miner,	do	do
Withers James, miner,	do	do
Woodward J. E. miner,	do	do
White J. H. miner,	do	do
Whitacre Thos. miner,	do	do

Ware W. H. miner,	Todd's Valley
Wyly O. H. P. miner,	do do
Wyly Robt. miner,	do do
Ward J. H. dairyman,	do do
Woodward E. A. miner,	do do
Wakeman W. miner,	do do
Wasberger L. merchant,	do do
Wasberger Joseph, merchant,	do do
Wallace Wm. miner,	do do
Winchester, H. hotel keep'r, [Wis. Hill]	do do
Ward B. F. miner,	do do
Walker Wm. miner,	do do
Witt Enoch, miner,	do do
Wiskgiber S. miner,	do do
Ward Wm. T. miner,	do do
Winslow P. miner,	Iowa Hill
Wheeler James, miner,	do do
Wheeler M. ditch owner,	do do
Willman Louis, miner	do do
Woods Geo. miner,	do do
Wiesler Wm. miner,	do do
Williams P. miner,	do do
Wookendoff Fred. miner,	do do
Witt E. B. miner,	do do
Williams Joseph, miner,	do do
Welsh James, miner,	do do
Wilson John, stage driver,	do do
Wilson P. miner,	do do
Warner J. E. miner,	do do
West J. miner,	do do
Waffle P. miner,	do do
Willard C. miner,	do do
Williams H. T. miner,	do .do
Watkins C. D. miner,	do do
Wash W. miner,	do do
Wigdon A. J. miner,	do do
Wood J. L. miner,	do do
Walsott U. S. miner,	do do
Waters J. M. miner,	do do
Wesegiver S. farmer,	do do

Y

Young John, merchant, C. & Y.	Main st, Gold Hill
Young John, miner,	Virginia,
Yokom Wm. laborer,	Illinoistown
Young Sam. news agent,	Forest Hill
Yule John, butcher,	do do
Young Thos. A. surveyor,	do do
Young Dan. miner,	do do
Young Thos. miner,	do do
Young O. H. carpenter,	Iowa Hill

Young S. M. miner,   Iowa Hill
Yarrington —, ditch owner,   Michigan Bluff
Yaw Wm. miner,   do   do
Yule James, miner,   Michigan Bluff
Yager Fred. saloon keeper,   Yankee Jim's
Yorkich Geo. hotel keeper,   Fox's Flat

Z

Zentmyer J. J.   bds Empire Hotel, Auburn
Zeginbine John, merchant,   Danesville
Zinwalt Chas. miner,   Rattlesnake
Zerr John, saloon keeper,   Dutch Flat
Zagenbien Wm. merch't, [Last Chance] Michigan Bluff

APPENDIX.

ADDITIONAL HISTORICAL SKETCHES OF TOWNS.

VIRGINIA.

A sketch of this enterprising mining town cannot be written in detail without re-stating many similar points described in the sketch of Gold Hill. Both towns being cotemporaneous in time of discovery and settlement, a history of one is almost essentially a history of the other. The parallel goes still further; many of the earliest settlers prospected and worked in both towns at about the same time.

Virginia was opened to mining in the year 1852, by the discovery of gold on the adjoining hills and ravines. The want of water during the dry season retarded the work of miners for two or three years subsequent, which was finally remedied by the introduction of water by the same canal which conveyed water into the Gold Hill district.

In 1853, a company of miners, of which Capt. John Birston was an active member, built a railroad track from Virginia Hill to the Auburn ravine, for the transportation of mineral earth; and mining was successfully carried on by the means of this road for several months of this summer. This road was certainly the pioneer railroad of Placer, if not the first laid down in the State for any purpose. This work was finally abandoned by the company, and its labor was better and more properly directed towards the introduction of water, through canals, direct to the tops of the various hills lying in and composing the Virginia district.

In the same summer a wild project was inaugurated, and a stock company organized, to build a railroad from Virginia to some point on Bear river, twenty or twenty-five miles from the town, for the purpose of carrying the "pay dirt" for washing. Stock was issued by the grand financiers of this extensive mining company, and several persons invested money in the chimerical movement. But the project was so impracticable that the bubble soon exploded of its own absurdity.

On the completion of the Gold Hill and Bear River Ditch, this town began to assume an importance as one of the safest and surest mining localities in the State. Thousands upon thousands of dollars were mined from the hills and ravines of Virginia, and subsequently paid in as assessments to tunnel companies, prospecting the hills at Iowa Hill, Dutch Flat, Todd's Valley, Forest Hill, and other successful mining camps in the upper end of the county. Virginia and Gold Hill were the "banks," where for years the honest and industrious miner recuperated his wasted means, and from which, annually, he returned back in the fall, to the mountains, to prosecute his

labors to obtain possession of a more permanent and lasting "paying" claim.
The miners in and about Gold Hill, Virginia, Ophir and Doty's Flat, were
as migratory as the antelope, who came down upon the foot hills and plains,
after the subsidence of the rainy and snowy seasons. The miners, after a
summer's labor in these sure diggings, returned to the hills with a well filled
purse, and with light hearts and strong arms, re-entered upon their prospecting labors. So time passed along with the early settlers of Virginia, and in
this manner many of those rich hills in upper Placer became early developed
of their mineral wealth. Early settlers of Virginia thus also became permanent residents of the mountain towns.

After the exhaustion of the more prominent and first opened hills in this
district, the attention of miners was called more particularly to the Auburn
ravine and to the large and small flats in the vicinity. Auburn ravine, as at
Gold Hill, was considered too deep to be mined with profit, but as the gold
placers most easily worked became in a great measure exhausted, companies
of miners were organized with the view of opening up drain ditches through
this ravine, and preparations made for removing the surface, either by water
or by the hand barrow. On some of the claims the horse scraper was ad-
vantageously used as early as the year 1854. Where draining was considered
impracticable, water wheels were erected and large pumps put into motion
for the purpose of keeping the claim dry while the rich bottom dirt was
lifted with a shovel into the tom or sluice box. In this district, at about this
time, the "sluice box" was first introduced, and which soon supplanted the
celebrated "long-tom," and which improvement contributed so much to the
value of shallow and easily mined surface diggings.

"Quartz Flat," a large territory lying under the very eaves of the town,
also about this time began to be prospected; and subsequently was found
to be extensive and profitable mining ground. This flat being covered with
a hard conglomerated gravel, cemented together by a clayish compound, it
was found to be safe to tunnel, especially when timbered with light material.
The pay dirt being near the rocks, this mode of mining Quartz Flat was
generally adopted, the miner drifting his subterranean chambers with a view
to labor-saving and not with due reverence to the dignity and importance of
his lungs. This flat contributed its full quota towards the fair mining
reputation of Virginia, although the Auburn ravine to-day still tenaciously
contends to contribute its share in holding good its original claim.

The Auburn ravine, it will not be disputed by any intelligent man, has
contributed more gold dust, *pro rata* with its area, than any auriferous ravine
in the Golden State; and its wealth has been the main-spring of building
up town after town, from its head at and near the high lands on the North
Fork of the American river, half a mile east of Auburn, to its terminus in
the plains, a few miles east of the Sacramento river, near the boundary line
of Sacramento and Placer counties. At its head, lump or coarse gold was
found, and gradually the gold diminishes in size and specific gravity, as the
miner follows the winding stream to the plains, where it is lost by its own
deposits. All these towns have passed the meridian of mining prosperity,
though Virginia, from her contiguity to the agricultural lands of the county,
perhaps, to-day wears her old garbs of prosperity, and is s ill, to use a
miner's phrase, "not played out."

Virginia No. 2, or Chinatown, ought not to be passed by without a notice.
For years after the first settlement, John Chinaman was not allowed to hold

a claim in this district, but latterly the cupidity of merchants, and the interests of ditch proprietors have forced John to amalgamate with the white man, and a large Celestial population is now found here. The error of this policy will grow more apparent as time progresses on its cycle.

The agricultural wealth bounding Virginia on the north and west will continue to add to the growth and prosperity of both Virginia and Gold Hill; and when this section shall fully recover from its miasmatic vapors, and its early reputation for health shall have been restored, a more permanent and steady growth will be inaugurated. S.

LAST CHANCE.

The village of Last Chance is situated high up in the mountains, on a ridge south of the main branch of the North Fork of the Middle Fork of the American river, at an altitude of nearly five thousand feet. Diggings were discovered in the cañons and gulches in the section of country in which Last Chance is situated, in the spring of 1850, but there was no permanent settlement made there until 1852. The general topography of the country is of the roughest description; the hills being precipitous, with here and there a large space of nothing in sight but bluff rocks, with scrub timber or chaparral growing out of the crevices. On the tops of the ridges, and on the benches of the hillsides, there is a heavy growth of excellent timber, of the various species most prized for lumber or fuel. On the ridge commencing immediately above the village, an open glade commences, and extends for several miles to the eastward; but on both sides of this bald spot is growing forests of the finest kind of timber, reaching far down upon the mountain sides towards the cañons.

The village is composed of about twenty-five houses upon the main street, and contains about seventy-five inhabitants, all of whom are industrious and steady miners, or careful and money-making traders. The mines are rich, and within the last two years have been paying well. In the summer of 1859, Messrs. Parkinson & McCoy succeeded in bringing water into the diggings from the main prong of the American river, in that part of the mountains, since which time the miners have been enabled to work their claims on the hillsides and in the heads of the cañons, by the hydraulic process; and as they have been supplied with water throughout the whole of the warm season, have never failed to make good wages.

Gold was discovered in the Last Chance diggings by a mere accident, the singularity of which is worth recording. A party of prospectors had encamped upon a small stream near where the town now stands, and having fire-arms with them, one or more of the party were generally sent out each day to hunt, and thus keep the party in meat, the balance of the company being engaged during the day in examining the gulches, ravines and cañons, and prospecting for gold. After being upon the ridge for several days, and the want of success having discouraged them, they were about to break up their camp and return to Bird's Valley, from whence they had set out on the tour, one of them remarking that that "was the *last chance* they would have to find gold on the west slope of the mountains," for they were so near the summit, he thought if they went further up they would have to pass over to the eastern side of the mountains before they could find any more auriferous soil. While this counsel was being held, one of the hunters, on his return to camp, and but a few hundred yards distant from it, finding a flock of grouse, fired at and killed one, which had taken refuge in a tall pine. The bird fell to the ground at the crack of the hunter's rifle, who, after re-loading his piece, proceeded to bag his game. On reaching the place where the bird lay he discovered that in its dying struggles it had scratched away the leaves, leaving the ground bare. In stooping down to pick up the bird he noticed a rock which drew his attention, and picking it up, on examination, discovered that it contained gold. He proceeded to the camp to report to his companions the success with which he had met, when, remembering the remark of one of the party who was in a most desponding mood during the consultation, they agreed to call the place Last Chance.

The diggings thus discovered was one of those outcroppings on the hillside, where, by some convulsions of nature, the rim rock has been broken off, leaving the rich gravel which contains the gold exposed to view. This discovery led to further prospecting and the discovery in the neighborhood of Little Duncan, Big Duncan and Miller's Defeat Cañons, and also other mines, which have been worked more or less during the last ten years.

For many years Last Chance was a kind of dernier resort for the "busted miner," and every season parties would repair thither to fish in the cañons, hunt and prospect for gold until the winter snows would drive them from the mountains and cause them to return to their homes in the old placers, lower down upon the divide. Among the first permanent settlers were Jack Hyland and his brother P. G. Hyland, the latter familiarly known as "Fip Hyland." These gentlemen for several years carried on the business of mining, milling and merchandizing; but the sparse settlement did not afford trade sufficient to keep up the business, and they quit trading and turned their attention solely to mining. They both yet reside in the village, and, like the balance of the working men of that vicinity, are making a good living.

Since the summer of 1858 the resources of the place have been gradually developing themselves, as the industrious and persevering population pushed forward their explorations, and at the present time there are few localities in the mining regions which have brighter prospects for the future, or in which miners are getting better paid for their labor than at Last Chance.

A little less than two years ago, a Division of the Sons of Temperance was organized at Last Chance, with upwards of twenty charter members, and in a very short time the Division made such rapid accessions to its numbers that at the end of the first year of its existence a splendid hall had been built by the society, and out of a voting population of about seventy fortytwo had renounced the use of intoxicating drinks and become members of the order; and to their credit be it said, very few have fallen from the high position which they assumed upon connecting themselves with that institution, by returning to the degrading habits of intemperance.

A saw mill has been built just above the village, capable of cutting a million feet of lumber per annum, the machinery of which is propelled by water power, which supplies an abundance of lumber, at reasonable prices, to answer all the purposes of the settlers.

The greatest backset to the rapid settlement of the place and development of its mining resources, is the great depth which the snow falls in the winter. During the winter season it is sometimes impossible for miners to obtain supplies, except by packing them themselves over the snow from Deadwood, a distance of seven miles. After the snows fall at the beginning of the winter season, it is sometimes months that the inhabitants have no intercourse with the *lower* world, except occasionally when an expressman travels over the snow to Michigan Bluff to procure letters and papers, which he takes to the people at the moderate charge of twenty-five cents for each letter and paper.

On the first day of December, 1857, was tried the first civil case which ever came before a Justice's Court in that Township, a graphic account of which is given by a correspondent of the Placer *Courier*, under the signature of " Dot," which we extract from that paper to show the way they did things there at that time. " Dot" speaks of the important event in the history of the village as follows : " To-day, (Dec. 1st, 1857,) although 'tis clear and fair without, 'tis blustery within. The Justice's Court is in session to try the first case by civil law in this township ; which is an action brought for the recovery of a *town lot* claimed by plaintiff to have been *jumped* by defendant. Mr. W. J. Harrison, of mining notoriety, appeared as counsel for the plaintiff, and Billy D. Smith, the celebrated butcher, as counsel for the defense. After hearing the evidence of witnesses until no more could be found of import to the case, His Honor quietly and calmly listened to the arguments of counsel, and immediately after gave judgment in favor of plaintiff. Notice of appeal was given. Hoor-rah for Last Chance !"

STONY BAR, HORSE-SHOE BAR AND BIRD'S VALLEY.

As the settlements at all these places were made at about the same time, and as they are but a short distance apart, we will notice them all conjointly.

Bird's Valley was first settled by a man named Bird, a packer, who built a log cabin for the purpose of storing his goods on his arrival from the city each week with his train of pack-mules. It was called Bird's Store, until the great influx of population from El Dorado in February and March, 1850, when quite a town was built up, and the name was changed to Bird's Valley. The diggings first discovered were in Dutch Gulch and Stitchner's Gulch, and a few dry ravines, which pitch off rapidly into the Middle Fork.

Below Bird's Valley about three miles are Stony Bar and Rester's Bar, on the North Fork of the Middle Fork, both of which were esteemed rich by the miners of '49 and '50. The diggings were shallow, and the greatest difficulty to contend with was the large stones which had to be removed by the miner in order to sink a hole to the bed-rock. Some of the stones were of immense weight, and as there were no blasting tools to be procured in that part of the country, and no blacksmith's forge at which to sharpen tools, they had to be removed by prying them up and rolling them out of the hole upon "skids." To obtain a few pans of earth off of the bed rock a company of a half dozen miners would often work a whole day to remove one of these stones, and yet the dirt was so rich under them that when removed the miners got well paid for the labor incurred.

Horse-shoe Bar is upon the Middle Fork of the American river, about two miles below Stony Bar, and about three miles from Bird's Valley. Here was cut the first bed-rock tunnel in the State. The work of cutting the Horse-shoe Tunnel was commenced in the month of February, by a company composed of seventeen men, under the leadership of a gentleman from

Maine, named Butterfield. The company was organized at a mining camp in El Dorado county, then called "Bald Hill," and known as the Horse-shoe Bar Tunnel Company. The object of the company was to turn the water through the narrow ridge into a race leading from the mouth of the tunnel to the lower end of the bar near the mouth of Mad Cañon, and thus drain the bed of the river for a distance of about one mile and a half. The company persevered in their undertaking until the first object—draining the water from the river bed—was accomplished, with the labor of the members, and at the completion of the work people had so much confidence in the success of the enterprise, shares were sold at $5,000 each. But the limited knowledge of the miners at that day of the science of mining, and the great disadvantages which they labored under for the want of proper tools and machinery to work with, together with the high prices of labor, caused the enterprise to fail, and the adventurous men who performed the vast labor of cutting a tunnel twelve feet wide and six feet high, through the hill, in solid slate of the hardest quality, were compelled to lose their whole year's work. In anticipation of the completion of the tunnel and the opening of the diggings in the bed of the stream to miners on the share, hundreds of them had flocked to the bar, and quite a town was built of tents, board shanties, etc. But the early rains of September of that year demolished the frail dam which had been thrown across the river when the water was low, and there being no mines open for the crowd of laborers, who had been lying around waiting for a chance to work among the boulders in the channels, where they could make their ounce per day, the camp was soon deserted and the miners scattered off to the mines on the hills and in the gulches of El Dorado and Placer counties.

The river has been worked every year since with varied success; but the prospects obtained one year were never sufficient to induce the miner of one year, whether successful or not, to "try the river again the next year." At the present time there are a large number of permanent settlers upon the different bars upon this part of the river, from the mouth of Mad Cañon to Stony Bar, and the miners are making good wages the whole year round. The diggings are extensive and rich, but require considerable capital to work them properly. There are several stores along here for the sale of miners' supplies, and quite a number of excellent gardens, orchards and vineyards.

TODD'S VALLEY.

Todd's Valley was first settled by Dr. Todd, who built a log house for a store and hotel, on the site of his present residence, at his ranch in the lower suburbs of the town, in June, 1849. The location at that time was the most eligible one to be found north of the Middle Fork of the American, and was the proper distance from the river to catch all the travel from the old diggings in El Dorado county to the new placers at Stony Bar, Horse-shoe Bar and Rester's Bar. The doctor also built a corral near his house in which to drive horses when he desired to catch them for his own or his customers' use, and took horses to ranch at the moderate sum of five dollars per week, cash; the owners to run all risks and hunt up their stock, themselves, when they desired to use them. The stand as a ranch and trading post was valuable, and perhaps could have been sold in the fall of '49, or spring of '50, for $10,000, or $15,000.

Although Todd's ranch was much resorted to by miners from the river and gulches adjacent to it, for the purpose of purchasing their supplies, and obtaining their letters and papers upon each arrival from the " city " of the expressman, yet the town of Todd's Valley did not commence to grow up until 1852, after the discovery of rich diggings in the "flat," at the head of the little stream upon which the Doctor's house was situated. The discovery of these mines drew the attention of miners and traders to the place and a town was laid off on the ridge, midway between, and at a convenient distance from the "flat" and " Poker Hill." The mines were rich, and although Yankee Jim's, the nearest town and rival of Todd's Valley, was *the* place of the Divide, yet it flourished until eventually it became the most populous town of the two. In the early part of the fall of 1859, a fire broke out in the town which destroyed the whole of the business part of the place except the provision and grocery stores of A. A. Pond & Co., and Reed & Benedict, which, being fire-proof, escaped damage by the conflagration. The property destroyed was estimated to be worth nearly two hundred thousand dollars. After the fire, the town was again re-built, and soon presented a better appearance than before the conflagration. There are now in the place twenty-five business houses of all kinds, among which are two hotels, three grocery and provision stores, several dry goods and clothing establishments, one banking office, one livery stable, three variety stores, two butcher shops, one brewery, etc., etc. Since the fire in 1859, the town has been gradually improving in appearance and increasing in population. There are in the place a Masonic Lodge, an Odd Fellows' Lodge, and two Temperance orders, all of which are in a flourishing condition and constantly increasing in membership. The mining here is both tunnelling and hydraulic mining, and both methods prove remunerative to those who own claims. Some of the richest mines upon the Forest Hill Divide are located near this place, and the trade of the miners is divided between the two towns. The Dardanelles tunnel and the Big Spring tunnel are situated about midway between Todd's Valley and Forest Hill, and until the last two years Todd's Valley commanded the whole of the trade of this vastly rich section. The Independent Bedrock Claims, No. 1 and No. 2, situated at the foot of Parker Hill, are very rich hydraulic claims, and have paid their owners immense sums every year since they were opened. Some of the longest tunnels that pierce the main divide are run in here ; one of them is now just completed and has been run through bed-rock a distance of 1800 feet. It is intended to drain the large flat at the back part of the town, and will open by the next year a large extent of mining ground that is known to be rich, but could not be worked to advantage for want of sufficient fall for drainage, which this tunnel was run for the purpose of supplying.

COUNTY, DISTRICT, TOWN AND TOWNSHIP OFFICERS,

FOR THE YEAR 1861.

COUNTY OFFICERS:

E. H. VANDECAR,..*County Judge.*
L. L. BULLOCK,..*Sheriff.*
H. GOODING,...*Clerk.*
W. A. SELKIRK,......................................*County Recorder.*
JO. HAMILTON,......................................*District Attorney.*
E. M. BANVARD, ...*Treasurer.*
JAMES PLATT,..*Coroner.*
RUFUS SMITH, ...*Public Administrator.*
H. S. GREENWOOD,...................*Superintendent of Public Schools.*

District Court, Eleventh Judicial District.—Hon. B. F. MYRES, Judge. Meets at Auburn on the second Monday in January, April and July, and the third Monday in October.

County Court.—Hon. E. H. VANDECAR, Judge. Meets on the fourth Monday in January, April and July, and third Monday in October.

Court of Sessions.—Hon. E. H. VANDECAR, presiding Judge; A. S. GRANT and SAMUEL M. JAMISON, associates. Meets on the second Monday in September, and the fourth Mondays in January and May.

Supervisors.—District No. 1, S. B. Woodin; District No. 2, W. H. Patton; District No. 3, Michael Fannon.

TOWN AUTHORITIES OF AUBURN.

Trustees.—Hiram R. Hawkins, President; E. W. Hillyer, Moses Andrews; Amos Gove, Tabb Mitchell.
Marshal, John C. Baggs; *Treasurer,* Julius P. Brooks; *Clerk,* A. S. Grant; *Assessor,* T. B. Hotchkiss.

TOWNSHIP OFFICERS.

Township No. 1.—Collector, G. L. Grilley; Assessor, J. D. Pratt; Justices of the Peace, G. M. Greer and P. H. Hall; Constables, W. Van Meter and N. W. Shepherd; Road Commissioners, Thos. Dudley, J. C. Hampton, and James Hovey.
Township No. 2.—Collector, Daniel Choate; Assessor, T. Goodrich; Justices of the Peace, S. Reno and W. R. Curtis; Constables, T. A. Wright and John T. Owens; Road Commissioners, F. W. Henn, G. Perry and J. P. Hopper.
Township No. 3.—Collector, John Connor; Assessor, George Russell; Justices of the Peace, A. S. Grant and Wm. Sexton; Constables, Wm. Osborne and Geo. H. Merrill; Road Commissioners, Wm. Turner, A. C. Neill and L. E. Miller.

Township No. 4.—Collector, N. W. Blanchard; Assessor, A. B. Gallatin; Justices of the Peace, H. Fellows and J. Brown; Constables, Jacob Keck and James T. Mathewson; Road Commissioners, A. Lowell, W. C. Richmond and E. J. Brickell.

Township No. 5.—Collector, J. L. Sanborn; Assessor, M. M. Crary; Justices of the Peace, A. B. Brown and S. M. Jamison; Constables, A. C. Haskell and W. H. Blank; Road Commissioners, W. H. Hardy, Wm. Duck and A. A. Pond.

Township No. 6.—Collector, E. Barrett; Assessor, D. Spear; Justices of the Peace, W. W. Cunningham and Wm. Cory; Constables, Robert Kennedy and J. D. McCormic; Road Commissioners, M. A. Powers, Wm. M. Leet and R. A. McDonald.

Township No. 7.—Collector, Jacob Neff; Assessor, C. P. Reno; Sustices of the Peace, Wm. Van Vactor and W. H. Davis; Constables, E. B. Priest and A. P. Cole; Road Commissioners, C. O. Trask, Lewis Smitzer, and S. L. Irish.

Township No. 8.—Collector, Jack Hyland; Assessor, R. C. McConnell; Justices of the Peace, E. H. Snyder and J.. B. Van Zandt; Constables, G. Ward and W. McPherson; Road Commissioners, P. G. Hyland, E. S. Tracy and C. J. Parker.

Township No. 9.—Collector, John White; Assessor, G. C. Newman; Justices of the Peace, S. J. Ray and E. Cook; Constables, S. C. Shaw and George W. Grew; Road Commissioners, E. H. Logan, D. Perkins and C. B. Harlan.

Township No. 10.—Collector, James Stewart; Assessor, John Bristow; Justices of the Peace, James Beck and Titus Ewing; Constables—J. Davidson and T. Spofford.

LIST OF POST OFFICES IN PLACER COUNTY.

Neilsburgh,..............J. C. Neil	Michigan Bluff,......F. S. Washeim
Lisbon,...........G. W. Applegate	Grizzly Bear House,.E.D.C. Faskett
Illinoistown,............B. Brickell	Yankee Jim's...........Wm. Duck
Rattlesnake,............D. S. Beach	Ophirville,...............D. Choate
Dutch Flat,..........Chas. Seffens	Virginia,..............A. W. Lyons
Mountain Springs,.....H. A. Brown	Auburn,................R. Gorden
Iowa City,............S. N. Cahin	Damascus,............T. Moreland
Forest Hill,..........R. Parkhurst	

POPULAR VOTE OF PLACER COUNTY.

MAY 26TH, 1851.

County Judge.—Hugh Fitz Simmons, 1261; James S. Christy, 722; H. Davenport, 763.

District Attorney.—R. D. Hopkins, 1474; W. B. Greer, 889; P. J. Hopper, 292.

County Clerk.—Wm. M. Jordan, 395; James S. Stewart, 1118; Hiram R. Hawkins, 961; John McNally, 219.

Sheriff.—Sam'l C. Astin, 1280 ; A. B. Hall, 1059 ; Wm. Kenniston, 453.
County Surveyor.—Sam'l B. Wyman, 1624 ; Lisbon Applegate, 129.
County Assessor.—Wm. E. Miller, 587; Alfred Lewis, 1073; E. T.
Menhall, 139.
County Treasurer.—Douglas Bingham, (died in 1851, and Abram Bronk
appointed to fill vacancy,) 1151 ; Hiram Jacobs, 679 ; Abram Bronk, 818.
County Coroner.—John C. Montgomery, 811 ; Enoch Fens, 706.
Total number of votes cast, 2792.

SEPTEMBER 3D, 1851.
State Senator.—Jacob Fry, 1204 ; W. Kennistar, 764.
Assembly.—Patrick Cannly, 1135 ; J. H. Gibson, 1198; Frederick Brad-
ley, 803 ; D. H. Stickney, 729.
County Treasurer.—Abram Bronk, 447 ; J. Lagdenby, 216.
Public Administrator.—Jonathan Roberts, 233 ; —— Coffryn, 38 ; E.
Hogan, 23.
District Judge.—S. B. Farwell, 1110 ; E. L. Sanderson, 732.
Total number of votes cast, 1968.

SEPTEMBER, 1852.
State Senator.—James E. Hale, 2164 ; Joseph Walkup, 2716.
Assembly.—John Hancock, 2274 ; Thomas White, 2269 ; Patrick Cann-
ly, 2706 ; Benj. F. Myres, 2474.
District Attorney.—R. D. Hopkins, 2125; P. W. Thomas, 2697.
Sheriff.—Wm. T. Henson, 2135 ; S. C. Astin, 2726.
County Clerk.—A. S. Grant, 2056 ; Wm. A. Johnson, 2658 ; H. R.
Hawkins, 175.
County Treasurer.—Henry Hubbard, 2189 ; Ed. G. Smith, 2681.
Assessor.—John Bristow, 2178 ; William Gunn, 2682.
Coroner.—W. J. Patterson, 2148; Doctor Pinkham, 2704.
Surveyor.—George M. Hill, 2127 ; N. O. Hinman, 2737.
Public Administrator.—Jonathan Roberts, 2148 ; Henry Barnes, 2733.
Total number of votes cast, 5102.

1853.
Governor.—Bigler, 1925 ; Purdy, 1747.
Senate.—Tuttle, 1948 ; Longley, 1643.
Assembly.—Myers, 1729 : Fairfield, 1890 ; Van Cleft, 1775 ; O'Neill,
1719 ; Crary, 1700 ; Evans, 1612 ; Trask, 1513 ; Wilson, 1646.
Assessor.—McCarty, 1709 ; Dewey, 1371.
Surveyor.—Finley, 1926 ; Elinson, 1462.
Public Administrator.—Jordon, 1980 ; Finley, 1498.

1854.
Senate.—W. H. Gray, 1831; G. C. Newman, 1211; J. C. Hawthorne, 2347.
Assembly.—J. H. Baker, 1805 ; D. B. Curtis, 1840 ; B. F. Parsons, 1844.
J. L. Bennett, 1734 ; L. N. Kitchum, 1247 ; J. N. Smith, 1237 ; P. H. Clay-
ton, 1226 ; J. C. Duell, 1183 ; Thomas Moreland, 2394 ; R. F. Gragg, 2312;
Wm. Corey, 2303 ; Mose Andrews, 2316.
County Judge.—A Bronk, 1904 ; H. Fitzsimmons, 1225 ; James E.
Hale, 2284.

Sheriff.—Samuel Todd, 1733; N. A. Dillingham, 1190; W. T. Henson, 2514.

District Attorney.—Philip W. Thomas, 1767; Joseph W. Scobey, 1224; M. E. Mills, 2452.

County Clerk.—W. C. Johnson, 1858; Wiley A. Parker, 1232; A. S. Grant, 2348.

County Treasurer.—E. G. Smith, 1822; George W. Applegate, 1269; J. R. Crandall, 2330.

County Assessor.—H. W. Starr, 1922; J. E. Stewart, 1241; A. S. Smith, 2261.

Public Administrator.—James Anderson, 1863; James Bowen, 1225; Jno. R. Gwynn, 2159.

Coroner.—Jno. P. Harper, 1913; J. L. Finley, 2276.

Surveyor.—C. W. Finley, 1364; G. H. Colby, 2436.

1855.

Senate.—Abram Bronk, 2428; Charles Westmoreland, 2955.

Assembly.—A. P. K. Safford, 2362; Albert Thorndike, 2385; B. K. Davis, 2306; Samuel B. Wyman, 2381; Silas Selick, 2978; Lansing Stout, 3017; T. H. Read, 3009; R. L. Williams, 2981.

Superintendent Common Schools.—Wm. A. Johnson, 2342; H. E. Force, 3002.

Total number of votes cast, 5554.

1856.

Senate.—H. R. Hawkins, 1913; Joseph Walkup, 2738; C. J. Hillyer, 1016.

Assembly.—Lansing Stout, 2183; C. J. Brown, 2024; P. B. Fagan, 2073; M. M. Robinson, 2013; W. W. Caperton, 2724; A. P. K. Safford, 2718; S. B. Wyman, 2720; James O'Neill, 2568; Burrows, 884; Bradley, 796; Lawrence, 925; Sheldon, 874.

Sheriff.—Wm. T. Henson, 2515; Richardson, 531; Chas. King, 2619.

District Attorney.—R. D. Hopkins, 1995; P. W. Thomas, 2711; F. B. Higgins, 908.

County Clerk.—B. F. Moore, 2302; Tabb Mitchell, 2576; Wm. Cony, 776.

Treasurer.—T. B. Hotchkiss, 2246; Philip Stoner, 2632; Matoon, 750.

Assessor.—A. S. Smith, 2129; J. W. Spann, 2679; Frary, 845.

Public Administrator.—H. T. Holmes, 1998; James M. Gaunt, 2753; Otis, 902.

Surveyor.—C. W. Finley, 1990; Phelps, 2789; Wagner, 869.

Coroner.—Jno. P. Gaines, 2081; H. M. House, 2586; Towle, 908.

Superintendent Common Schools.—S. R. Case, 2013; P. C. Millett, 2708; Albert Hart, 933.

1857.

Senate, full term.—J. C. Baker, 1841; T. P. Slade, 1474; P. H. Sibley, 704. *Short term.*—James Anderson, 1977; Jno. Barnes, 1388; S. R. Bradley, 640.

Assembly.—D. B. Curtis, 2005; A. P. K. Safford, 2007; N. Kabler, 1968; W. C. Stratton, 2001; James H. Toole, 1330; F. J. Frank, 1400; H. S. Wooster, 1379; W. Whittier, 1434; A. G. Read, 604; A. H. Goodrich, 634; A. C. S. Kull, 622; W. H. Hilton, 635.

Superintendent Common Schools.—P. C. Millett, 1970; J. P. Brooks, 1485.
County Surveyor.—S. G. Elliott, 2018.
Public Adminstrator.—Thos. Coffey, 1935; C. T. Palmer, 1578.
Coroner.—W. J. Esmond, 2071; Dr. Page, 1457.
Total number of votes cast, 4219.

1858.

Senate.—Anderson, 1909; Wooster, 1392; Ball, 1290.
Assembly.—Stratton, 1948; Barclay, 2130; Lynch, 1989; Wing, 1817;
Robinson, 1214; Franks, 1314; Henderson, 1358; Collins, 1301; Shell-
house, 1287; McDonald, 1256;Kavanaugh, 1285; Lowell, 1278.
County Judge.—Vandecar, 1957; Hawkins, 1418; Arnold, 1209.
Total number of votes cast, 4720.

1859.

Senate.—Samuel T. Lent, 1765; H. Fitz Simmons, 706; C. J. Hillyer,
809; Thomas P. Slade, 1110.
Assembly.—S. W. Lovell, 1905; James N. Makins, 2031; D. S. Beach,
2056; J. W. Harville, 2059; L. L. Deming, 522; E. W. Nevers,567; D.
Louderback, 485; D. H. Gray, 561; S. R. Bradley, 865; Jno. Yale, 934;
W. D. Harriman, 854; G. D. Aldrich, 848; S. E. Barrett, 913; D.B. Goode,
353; S. M. Jamison, 898; W. G. Monroe, 982.
Superintendent Common Schools.—S. S. Greenwood, 1717; E. M. Barnard,
565; A. H. Goodrich, 885; W. C. Howe, 1064.
Public Administrator.—Dr. Traphagan, 1804; M. P. H. Love, 2098.
Whole number of votes 4670.

1860.

Senate.—Thomas, (D.,) 1788; Walkup, (B.,) 1372; Higgins, (R.,) 1757;
Longley, (Union,) 700.
Assembly.—Lovell, 1318; Vance, 1400; Beach, 1419; Makins, 1364;
Ball, 1737; Smith, 1863; Harrison; 1852; Mundy, 1801; Harriman, 1764;
Densmore, 1670; Case, 1696; Hubbell, 1677.
Sheriff.—Miller, 1347; Bullock, 1612; Garland, 1188; Boggs, 1509.
Clerk.—Johnson, 1358; Gooding, 1974; Aldrich, 1603; Hosmer, 719.
Treasurer.—Starr, 1408; Barnard, 1761; Stanford, 1693; Brooks, 768.
Recorder.—Moffat, 1400; Stewart, 1761; Selkirk, 1763; Bull, 703.
District Attorney.—Anderson, 1358; Hamilton, 2304; Hillyer, 1665;
Mills, 247.
Surveyor.—Finley, 1407; Elliott, 1826; Davidson, 1687; Whitcomb, 737.
Public Administrator.—Love, 1486; Smith, 1770; Hotchkiss, 835.

The following two pages are reproductions of the actual front and back cover of the original 1861 Placer County Directory.

AMERICAN HOTEL

AND GENERAL

STAGE OFFICE,

AUBURN, CAL.

GUIOU & LEIGETON, - PROPRIETORS.

Having opened this fine Hotel, the Proprietors desire to return thanks to their numerous friends for their former patronage while engaged in the Hotel Business in other portions of the county, and invite a continuance of their favors. The AMERICAN is new, fire-proof, and splendidly furnished throughout in

Parlors, Bed Rooms, Dining Room & Bar.

From a long experience in the Business, they believe they can give entire satisfaction to those who may favor the House with their patronage.

☞ The TABLE will be supplied with the best to be had in the market.

☞ The BAR always furnished with the best LIQUORS and CIGARS, and the BEDS neatly kept.

THE OFFICE OF THE

CALIFORNIA STAGE COMPANY

IS KEPT AT THIS HOTEL,

Where passengers can take the Stages daily for Sacramento, and all parts of the State.